Supporting English Language Learners in Math Class

Grades 6-8

Kathy Melanese

Luz Chung

Cheryl Forbes

Math Solutions
Sausalito, California, USA

Math Solutions
150 Gate 5 Road
Sausalito, California, USA 94965
www.mathsolutions.com

Library of Congress Cataloging-in-Publication Data
Melanese, Kathy.
  Supporting English language learners in math class, grades 6/8 / Kathy Melanese, Luz Chung,
Cheryl Forbes.
      p. cm.
  Includes bibliographical references.
  ISBN 978-1-935099-18-5
  1. Mathematics—Study and teaching (Middle school) 2. English language—Study and teaching
(Middle school)—Foreign speakers. I. Chung, Luz. II. Forbes, Cheryl. III. Title.
  QA135.6.M45 2012
  510.71'2—dc22   2011005083

Editor: Jamie Ann Cross
Production service: Element LLC
Production coordinator: Melissa L. Inglis-Elliott
Cover design: Jan Streitburger
Interior design: Element LLC
Cover and interior images: Melanie Rossi and Mrs. Rowan's sixth-grade class at Kennedy-Longfellow
   School, Cambridge, Massachusetts. Videographer: Friday's Films, www.fridaysfilms.com
Composition: Element LLC

SUSTAINABLE FORESTRY INITIATIVE
Certified Fiber Sourcing
Label applies to the text stock   www.sfiprogram.org

Printed in the United States of America on acid-free paper
15 14 13 12 11   ML   1 2 3 4 5

A Message from Math Solutions

We at Math Solutions believe that teaching math well calls for increasing our understanding of the math we teach, seeking deeper insights into how students learn mathematics, and refining our lessons to best promote students' learning.

Math Solutions shares classroom-tested lessons and teaching expertise from our faculty of professional development consultants as well as from other respected math educators. Our publications are part of the nationwide effort we've made since 1984 that now includes

- more than five hundred face-to-face professional development programs each year for teachers and administrators in districts across the country;
- professional development books that span all math topics taught in kindergarten through high school;
- videos for teachers and for parents that show math lessons taught in actual classrooms;
- on-site visits to schools to help refine teaching strategies and assess student learning; and
- free online support, including grade-level lessons, book reviews, inservice information, and district feedback, all in our Math Solutions Online Newsletter.

For information about all of the products and services we have available, please visit our website at *www.mathsolutions.com.* You can also contact us to discuss math professional development needs by calling (800) 868-9092 or by sending an email to *info@mathsolutions.com.*

We're always eager for your feedback and interested in learning about your particular needs. We look forward to hearing from you.

Math Solutions.
FOUNDED BY MARILYN BURNS

SCHOLASTIC

Contents

Foreword

The authors of *Supporting English Language Learners in Math Class, Grades 6–8* are uniquely qualified to write this resource. As bilingual teachers and current and past regional directors of the California Reading and Literature Project, Kathy Melanese and Cheryl Forbes bring to the resource their extensive knowledge of English language development and their keen awareness of how to support English learners in all the content areas. Luz Chung, a native of Ecuador, is an English learner herself. Having been schooled in her native country, she came to the United States as a college student and experienced firsthand what it means to learn about academic content in a language that is unfamiliar. The authors have combined Luz's years of experience as a middle school bilingual math teacher and knowledge of math content and pedagogy with Kathy and Cheryl's expertise in the area of English language development to create this important and timely resource. It is their passion for social justice and interest in issues of access and equity that motivated them to write this book.

The lessons and strategies in this resource are founded on the premise that communication is a vital process in developing mathematical understanding, and is, of course, key to progress in learning English as a second (or third) language. Through sample vignettes, the authors clearly make the case that middle school students can, with the right support, simultaneously develop their English language skills while using English to deepen their understanding of mathematical ideas. The lessons in this book place language at the forefront of math instruction, reminding us that when we teach math, we must also teach English, not just teach *in* English.

Teachers, staff developers, coaches, and university faculty can easily use this resource to learn how to implement strategies in three key areas: (1) making math content comprehensible to middle school students, (2) providing opportunities for them to communicate, and (3) supporting them as they communicate their mathematical ideas both orally and in writing. The strategies outlined in this resource are effective for all students, and are essential for English learners.

In this era of high-stakes testing and accountability, there is a loud call from stakeholders for schools to improve student achievement. Teachers are under increased pressure to make sure that their students meet standards that are ever more rigorous and demanding. This resource answers the call from stakeholders by providing educators with concrete ways to help all students, but especially English learners, experience success in mathematics.

—RUSTY BRESSER
UNIVERSITY OF CALIFORNIA, SAN DIEGO

Acknowledgments

We'd like to thank the following people for making this book possible: Jamie Cross and Rusty Bresser for their editorial expertise, Denise Botelho for her work on the book's production, Marilyn Burns for her support, and the California Reading and Literature Project and Susana Dutro for their groundbreaking work with English learners.

We'd like to acknowledge the authors of the Supporting English Language Learners in Math Series—Rusty Bresser and Christine Sphar. Their innovative and powerful work in the elementary series provided us with a solid framework upon which to write this book.

We'd also thank the following principals and teachers for allowing us to work at their schools and in their classrooms: from Emerson Elementary School, San Diego, CA: Principal Mirna Estrada, Sandra Jasso; from Montgomery Middle School, San Diego, CA: Principal Jonathan Ton, Laura Williges; from Wagenheim Middle School, San Diego, CA: Principal Lamont Jackson, Genevieve Esmende; from Memorial Preparatory for Scholars and Athletes, San Diego, CA: Principal Georgina Barajas-Aguirre, Claudia Aguilar.

Luz Chung would like to thank her husband, Tarek, for his unwavering love and support; her students for their wonderful energy; and her coauthors for sharing their incredible wisdom and for their admirable work toward teaching for social justice.

Cheryl Forbes would like to thank her students, past and present, for teaching her so much; her extended family for their enduring encouragement, especially Dan for love and companionship and Frankie for moral support during this project; and her coauthors for their dedication, extraordinary insights, and generous collaboration.

Kathy Melanese would like to thank the amazingly dedicated teachers and students with whom she works and who provide her with endless inspiration; her colleagues and directors at EDS and CRLP; her coauthors for an incredible experience in collaboration; and, as always, her family: Steve, Trevor, Amanda and Nicholas—her heart and soul.

How This Resource Is Organized

Section I presents an overview of teaching math to English learners: the research, the challenges, how to determine the linguistic demands of a math lesson, and specific strategies and activities that simultaneously support learning English and learning math. In addition, we present the Correlations with Curricula table on pages xviii–xxii that indicates how the lessons contained in this book correlate with current mathematics curricula.

Section II features six math lessons modified for English learners. The lessons are designed to help students understand math content and develop their English language skills. Although the lessons span the math curriculum, the resource isn't intended to provide all the needed lessons for English learners. Rather, the lessons are meant to serve as examples of how best to provide the necessary support these students require.

Topics for lessons in the book include geometry, algebra, the number system, data analysis, and probability and measurement. Each of the lessons addresses one or more of the Common Core Standards for Mathematics, which are referenced at the beginning of the lesson. The lessons were taught to students in grades 6 through 8 from a variety of ethnic and socioeconomic backgrounds whose native languages included English, Spanish, Filipino, Chinese, Vietnamese, Arabic, and Turkish.

Each lesson in the resource contains the following:

Lesson Framework

+ An overview of the lesson
+ Connections with the Common Core State Standards
+ The math goal of the lesson
+ The language goal of the lesson

- ✦ Key vocabulary developed
- ✦ A list of materials needed
- ✦ Sentence frames
- ✦ An activity for introducing academic language
- ✦ An activity for introducing the new math concept
- ✦ A vignette describing implementation of the lesson in a middle school classroom
- ✦ Samples of student work, including reproducibles as appropriate
- ✦ A summary of the strategies used for teaching language and mathematics
- ✦ Description of a writing activity for students
- ✦ Suggestions for extending the lesson
- ✦ Corresponding reproducibles

The introduction of new math concepts in each lesson is preceded by an activity to introduce the academic language that students will need to understand and use to build and demonstrate understanding. During the introductory activity, sentence frames are introduced. The sentence frames are crucial and serve a variety of purposes. Sentence frames provide the support English learners need to participate fully in math discussions. They serve to contextualize and bring meaning to the vocabulary, they provide a structure for practicing and extending English language skills, they help students use the vocabulary they learn in grammatically correct and complete sentences, and they allow for differentiated learning opportunities within a whole-group lesson because they are designed for different levels of English language proficiency. For example, the following frames support students at varied language levels in their discussions about polygons:

Beginning

This is a _____. *It is/has* _____.

This is not a _____. *It is/has* _____.

Intermediate/Advanced

> This is a _____, because _____.

> This is not a _____, because _____.

> This shape has _____, _____, and
> _____.

> This shape has _____, _____, and
> _____; therefore, it is a polygon.

After the activity to introduce academic language, instruction on the new math concept begins. Now the English learners in the class have the support they need to participate fully in class discussions, using language to develop their understanding of math content.

Throughout the lessons, students practice using different language functions, depending on the mathematics that is being taught and the sentence frames used. For example, the following sentence frame helps students describe nouns, such as polygons:

> This is a _____. It is/has _____.

This sentence frame helps student compare and contrast:

> A _____ has _____, but a
> _____ has _____.

Other frames assist students in describing a sequence of procedures:

> First, _____.

> Next, _____.

> *Then,* _____ .

> *After that,* _____ .

> *Finally,* _____ .

Other frames help students make predictions:

> *I predict that* _____ *because* _____ .

For more on sentence frames, see Chapter 8: How to Modify Math Lessons to Support English Learners.

The lessons in this resource help students learn to use a variety of language functions while discussing their mathematical ideas in English. These functions include making comparisons, sequencing, describing, hypothesizing, categorizing, explaining cause and effect, predicting, making inferences, and drawing conclusions.

In Section III we take a detailed look at how to modify math lessons to support English learners. Here, we describe our thinking and planning behind each lesson—how we identified the language demands and developed the sentence frames, and why we chose particular instructional strategies. We then give you the opportunity to try out modifying your own lessons.

Last, in the Appendix, we include the following:

✦ FAQs (we address teachers' concerns and frequently asked questions about supporting English learners in math class)
✦ Multiple-Meaning Words in Mathematics (we include a list of words that are commonly used in everyday English, but have a specialized meaning in mathematics)

Meeting the Challenge

Mathematics is the gatekeeper to higher education. In fact, the more mathematics that students take in middle school and high school, the more likely they are to go on to college (U.S. Department of Education 2000). Because English learners are not achieving at the same levels in math as their native English-speaking counterparts, many are at risk of having the gate to higher education closed to them. Fortunately, math teachers *can* make a difference and address this inequity by providing well-designed support so that English learners can develop proficiency in English *and* develop their mathematical understanding.

The prospect of leveling the playing field so that all students have equal access to the math content being taught is exciting yet challenging. Meeting this challenge will require extra support, the kind of assistance that this resource describes. It is our hope that teachers view the lessons in *Supporting English Language Learners in Math Class, Grades 6–8* as models and apply the strategies to their own experiences as they help *all* their students succeed in mathematics.

Common Core State Standards: Lesson Correlations

Authors' Note: All lessons were implemented in a specific grade-level class (for example, eighth-grade algebra). However, with the appropriate language and content scaffolds, and with the appropriate grade-level differentiation, all lessons included in this resource can be implemented in grades 6 through 8. For example, *Cats and Birds* (Chapter 4) is a lesson that focuses on problem-solving strategies that lead to algebraic reasoning. This lesson requires prior understanding as well as a review of arithmetic concepts and basic knowledge of expressions to decipher the clues for *Cats and Birds*. Such concepts are covered in the common core standards for grades 6 and 7 (*Expressions and Equations*).

We determined the correlations between the lessons and the Common Core State Standards by examining the math goals, the math content knowledge required, as well as the receptive and productive tasks related to the language goals for each lesson. These correlations are presented in the following table.

Lesson	Page	Grade 6	Grade 7	Grade 8
Secret Number Puzzles	22	The Number System *Compute fluently with multidigit numbers and find common factors and multiples.*	The Number System *Apply and extend previous understandings of operations with fractions to add, subtract, multiply, and divide rational numbers.*	

(Continues)

Lesson	Page	Grade 6	Grade 7	Grade 8
Guess the Function	47			Functions *Define, evaluate, and compare functions.*
Cats and Birds	70	Expressions and Equations *Apply and extend previous understandings of arithmetic to algebraic expressions. Write, read, and evaluate expressions in which letters stand for numbers.*	Expressions and Equations *Use variables to represent quantities in a real-world or mathematical problem, and construct simple equations to solve problems by reasoning about the quantities.*	Expressions and Equations *Analyze and solve pairs of simultaneous linear equations. Solve real-world and mathematical problems leading to two linear equations in two variables.*
The Game of *SKUNK*	98		Statistics and Probability *Investigate chance processes and develop, use, and evaluate probability models.*	
Scaling Up!	121		Ratios and Proportional Relationships *Analyze proportional relationships and use them to solve real-world and mathematical problems.*	
Archimedes' Puzzle	144	Geometry *Solve real-world and mathematical problems involving area.*	Geometry *Solve real-life and mathematical problems involving angle measure and area.*	

Correlations with Curricula

The lessons in *Supporting English Language Learners in Math Class, Grades 6–8* are herein directly correlated to three of the leading middle school mathematics programs—Pearson: Connected Mathematics 2; Prentice Hall: Mathematics Course 1, 2, 3; and Holt McDougal: Mathematics Course 1, 2, 3. Use these tables to further facilitate the use of these lessons with your curricula.

Correlation with Pearson: Connected Mathematics 2			
Supporting English Language Learners in Math Class, Grades 6–8	*Grade 6*	*Grade 7*	*Grade 8*
Chapter 2 *Secret Number Puzzles* Numbers and Operations	Bits and Pieces I: Investigation 3		Growing, Growing, Growing: Investigation 1
	Bits and Pieces II: Investigation 3, 4		
	Bits and Pieces III: Investigation 1, 2, 3		
	Prime Time: Investigation 1, 2, 3		

Chapter 3 *Guess the Function* Algebra		Variables and Patterns: Investigation 3	Say It with Symbols: Investigation 1
		Moving Straight Ahead: Investiga- tion 1, 2, 3	Thinking with mathematical models Investigation 1, 2
Chapter 4 *Cats and Birds* Reasoning and Problem Solving	Prime Time: Investigation 1, 3	Moving Straight Ahead: Investigation 2, 3	The Shapes of Algebra: Investigation 2
		Variables and Patterns: Investigation 3	Say It with Symbols: Investigation 2, 3
Chapter 5 *SKUNK* Probability	How Likely Is It?: Investigation 2, 3	What Do You Expect?: Investigation 1	
Chapter 6 *Scaling Up!* Measurement– Ratios and Proportions	Shapes and Designs: Investigation 1	Stretching and Shrinking: Investigation 1, 2	
		Comparing and Scaling: Investigation 1, 4	
Chapter 7 *Archimedes' Puzzle* Geometry	Shapes and Designs: Investigation 1, 4		
	Covering and Surrounding: Investigation 1, 3		

Correlation with Glencoe/McGraw-Hill: Math Connects: Concepts, Skills and Problem Solving Course 1, 2, 3			
Supporting English Language Learners in Math Class, Grades 6–8	*Math Connects: Course 1 Grade 6*	*Math Connects: Course 2 Grade 7*	*Math Connects: Course 3 Grade 8*
Chapter 2 *Secret Number Puzzles* Number and Operation	Chapter 3: Operations with Decimals	Chapter 5: Applying Fractions	
	Chapter 4: Fractions and Decimals		
	Chapter 5: Operations with Fractions		
Chapter 3 *Guess the Function* Algebraic Reasoning	Chapter 1: Algebra: Number Patterns and Functions	Chapter 1: Introduction to Algebra and Functions	Chapter 1: Algebra: Integers
		Chapter 3: Algebra Linear Equations and Functions	
Chapter 4 *Cats and Birds* Math Reasoning and Problem Solving	Chapter 12: Algebra: Properties and Equations	Chapter 3: Algebra Linear Equations and Functions	Chapter 8: More Equations and Inequalities
Chapter 5 *SKUNK* Probability	Chapter 7: Percent and Probability	Chapter 9: Probability	Chapter 12: Probability
Chapter 6 *Scaling Up!* Ratio and Proportion	Chapter 6: Ratio, Proportion, and Functions	Chapter 6: Ratios and Proportions	Chapter 4: Ratios and Similarity

Chapter 7 *Archimedes' Puzzle* Geometry	Chapter 9 Geometry: Angles and Polygons	Chapter 10: Polygons	Chapter 7: Measurement: Area and Volume
	Chapter 10: Measurement: Perimeter, Area, and Volume	Chapter 11: Measurement: Two- and Three- Dimensional Figures	

Correlation with Prentice Hall: Mathematics Course 1, 2, 3			
Supporting English Language Learners in Math Class, Grades 6–8	*Mathematics Course 1 Grade 6*	*Mathematics Course 2 Grade 7*	*Mathematics Course 3 Grade 8*
Chapter 2 *Secret Number Puzzles* Number and Operation	Chapter 1: Whole Numbers and Decimals	Chapter 1: Decimals and Integers	Chapter 2: Rational Numbers
	Chapter 11: Integers	Chapter 2: Exponents, Factors, and Fractions	
		Chapter 3: Operations with Fractions	
Chapter 3 *Guess the Function* Algebraic Reasoning	Chapter 3: Patterns and Variables	Chapter 4: Equations and Inequalities	Chapter 1: Integers and Algebraic Reasoning
		Chapter 9: Patterns and Rules	Chapter 11: Functions
		Chapter 10: Graphing in the Coordinate Plane	
Chapter 4 *Cats and Birds* Reasoning and Problem Solving	Chapter 12: Equations and Inequalities	Chapter 4: Equations and Inequalities	Chapter 6: Equations and Inequalities
	Chapter 3: Patterns and Variables	Chapter 9: Patterns and Rules	Chapter 11: Functions
		Chapter 10: Graphing in the Coordinate Plane	

Chapter 5 *SKUNK* Probability	Chapter 10: Exploring Probability	Chapter 12: Using Probability	Chapter 10: Probability
Chapter 6 *Scaling Up!* Ratio	Chapter 7: Ratios, Pro- portions, and Percents	Chapter 5: Ratios, Rates, and Proportions	Chapter 4: Applications of Proportions
Chapter 7 *Archimedes' Puzzle* Geometry	Chapter 8: Tools of Geometry	Chapter 7: Geometry	Chapter 7: Geometry
	Chapter 9: Geometry and Measurement	Chapter 8: Measurement	

Correlation with Holt McDougal: Mathematics Course 1, 2, 3			
Supporting English Language Learners in Math Class, Grades 6–8	Mathematics Course 1 Grade 6	Mathematics Course 2 Grade 7	Mathematics Course 3 Grade 8
Chapter 2 *Secret Number Puzzles* Number and Operation	Chapter 1: Whole Numbers and Patterns	Chapter 3: Applying Rational Numbers	Chapter 2: Rational Numbers
	Chapter 3: Decimals		
	Chapter 5: Fraction Operations		
Chapter 3 *Guess the Function* Algebraic Reasoning	Chapter 2: Introduction to Algebra	Chapter 1: Algebraic Reasoning	Chapter 1: Principles of Algebra
			Chapter 3: Graphs and Functions
Chapter 4 *Cats and Birds* Reasoning and Problem Solving	Chapter 13: Functions, Equations, and Inequalities	Chapter 12: Multi-Step Equations and Inequalities	Chapter 11: Multi-Step Equations and Inequalities
Chapter 5 *SKUNK* Probability	Chapter 12: Probability	Chapter 11: Probability	Chapter 10: Probability
Chapter 6 *Scaling Up!* Ratio	Chapter 7: Proportional Relationships	Chapter 4: Proportional Relationships	Chapter 5: Ratios, Proportions, and Similarity

Chapter 7 Archimedes' Puzzle Geometry	Chapter 8: Geometric Relationships	Chapter 8: Geometric Figures	Chapter 7: Foundations of Geometry
	Chapter 10: Measurement: Area and Volume	Chapter 9: Measurement: Two-Dimensional Figures	Chapter 8: Perimeter, Area, and Volume

Teaching Math to English Learners 1

Consider the following scenario. Early one Monday morning, a group of seventh-grade math students in Linda Escamilla's first-period class is preparing for the day's lesson. At one table, Halat takes out her notebook and the small dictionary that has become her constant companion since beginning school in the United States a few weeks earlier. She is used to needing a dictionary on occasion. After all, in Iraq her teachers used Arabic to conduct lessons instead of the Kurdish she spoke at home. Although she studied Arabic at the mosque, some of the words used in her school classes were unfamiliar. Halat eagerly wonders what the class will be doing today. She is happy to be in school again after the long months in the refugee camp in Jordan, where she began to wonder if she would ever realize her dream of studying hard to become a pediatrician. She likes her new school, although it has taken some time to get used to things. Back in Iraq, her teachers primarily lectured, and the girls in her class did not often talk together. Here it seems that the teacher talks very little. However, she is getting used to conversing with the other girls and boys in her group, and some of them have even begun to learn a few Arabic words.

Javier and Bao place their backpacks near the wall, playfully shoving each other as they return to their seats next to Halat. The boys have known each other since fourth grade, when they were in the same small group that met with Mr. Mendoza, the English as a Second Language (ESL) teacher, several times a week. Although they had attended the same elementary school since kindergarten, Javier had been in bilingual classes off and on, so they didn't meet until upper grades when they began the ESL group together. Javier liked math. It had always been one of his favorite subjects and he especially liked working with the cubes or other materials that his teachers set out. However this year, he was beginning to change his mind. He found himself becoming sleepy when the teacher gave the class problems to read. The words just didn't make sense, even though he knew he could say most of them aloud. Bao, on the other hand, had never liked math very much. He decided he just wasn't good at it the way some people are. He particularly disliked the worksheets his sixth-grade teacher had sent home nearly every night with lots of story problems. Bao's parents spoke only Vietnamese, and although they tried, they were not able to help him often with those problems. He was even having more trouble understanding when his parents tried to explain some of the computation problems, too. Lately, he realized he was beginning to forget words in Vietnamese at times.

As the class gets underway, Bao looks at the clock. The students are taking an unusually long time this morning to settle in. Bao estimates that it won't be long until the 50-minute period will be over and it will be time to pack up his things again. He catches Javier's eye, points to the clock, and both boys give a thumbs-up sign.

Seated on the other side of Halat, Hugo also anxiously awaits the day's activity. Like Javier, Hugo has always loved math, and he excelled in math back home at school in Mexico. When he arrived in school in the United States in fifth grade, he was surprised to find that the students did not know how to do some of the problems he completed with ease. Even though he had been in school here a short time, he had made rapid progress in English in his bilingual classroom. When his teacher realized how quickly and accurately he completed his math lessons, she began to let him try more advanced problems in a math book written in Spanish. That makes him very happy, because if he is going to become an engineer like his uncle back in Mexico, he knows he is going to need to learn a lot of math. The only thing Hugo dislikes about math these days are those times when he has to work with other students. He hopes today isn't going to be one of them. He grows tired of the ways that Bao and Javier often play around, for example, and thinks that he would learn a lot faster if he could work by himself.

The remaining two girls at the table, Andrea and Kristin, also take out their notebooks and pencils. Andrea leans forward, her eyes scanning the board for instructions for the day's work. Like Hugo, she has always found math easy, and this year is no exception, so far. Learning English, too, had come easily for her. Although her family immigrated to

New York City when she was a young child, Andrea has always heard both English and Spanish at school and at home, and she even began her school years in a bilingual kindergarten in Puerto Rico. In fact, Andrea knows that many of her teachers this year in seventh grade do not even realize that she speaks Spanish. Sometimes she has begun to worry lately, however, when she finds herself unable to express her ideas in English as well as she knows she would be able to do in Spanish. Andrea is a very lively and outgoing girl. She becomes particularly frustrated when she senses that her English-speaking friends don't always understand her when she explains a math problem. She is even beginning to wonder if she really understands the problems herself.

Kristin, seated next to Andrea, slouches in her seat. Kristin is the lone member of the group who is a native English speaker. Like Javier, Kristin always loved math in elementary school. This year, however, she, too, has begun to dread math class, even though sometimes she is not sure why she feels that way. Usually, she understands what she is supposed to do, and on occasion is excited when she solves a complicated problem that stumps some of her friends. Yet she often feels embarrassed when she has to speak in class, and sometimes she fumbles when pronouncing some of the longer words. She finds herself nervously hoping that today will not be one of those days.

If you are a middle school math teacher, it is likely that you recognize aspects of this scenario from your own experience. Adolescent students bring a variety of skills and experiences to the mathematics classroom. The ways in which they learn and see themselves as students are influenced by factors ranging from the instructional practices of their elementary school teachers, their linguistic and experiential backgrounds, the goals they and their families have set for their futures, and the opportunities they have had to acquire academic language in English, or the kind of language that is used in secondary school-content classrooms and textbooks.

In addition, adolescent students are grappling with the development of their own identities at a time when peer relationships become even more important. Although they may be unable to articulate or even be fully aware of their perceptions, many students may begin to experience a host of societal pressures. These include the often-unspoken expectations of their teachers and their peers based on their gender, ethnicity, and individual personalities as well as on the socioeconomic status and educational backgrounds of their families. Within this complex landscape, students' facility with academic English plays a critical role. Language is intricately tied

> Language is intricately tied to students' sense of self as well as to the ways in which they are perceived by others. These perceptions influence adolescent students' engagement in mathematics.

to students' sense of self as well as to the ways in which they are perceived by others. These perceptions influence adolescent students' engagement in mathematics, as the opening scenario illustrates. Access to academic English also clearly impacts students' opportunities for conceptual development in middle school settings where content instruction occurs in English. Although all these factors affect native English-speaking students (like Kristin in our scenario), students for whom English is a second (or third) language rely on school to develop both content understanding and academic English. For this reason, attention to language in the math classroom is helpful for all students, but is critical to the success of English learners.

> Achievement data show that the performance of ELs in mathematics actually decreased between 2007 and 2009 (National Assessment of Educational Progress 2009). This inequity is of grave concern. . . .

Like most teachers, you have probably seen the numbers of English learners (ELs) increase at your school. It is also likely that the majority of these students are struggling with the content demands of mathematics for a variety of reasons. Although the overall math achievement of middle school students has improved steadily during the past few years, the same cannot be said for ELs. In fact, achievement data show that the performance of ELs in mathematics actually decreased between 2007 and 2009 (National Assessment of Educational Progress 2009). This inequity is of grave concern, especially given the critical importance of mathematics to students' future academic success and life chances. It is an issue that can be addressed if teachers provide well-designed linguistic and conceptual support for their students.

Why should math teachers address English language development (ELD) during precious instructional time? After all, in most secondary schools across the United States, ELD has its own class period. And content-area teachers have learned strategies for helping ELs understand their lessons. Isn't the incorporation of visuals, the use of manipulatives, and a conscious effort to read word problems or other written materials aloud sufficient to address the needs of these students?

ELs do need to learn the content of their mathematics courses, but learning is mediated through language—in our case, the English language. Every part of learning is dependent upon language, from the arousal of curiosity, to the teacher's explanation of a concept, to the formation of an understanding and the verbalization or written expression of that understanding. Along the path from curiosity to demonstrated understanding, a learner—any learner—needs to clarify her developing understanding, test hypotheses, and solicit confirmation of her thinking. All these activities are conducted through the medium of language.

Because of the importance of language in mathematical reasoning, the instructional strategies presented in this resource foster deeper understanding for native English speakers as well as for ELs. However, although the strategies are helpful for students who are proficient in English, they are essential for ELs. When a student is carrying out intensive cognitive work in a second language, limitations in language can lead to limitations in opportunities to learn. Therefore, the more linguistic support given to ELs in math class, the sooner they can enter and appreciate the world of mathematics, along with their native English-speaking peers.

This resource is intended to assist middle school math teachers in helping their students accomplish two goals: to develop proficiency in English and to develop mathematical understanding. To that end, the lessons in this resource seek to amplify rather than simplify the role of language in math class. The lessons and vignettes show different ways that teachers can explicitly structure experiences so that all students, especially ELs, can engage in conversations about math in English that promote better understanding of the content being taught.

To accomplish these goals, it is important for teachers to be aware of the factors that contribute to ELs' success in mathematics. These include the backgrounds and experiences that adolescent ELs bring to the classroom, how middle school-age students acquire a second language, the challenges ELs face when learning mathematics, the determination of the linguistic demands of a math lesson, and specific strategies and activities that simultaneously support learning English and learning mathematics with understanding.

> The lessons in this resource seek to amplify rather than simplify the role of language in math class. The lessons and vignettes show different ways that teachers can explicitly structure experiences so that all students, especially English learners, can engage in conversations about math in English that promote better understanding of the content being taught.

The Research: Backgrounds of Adolescent English Learners

There are approximately five million English learners enrolled in public schools in the United States (National Clearinghouse for English Language Acquisition 2010). That is more than 10 percent of the school population. In some states, ELs represent a far larger portion of the school population. In California, for example, more than 25 percent of students are ELs (California Department of Education 2008–2009). Texas, New York, Florida, Illinois, and Arizona also have substantial numbers of students who are learning English as a new language. In some states, the school population of ELs is not relatively as large, but the percent increase in recent years is significant. In the southern United States, for example, the EL population in schools has increased more than 400 percent during the past 10 years (National Clearing-house for English Language Acquisition 2010).

What is more, approximately one-third of all ELs are found in grades 7 through 12, representing the fastest-growing segment of the total population (National Center for Education Statistics 2005). Students in secondary school have far less time to acquire the kind of academic English necessary for success in content classrooms while simultaneously learning new content.

The profiles of secondary school ELs vary in the time they have been in the United States as well as in the amount and quality of schooling they have received. The educational backgrounds of ELs range from recent arrivals with little or no schooling to those whose educations may have been interrupted, like Halat. Still others, like Hugo, enter U.S. schools with a high degree of literacy in their native language. Some students, many of whom have benefited from bilingual education in elementary school, may have acquired enough proficiency in English to be reclassified as fully English proficient, like Andrea, and yet may still struggle with acquiring the more advanced academic language necessary for them to reach their full conceptual potential. And there are those students whose families have been in the United States for one or two generations but who have not yet acquired enough English to be proficient in academic settings. In fact, the majority of secondary ELs in many states have been in U.S. schools for more than six years, like Javier and Bao in the opening scenario. For example, in nearly one-third of California schools, as many as 75 percent of EL students could be called "long-term ELs" (Olsen 2010). Similar data have been reported from other states with large EL populations, such as New York and Texas. The situation of these students is particularly critical as they enter secondary school with academic deficits and without achieving full English proficiency. ELs are disproportionately represented in dropout rates between tenth and twelfth grades.

A variety of factors contribute to the amount of time it takes for individual ELs to develop academic language proficiency. These factors include the types of school programs in which they have been enrolled and whether they have received any specialized language instruction at all. Many ELs whose progress stalls at an intermediate proficiency level have experienced inconsistent or weakly implemented ELD programs. ELs are enrolled in different types of programs in school, depending on the resources and philosophies of the state or district in which they are educated. Some middle school students may have been educated in elementary school in states where bilingual education is offered in a student's primary language as well as English. Well-designed bilingual programs allow students to continue their conceptual growth and literacy skills in their primary language while adding English. When children are provided an education in their first language, they receive two benefits: (1) they pick up academic knowledge and (2) they acquire literacy skills. Both the knowledge and the literacy skills students develop in their first language help ELD and transfer across languages to facilitate learning of new content (Goldenberg 2008). Teachers of English to speakers of other languages see the maintenance and promotion of students' native language as an important part of effective education for students who are learning English (Teachers of English to Speakers of Other Languages 2006).

In locations where bilingual education is unavailable for various reasons (no teachers speak the students' language, or district or state policies restrict bilingual education, for example), elementary school ELs are placed in English-only classrooms, and in some schools or districts they may receive ELD as part of the school day. Some districts offer newcomer programs for recent immigrants to help them learn some basic survival English and become better acquainted with American culture.

The length of time English language learners have been in the United States and the kinds of educational support they have received affect their progress in acquiring English. In addition, any instruction, including math, that is delivered in English affects students' ELD. Many ELs may arrive in middle school mathematics classrooms with a solid foundation in content and then learn they need to transfer that content to a new language. However, many other ELs, especially those who have not had the opportunity to acquire academic English as well as mathematics knowledge in well-designed instructional programs, may become discouraged.

> Middle school math teachers who are able to assist adolescent English learners learn both language and content play a crucial role in helping these students develop confidence in their own abilities and a positive mathematics identity (Anderson 2007).

Such students may adopt the notion that they "aren't good" at math or other academic subjects. Interviews with struggling secondary English language learners suggest that patterns of disengagement and disinterest begin around fifth grade (Olsen 2010). Middle school math teachers who are able to assist adolescent ELs learn both language and content play a crucial role in helping these students develop confidence in their own abilities and a positive mathematics identity (Anderson 2007).

The Research: English Language Development in the Content-Area Classroom

Considering the importance that acquiring English has on learning in the content areas, instruction that combines ELD and math instruction should be based on sound theoretical principles of how students acquire a second language as an outcome of schooling. Dutro and Moran (2003) discuss the differences between theories that posit that a second language can be best acquired through meaningful interaction (Krashen and Terrell 1983) and those that call for a greater role for direct instruction (McLaughlin 1985). Dutro and Moran (2003) argue for a balance between these two theories, stating that "a comprehensive theory of classroom instruction should incorporate both informal and formal language-learning opportunities" (228).

> Instruction that combines English language development and math instruction should be based on sound theoretical principles of how students acquire a second language as an outcome of schooling.

Fillmore and Snow (2000) echo this idea by explaining that certain conditions must be present for students to be successful in learning English in school. They state that ELs must interact directly and frequently with people who are expert speakers of English, which mirrors the natural process of language acquisition. However, if that condition is not met for any reason, then direct instruction in English is essential for language learning. Therefore, regardless of students' primary language or school experience, they need systematic, direct instruction for learning. Furthermore, this instruction needs to be embedded in a natural, meaningful context with many opportunities for practice. The lessons in this resource were developed to include both informal and formal language-learning opportunities in math class.

Another aspect of instruction for ELs is that teachers need to use strategies that provide students access to grade-level content in mathematics, and that help them acquire the sophisticated vocabulary and language structures required in that academic setting. This focus on English as a language, not just as a means of instruction, should be at the forefront of teachers' thinking when planning a lesson. In other words, when we teach math to English language learners, we are also teaching English, not just teaching *in* English. Dutro and Moran (2003) have called this teaching of language prior to content instruction *frontloading*. Dutro, in conjunction with the California Reading and Literature Project (2003), developed frontloading approaches for language arts curricula in California. We offer here an approach to frontloading English academic language in the secondary math classroom.

> When we teach math to English language learners, we are also teaching English, not just teaching *in* English.

The Challenge: Developing Academic English Language in Middle School

Many educators share the misconception that because it uses symbols, mathematics is not associated with any language or culture and is ideal for facilitating the transition of recent immigrant students into English instruction (Garrison 1997). To the contrary, language plays an important role in learning mathematics (National Council of Teachers of Mathematics 2000). Teachers use language to explain mathematical concepts and to carry out math procedures. While solving problems in mathematics, we often use specialized technical vocabulary (*equation, congruent, decimal, integer*). Researchers of mathematical learning have found that students deepen their understanding of mathematics by using language to communicate and reflect on their ideas, and cement their understanding. Classroom talk causes misconceptions to surface, helping teachers recognize what students do and do not understand. When students talk about their mathematical thinking, it helps them improve their ability to reason logically (Chapin and Johnson 2006, Cobb et al. 1997, Khisty 1995, Lampert 1990, Wood 1999). Classrooms that invite and support ELs in using language to become full participants in a mathematical community of practice have been shown to be particularly effective for teaching both content and language at the secondary level (Faltis and Coulter 2008).

> Many educators share the misconception that because it uses symbols, mathematics is not associated with any language or culture and is ideal for facilitating the transition of recent immigrant students into English instruction (Garrison 1997).

The challenge of teaching math to ELs lies not only in making math lessons comprehensible to students, but also in ensuring that students have the language needed to understand instruction and express their grasp of math concepts both orally and with written language. As mentioned, ELs have the dual task of learning a new language and content simultaneously. For this reason, "it is critical to set both content and language objectives for [English language learners]. Just as language cannot occur if we only focus on subject matter, content knowledge cannot grow if we only focus on learning the English language" (Hill and Flynn 2006, 22).

ELs are faced with some common obstacles when learning math. One challenge they face is unknown or misunderstood vocabulary. For example, they can become confused during a discussion if the mathematical terms have different meanings in everyday usage, as *even*, *odd*, and *function*. They may also be confused if the same mathematical operation can be signaled with a variety of mathematical terms, such as *add*, *and*, *plus*, *sum*, and *combine*. A word such as *left*—as in "How many are left?"—can be confusing when the directional meaning of the word is most commonly used in everyday English. The words *sum* and *whole* can also cause confusion because they have nonmathematical homophones (*some* and *hole*).

A second obstacle is an incomplete understanding of syntax and grammar. For example, math questions are often embedded in language that makes the problems unclear or difficult to comprehend even when the mathematical content is not especially complex. Consider the following problem:

> *Samuel bought 3 bags of oranges with 7 oranges in each bag.*
> *How many oranges did he buy?*

This word problem uses both the past and present tense of the irregular verb *to buy* in one question, which may cause difficulty for an English language learner, depending on the student's English language proficiency and native language background. Consider another problem:

> *Lisa gave a total of 12 treats to her cats.*
> *She gave her large cat 2 more treats than she gave her small cat.*
> *How many treats did she give to each cat?*

Here, students need to understand or figure out the meanings of words such as *total* and *treats*. They also need to understand words that convey a mathematical relationship such as *more . . . than*. In addition, students need to infer that Lisa has only two cats.

ELs typically experience difficulty understanding complex and abstract written instructions included in textbooks, as well as word problems, even relatively simple word problems such as those just analyzed. These difficulties increase throughout elementary school as textbook language and word problems become more linguistically and conceptually dense (Cummins 2004). Difficulty with grammar, syntax, and vocabulary lies in both understanding math instruction and having the ability to engage in discussions about math.

> Difficulty with grammar, syntax, and vocabulary lies in both understanding math instruction and having the ability to engage in discussions about math.

Many teachers now use strategies to help middle school students understand the content in their math lessons. Scaffolds for learning may include manipulatives, visuals, and graphics. These supports are all essential for building a cursory understanding of math concepts, but they may not provide enough linguistic support for them to discuss their thinking, which would lead to a deeper understanding of content. For example, let's say that a student's understanding of polygons is based on a two-column chart with drawings that distinguish polygons from shapes that are not polygons. After the chart is put away, the student may not have internalized enough of the linguistic elements of the lesson to be able to continue his learning in subsequent lessons on polygons. Having the language to talk about math concepts is crucial to developing an understanding of those concepts.

Classroom discussions about math have been shown to deepen students' conceptual understanding. These discussions are a critical aspect of the development of language and content, providing a setting for ELs to negotiate meaning in daily instructional interactions (García 2003). However, if the language needed to engage in these discussions is not made explicit, ELs are less likely to benefit from mathematical discussions and can fall further behind their peers. Students need to learn not only important mathematical vocabulary and the grammatical forms for expressing ideas but also need to have opportunities for practice with the ways in which words are used and pronounced (Scarcella 2003). Adolescent students are particularly sensitive to the linguistic judgment of their peers, and support for the development of ELs' oral language development is an often-overlooked area in content-area classrooms (Gibson, Gándara, and Koyama 2004).

The challenge for teachers is to focus on math concepts *and* the academic language that is specific to mathematics. Teachers must be cognizant of the linguistic demands of their lessons and how they will address those demands explicitly during instruction so that ELs can fully participate.

The Challenge: Determining the Linguistic Demands of a Math Lesson

Before providing specific support for ELs in mathematics, we first need to consider the linguistic demands of a math lesson. This involves determining what academic language students will need to understand and use, and knowing how much of the English language students are capable of understanding and producing.

Social or conversational language is the language that students use in familiar, face-to-face situations. Many middle school-age ELs will have developed a fairly high degree of social language, which can lead teachers to assume that these students understand more than they do. Social language is different than academic language, which includes knowledge of technical and less frequently used vocabulary, and ways of speaking English that are not usually heard or used in everyday conversation. The academic language of mathematics includes specialized vocabulary (*polygons, sides, vertices, corners, open, closed, straight, curved*), and the language structures and grammar needed to use the vocabulary (*The* shape *is not a* polygon *because it has* curved sides *and it is* open).

> Social language is different than academic language, which includes knowledge of technical and less frequently used vocabulary, and ways of speaking English that are not usually heard or used in everyday conversation.

The publishers of math textbooks and curriculum materials often make note of the academic vocabulary being introduced in a particular lesson. Frequently, however, there is no direction provided, either to the teacher or to the students, on how to use the new terms correctly. Just because an EL is told the meaning of a new word does not mean that she can construct a coherent sentence (thought) using that term. Simply knowing the term does not allow the learner to use it to express or develop understanding or learning related to the concept. For example, an EL might be taught the definition of the term *polygon*, but that does not mean he can draw conclusions, either orally or in writing, about a particular shape and determine whether it is a polygon. And if the EL cannot construct the sentences necessary to talk about particular figures, how will the teacher know what the student has learned?

After teachers have identified what academic language students will need to know and understand in a particular math lesson, they can then plan strategies for supporting students' ability to use the language to conduct mathematical discussions in English. To provide appropriate support, teachers must be aware that there are varying levels of proficiency with language acquisition.

Given that middle school math teachers may have a wide range of proficiency levels in their classes, from beginning ELs to fully proficient native English speakers, it can be overwhelming to figure out how to meet the needs of all their students in one math lesson. In this resource, we illustrate lessons that help teachers provide differentiated language instruction within one math lesson, rather than separate lessons for varied language proficiency levels. It is important, then, for math teachers to know their students' levels of English proficiency. Descriptions of the levels of English language proficiency differ from state to state. In California, for example, the CELDT (California English Language Development Test) identifies the levels as beginning, early intermediate, intermediate, early advanced, and advanced. In the state of Washington, the levels of English language proficiency are beginning, advanced beginning, intermediate, advanced, and transitional. In Illinois, the levels are described as follows: beginning, developing, expanding, and bridging.

In this resource, we provide language supports for students at two broad proficiency levels: (1) those who are beginners, or newcomers to English, and (2) those students who are at intermediate and advanced English proficiency levels. What's important is that teachers recognize that there *are* different levels of English language proficiency, and that the kind of support they give to students often depends upon how much of the second language students are currently capable of understanding and producing.

> What's important is that teachers recognize that there *are* different levels of English language proficiency, and that the kind of support they give to students often depends upon how much of the second language students are currently capable of understanding and producing.

The Action: Using Specific Strategies and Activities That Simultaneously Support Learning English and Learning Math

There are a variety of effective strategies and activities that teachers can use in a lesson that will help all students, particularly English language learners, understand math content and develop English language skills. The use of gestures, manipulatives, charts, and graphs, for example, helps students understand the math content when it is being taught in English. Other strategies and activities, such as using sentence frames (e.g., *This is a _____. It is/has _____.*) and allowing time for class discussions, provide students with the support and the opportunity to talk about their mathematical ideas in English, and to use actively the language of mathematics.

Although using the following strategies and activities in a math lesson can benefit all students, it is essential for ELs. The strategies are divided into sections according to their purpose in the middle school math classroom:

✦ Strategies that make content accessible
✦ Strategies that provide opportunities for students to communicate mathematical understanding
✦ Strategies that support student communication

Strategies That Make Content Accessible

✦ Activate prior knowledge.
✦ Make manipulative materials available.
✦ Connect symbols with words.
✦ Provide visuals.
✦ Pose problems in familiar contexts.
✦ Elicit nonverbal responses (e.g., thumbs-up or thumbs-down).
✦ Demonstrate and model.
✦ Modify teacher talk and draw attention to key concepts.
✦ Recast mathematical ideas and terms.
✦ Use native language as a resource.

Activate Prior Knowledge
Prior knowledge provides the foundation for interpreting new information and enables all students, especially ELs, to make inferences about the meanings of words and expressions to which they may not have been exposed before. The more connections we can make to students' experiences, interests, and prior learning, the more relevance math is likely to assume in students' minds and lives. Making instruction relevant is particularly critical for middle school students as they begin

to consider the importance of mathematics in their everyday life as well as in their future aspirations, at the same time that the curriculum becomes increasingly complex and abstract.

Make Manipulative Materials Available

Manipulatives serve a variety of purposes and are important tools that can make math content comprehensible to ELs. Manipulatives provide the means for students to construct physical models of abstract mathematical ideas, they build students' confidence by giving them a way to test and confirm their reasoning, they are useful tools for solving problems, and they make learning math interesting and enjoyable. Manipulatives can also facilitate effective communication by providing a referent for talking about mathematical ideas (Hiebert et al. 1997).

Connect Symbols with Words

When strategies for solving problems are described, write and point to the symbols you use (such as $<$, $\sqrt{}$, %), stressing the terms in English and providing students with an opportunity to pronounce the words as appropriate.

Provide Visuals

Visuals enable students to see a basic concept much more effectively than if we rely only on words. Among the visuals we use to present math content are pictures and photographs, real objects, graphic organizers, drawings displayed for the whole class to see, and charts.

Pose Problems in Familiar Contexts

When a problem is embedded in a familiar context, ELs have an easier time understanding the problem's structure and discussing how to solve it.

Elicit Nonverbal Responses

Nonverbal responses (such as a thumbs-up or thumbs-down) help teachers check for understanding without requiring students to produce language. ELs can participate and show that they understand a concept, or agree or disagree with someone's idea, without having to talk. This is especially important for students whose comprehension of English is more advanced than their ability to produce the language orally or in writing.

Demonstrate and Model

When teachers model their thinking aloud or demonstrate an example of how to do an activity in a clear and explicit manner, it helps ELs visualize and comprehend what to do.

Modify Teacher Talk and Draw Attention to Key Concepts

Reducing the amount of teacher talk, using a variety of words for the same idea, and exaggerating intonation can help ELs attend to important ideas more easily. You may also find it useful to slow the rate of your speech, to articulate clearly, and to use gestures to illustrate explanations, directions, and vocabulary when possible.

Recast Mathematical Ideas and Terms

Mathematics has many linguistic features that can be problematic for ELs. Use synonyms strategically so that students are exposed to key math vocabulary, such as *exponent, factor, integer,* but can also access important concepts. Keep in mind that using too many terms simultaneously can confuse ELs, particularly those at the beginning proficiency level.

Use Native Language as a Resource

Teachers who know the native language of their students can preview and review vocabulary in the native language. Teachers can also ask students to help others in the class who share a common language by asking them to translate, define, or clarify English terms. In addition, students who speak the same languages can collaborate at times in the native language during partner talk or group work, particularly when drawing upon prior knowledge or clarifying explanations. It is important to ensure that ELs have many opportunities to interact with English-proficient peers in math class so that they extend their grasp of the language for academic and social purposes. However, maximizing such opportunities does not need to preclude allowing students to draw upon a wide range of linguistic resources to advance their understanding of math concepts.

In addition, if the students' native language shares cognates with English, these cognates can be pointed out and used to help students understand both key vocabulary terms and other important words used in academic settings. Cognates are words that share the same linguistic origins and therefore are very similar in spelling, pronunciation, and meaning in two languages. For example, *function* and *función* are English and Spanish cognates. For cognates to be useful, students must know the meanings of the words in their primary language. Lists of cognates are available from a variety of sources. We recommend starting with *The ESL Teacher's Book of Lists* (Kress 1993).

Strategies That Provide Opportunities for Communication

✦ Facilitate whole-class discussions.
✦ Allow for small-group discussions.
✦ Utilize partner talk.
✦ Ask for choral responses from students.

Facilitate Whole-Class Discussions
During a whole-class discussion, the teacher should do more than deliver information or quiz students. Rather, effective whole-class discussions provide students with an opportunity to engage in sustained reasoning. The teacher can facilitate and guide, and the focus is on student thinking (Chaplin, O'Connor, and Anderson 2003).

Allow for Small-Group Discussions
In a small-group discussion, the teacher typically gives students a question to talk about among themselves, in groups of three to six. The teacher circulates, listening in on discussions, asking questions, and assisting when indicated. It is helpful to arrange the room so all members of the group can see and hear each other clearly.

Utilize Partner Talk
During partner talk, the teacher asks a question and then provides a minute or two for students to put their thoughts into words with a peer. Partner talk allows more students to participate in classroom discussions, and encourages active listening. ELs, in particular, may find it useful to write or draw their ideas briefly before engaging in partner talk. The use of sentence frames and vocabulary banks can be helpful in this endeavor.

Ask for Choral Responses from Students
When teachers ask students to repeat a word or phrase, students are exposed to new vocabulary. Although this practice may not seem challenging, ELs in particular benefit from the opportunity to hear and practice correct pronunciation, syntax, and grammar. Providing these opportunities for students to acquire phonological and grammatical as

well as conceptual understanding of academic vocabulary helps ELs build the confidence they need to engage in partner talk, small-group interaction, and whole-group discussion. This experience is especially helpful for adolescent ELs who may be sensitive to perceived or real negative linguistic judgments from their peers.

Strategies That Support Communication

- Create vocabulary banks.
- Use sentence frames.
- Ask questions that elicit explanations.
- Design questions and prompts for different proficiency levels.
- Use prompts to support student responses.
- Foster a positive learning community and a safe atmosphere.
- Practice wait time.
- Consider language *and* math skills, as well as social factors, when grouping students.
- Rephrase strategies and ideas.

Create Vocabulary Banks
Charts that contain key math vocabulary and phrases are helpful references for ELs when discussing or writing about their math thinking, especially if the words are accompanied with diagrams, examples, or illustrations.

Use Sentence Frames
Sentence frames serve a variety of purposes. They provide the support ELs need to participate fully in math discussions, they contextualize and bring meaning to vocabulary, they provide a structure for practicing and extending English language skills, and they help students use the vocabulary they learn in grammatically correct and complete sentences. Because they have opportunities to practice using the frames to express their mathematical thinking, students will also apply the use of the frames to writing.

Ask Questions That Elicit Explanations

Asking good questions can prompt ELs to discuss their thinking and elaborate on their ideas. Ask questions that elicit more than a yes-or-no response, such as these:

✦ What do you think the answer will be? Why do you think that?
✦ What is this problem about?
✦ What's the first thing you'll do to solve the problem?

Design Questions and Prompts for Different Proficiency Levels

Questioning students lets teachers know what students have learned and it can also identify areas of misconception. Answering questions allows students to test, confirm, or modify their own understandings. None of these goals can be met unless the questions are structured in a way that produces a response from the students. The following are examples of questions and prompts we use to support students at different proficiency levels.

Beginning Level ELs are not always able to answer the questions posed to them, especially when questions are open-ended. A teacher can provide support and improve participation of students with lower levels of English proficiency by using a prompt that requires a physical response:

✦ Give a thumbs up when you find a pattern.
✦ Point to the polygon.

Teachers can also ask a question with a yes-or-no answer:

✦ Is integer A larger than integer B?

When asking short-answer questions, the teacher can build the answer into the question for additional support:

✦ Is this a right triangle or a scalene triangle?
✦ Is the answer a negative number or a positive number?
✦ Should we divide or multiply?

Intermediate and Advanced Levels Students with intermediate and advanced levels of proficiency need less support to understand and respond to questions from the teacher, but carefully crafted questions can improve the quality of both their responses and their

Instead of asking an intermediate-level student, *"How did you solve the problem?"* you might phrase your question this way: *"What did you do first, second, and third to solve the problem?"* The second question models the structure of a well-crafted answer. . . .

English. For example, instead of asking an intermediate-level student, *"How did you solve the problem?"* you might phrase your question this way: *"What did you do first, second, and third to solve the problem?"* The second question models the structure of a well-crafted answer: *"First I decided which part of the picture I wanted to measure. Then, I measured the head of the figure. Finally, I tried different ratios."* Compare that with the response more likely from the first question: *"I measured."* Students with advanced fluency can respond to prompts and questions that are even more open-ended, such as *"Describe to me the steps you used to solve the problem and explain how you used them."*

Use Prompts to Support Student Responses
Prompts can help ELs learners get started when responding to a question.

✦ You figured it out by . . .
✦ It is a polygon because . . .
✦ First you simplified the fraction, and then . . .

Foster a Positive Learning Community and a Safe Atmosphere
Creating an environment in which students feel comfortable taking risks to express their mathematical thinking is essential for all students so they will come to see themselves as "good at" math. A safe atmosphere encourages students to view mathematical mistakes as opportunities for learning. Although the creation of a positive learning community assists all students in developing conceptual understanding and positive math identities, such an environment is particularly critical for ELs, who must seek to understand unfamiliar ideas, and to make their own ideas understood, in a language they don't yet dominate. The role of teaching academic language vocabulary and functions in math class is to provide a scaffold for ELs so they can express their understanding. Mistakes such as incorrect grammar should not inhibit the recognition of good mathematical thinking.

Practice Wait Time
After asking a question, it is helpful to wait for a while before calling on a volunteer. This practice gives all students, especially ELs, time to process the question and formulate a response.

Consider Language and Math Skills, as Well as Social Factors, When Grouping Students
There are times when grouping students with like abilities in math makes sense, especially when those students are all struggling with the

same concept or skill. Most of the time, however, students benefit from working in groups with peers who have varying skill levels.

ELs also benefit from working in groups in which students have different levels of English language competence. In addition, middle school teachers may find it helpful to allow students to choose their own partners or small groups at times, or to assign same-sex pairings. Whatever grouping strategies are used, it is critical for teachers to set clear expectations for student interaction and to monitor talk to ensure that all students have the opportunity to engage in mathematical conversations. Monitoring student interaction is especially important at the middle school level for a variety of reasons. Students may have come to expect that math class will primarily involve silent completion of individual seatwork and may be unsure of how to engage in talking about math. Adolescents are naturally sociable, and without a clear set of guidelines for discussion, talk can easily stray from the topic at hand. Providing students with engaging problems that elicit an authentic desire to communicate fosters effective conversations about mathematics, along with appropriate linguistic scaffolds such as sentence frames and vocabulary banks that facilitate participation.

Rephrase Strategies and Ideas
Rephrasing is when the teacher or a student explains a strategy or an idea, in English, that someone else has shared. Rephrasing allows ELs another opportunity to make sense of an idea. When students rephrase another student's idea or strategy, it helps clarify their thinking and cement their understanding.

2 Secret Number Puzzles

COMMON CORE STATE STANDARDS

Grade 6: The Number System

Compute fluently with multidigit numbers and find common factors and multiples.

- Fluently divide multidigit numbers using the standard algorithm.
- Fluently add, subtract, multiply, and divide multidigit decimals using the standard algorithm for each operation.
- Find the greatest common factor of two whole numbers less than or equal to 100 and the least common multiple of two whole numbers less than or equal to 12. . . . . Apply and extend previous understandings of numbers to the system of rational numbers.

Grade 7: The Number System

Apply and extend previous understandings of operations with fractions to add, subtract, multiply, and divide rational numbers.

- Apply properties of operations as strategies to add and subtract rational numbers.
- Solve real-world and mathematical problems involving the four operations with rational numbers.

Overview

In this lesson students work on solving secret number puzzles from clues presented by the teacher. They use their knowledge of basic arithmetic operations and number sense to discover the number or numbers that meet the specific criteria for the secret number. While they work to discover the secret number, students are engaged in problem solving, including making reasonable estimates and understanding relationships among numbers.

Math Goal: Students will use their understanding of numbers, operations, and number systems to discover the "secret number" from clues given to them.

Language Goal: Students will explain orally and in writing how they used the clues to find the secret number.

Adapted from *Math for All: Differentiating Instruction* by Linda Dacey and Karen Gartland (2009).

Key Vocabulary: between, clues, digit

Operations: add, subtract, multiply, divide

For more on determining key vocabulary, see page 180.

Number Values: ones, tens, hundreds, thousands versus tenths, hundredths, thousandths

Materials:

✦ Paper to record and solve problems

Sentence Frames

For more on creating sentence frames, see page 175.

Beginning

> *The secret number could be _____.*

Intermediate/Advanced

> *I think the secret number could be _____, because _____.*

> *I know the secret number is _____, because _____.*

> *I know that _____, so the secret number could be _____.*

> *I know that _____, so the secret number is _____.*

Secret Number Puzzles: Part 1

Luz Chung greeted the students in Ms. Escamilla's seventh-grade pre-algebra class. The room of 34 students was comprised of a diverse mix of native English speakers, ELs, and ELs who had been reclassified as fluent English proficient. In addition, students also had different prior experiences in mathematics and were at a variety of math proficiency levels. Luz knew that the varying levels of proficiency in English and in math could present her with many challenges, and that she would have to be very intentional and strategic in her instruction to ensure that she met the varied needs of the students with whom she would be working.

Introducing Academic Language

"Today we are going to be solving problems to get to a secret number," Luz told the class. The students' curiosity about the math lesson was piqued, because it was presented as a game. This type of lesson format can be motivating to students.

Luz prompted the students to think about what they do to solve a puzzle. By tapping their prior knowledge about solving puzzles, Luz immediately made the content more accessible.

"What do you need to do to solve a puzzle?" Luz asked the class. She then told them to take some think time before responding. A number of students suggested ideas for solving puzzles and Luz recorded them on chart paper.

"Use strategy," Minh said.

"What do you mean by strategy?" Luz probed, looking for Minh to expand on her response. Luz takes advantage of opportunities to push students to explain their thinking. She knows that by having students verbalize their thoughts, it gives them a chance to clarify their ideas and it gives her an opportunity to assess their under-standing.

"A way to put it together," Minh replied.

"Find clues," Luis said.

"What are clues?" Luz asked.

Lacey stated, "Something to figure out something else."

"Ways to help you solve a problem," Daniel said.

Su expanded on that idea by saying, "Information that tells you what you are trying to find out."

"So clues give us hints about what we are trying to find out," Luz paraphrased.

Restating or paraphrasing gives ELs a second chance to hear and process the ideas that have been shared. It gives students more than one opportunity to access and understand concepts, especially if the initial explanation is confusing or unclear.

"Are you ready for your first number puzzle?" Luz asked the class.

"Yes!" the students voiced enthusiastically.

After prompting the students to get out a piece of paper and a pencil, Luz referred back to the list of strategies the class had constructed about solving number puzzles. She reminded them that they could use any of the ideas listed on the chart paper to help them. Adolescent ELs benefit from having written directions or text to refer back to if they aren't able to process all the oral language that was used during a lesson.

Luz revealed the first clue, written on a separate piece of chart paper, to the students like this:

Clue 1: The number has 3 digits and is between 408 and 450.

Luz asked students if they knew the academic term *digits*. She added it to a vocabulary bank. Students volunteered a number of responses.

"Digits are like the numbers in your zip code," Katrina explained.

Jazmin added, "You also have digits in your area code. There are three."

Luis, a student for whom Spanish is his first language added, "Digits are *dígitos*. They can mean your fingers and numbers." Luis knew the cognate (words that share a Latin root and are similar in two languages) for digits in Spanish and this helped him understand the academic term *digits* in English. When teachers are aware of and use cognates during instruction in English, it can be a very powerful and effective strategy for ELs.

When Luz felt confident that the group understood the meaning of *digits*, she read the clue aloud to the students and asked them to give her some possible answers to the number puzzle based on the first clue.

"Who can share a number *between* four hundred eight and four hundred fifty with three *digits*?" Luz asked.

Luz asked the students to think silently of some possible answers to the number puzzle. After some quiet think time, Luz elicited some ideas.

"It could be four hundred nine, four hundred ten, four hundred eleven," Lacey suggested.

"It's greater than four hundred eight and less than four hundred fifty," Su replied.

"Correct, Su. The number is bigger than four hundred eight and smaller than four hundred fifty," Luz responded.

Luz restated Su's idea using synonyms for the academic terms *greater than* and *less than*. By using everyday language during her math instruction, Luz provides access for students who aren't yet proficient with some academic terms.

Luz reminded the students that they could not use 408 or 450 because the clue said that the secret number was *between* those digits. Clarifying this term was critical to being able to solve the number puzzle. Luz took the time to model what *between* meant. Luz recorded the word *between* on the vocabulary bank.

At this time, Luz introduced the first sentence frame to help students justify their thinking.

"It is important for us to explain or justify why we think certain numbers could be the secret number. Here is a sentence frame to help you explain yourself." Luz placed the first sentence frame on the board:

> *I think the secret number could be _____ because _____ .*

Luz modeled how to use the frame to express her thinking. She said, "I think the secret number could be four hundred thirty because it is between four hundred eight and four hundred fifty and it is a three-digit number."

She asked for a student to volunteer to use the frame to give another possible answer to the number puzzle.

Daniel volunteered, "I think the secret number could be four hundred sixteen because it would be possible."

"What do you mean that it would be possible?" Luz probed.

"It is possible because it matches the clues," Daniel said.

Luz pushed Daniel to be more precise in his explanation, "How does it match the clues?"

Looking back at the board with the written clues, Daniel explained, "It has three digits and it is between four hundred eight and four hundred fifty."

"Right. Remember that the clues give you ideas to what the possible number is. We have to be sure the use them to figure out the secret number," Luz replied.

Luz called on Jessica. "I think the secret number could be four hundred twenty-seven, because it is a number between four hundred eight and four hundred fifty," Jessica replied.

Luz prompted the students to nod in agreement if the number suggested was in fact a number that fit the criteria. Nonverbal responses, such as nodding or giving a thumbs-up to demonstrate agreement, are effective ways to engage ELs in discussions.

Luz directed the students to turn to a partner to share a possible secret number and to use the clues and the sentence frame to help them justify their ideas. Luz knows that for students to internalize new language, they need structured opportunities to practice the new linguistic structures. When she was confident that the students were making plausible guesses based on the first clue, she presented the next one to the class.

> Luz knows that for students to internalize new language, they need structured opportunities to practice the new linguistic structures.

"I heard a lot of good ideas about the secret number, but there are more clues to help you solve this number puzzle. Here is the next clue." Luz showed them this:

Clue 1: The number has 3 digits and is between 408 and 450.

Clue 2: All of the digits are even numbers greater than 2.

Although there was a lot of excitement generated by this clue, Luz wanted to ensure that the students understood it before letting them begin to make their guesses.

"What does this clue mean? What are digits that are greater than two?" asked Luz.

"Anything higher than two," Katrina said.

"Three, four, five, six, seven, eight, nine," Luis replied.

"It can't be zero, one, or two," Bryan added.

"What are even numbers that are greater than two?" Luz asked. Although Luz knew that this was familiar content for her students, she wanted to review these basic concepts to help them with their problem-solving skills and in using the academic language.

"Four, six, or eight," Kristopher suggested.

"Correct," Luz responded and wrote these digits on the board.

"Could the secret number be four hundred seventeen?" Luz prompted. "Talk with a partner about whether the secret number could be four hundred seventeen."

While circulating, Luz heard the following comments:

"It can't be four hundred seventeen, because there is a one and a seven," Su stated.

Minh said, "The clue says that the digits are greater than two and are even, so this can't be the secret number."

"Give me a thumbs-up if you agree that the secret number is not four hundred seventeen and a thumbs-down if you disagree," Luz directed the class.

All of the students gave a thumbs-up, so Luz continued with the lesson.

"I want to share with you another sentence frame to help you explain your thinking" Luz stated. She had the students chorally read the following sentence frame with her.

> I know that _____ so the number could be _____.

In order to not limit or restrict language use and to model multiple ways to express ideas, Luz often provides at least two sentence frames in each lesson.

Luz explained, "The second sentence frame is a bit different than the first one. I will model for you how to use it." Providing a model for how to use the sentence frame is essential to ensuring that students use them during the lesson.

Providing a model for how to use the sentence frame is essential to ensuring that students use them during the lesson.

"I know that four, six, and eight are even digits greater than two, so the number could be four hundred forty-four," Luz modeled.

She continued, "Talk at your tables about what the secret number could be. Remember to use the frames and the clues to talk about your thinking."

Students approached the task differently. Some started random lists of numbers that fit the clues. (See Figure 2–1.) Others took a more systematic approach to finding the possible numbers that fit the criteria. (See Figure 2–2.) Luz is cognizant to give her students opportunities to approach their work in a variety of ways. She values the problem solving and reasoning skills students develop in this type of environment.

After a few minutes, Luz called the class back together. "Who would like to guess the secret number?"

"I think the secret number is four hundred forty-six. All of the digits are greater than two. It is between four hundred eight and four hundred fifty and it has three digits," Miguel said, using the first sentence frame.

"The number is between four hundred forty and four hundred forty-eight," Jessica volunteered.

"How do you know that?" Luz asked.

"All the numbers below four hundred forty have a zero, one, two, or three, so they can't be the secret number, and the secret number

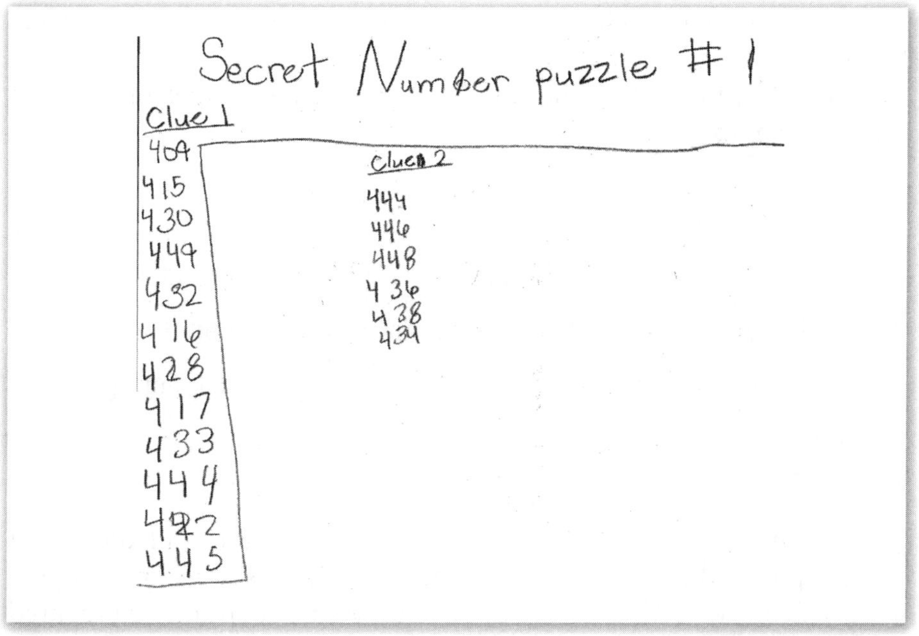

![Secret Number puzzle #1 handwritten chart]

Secret Number puzzle # 1

Clue 1
409
415
430
449
432
416
428
417
433
444
422
445

Clue 2
444
446
448
436
438
434

FIGURE 2-1. *Some students wrote numbers that didn't seem to have much organization.*

isn't higher than four hundred fifty, so it can only go up to four hundred forty-eight."

"What about four hundred forty-one and four hundred forty-two?" Francine asked.

"You're right!" Jessica said. "I forgot about the digits in the ones place. I guess it can't be four hundred forty, four hundred forty-one, or four hundred forty-two."

"What numbers could it be?" Luz probed.

"It could be four hundred forty-four, four hundred forty-six, or four hundred forty-eight," Francine said.

Luz wrote the numbers on the chart paper that Francine shared to provide a visual of the numbers. Most students recorded the numbers Luz wrote on the board on their paper.

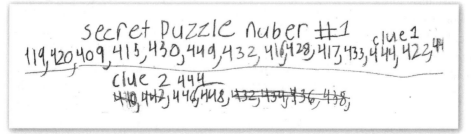

FIGURE 2-2. *Other students created lists of numbers and crossed out some based on the clues to determine the secret number.*

"We are getting closer to finding the secret number," Luz said. "Let's look at the last clue.

Luz added the third and final clue to the chart paper underneath the first two like this:

Clue 1: The number has 3 digits and is between 408 and 450.

Clue 2: All of the digits are even numbers greater than 2.

Clue 3: The sum of the first 2 digits is equal to the last digit in the number.

"With the last clue, you should be able to figure out the secret number puzzle. I don't want you to shout out the answer when you find it, but instead write down your answer on your paper and be prepared to explain how you know.

"Before you begin, who can tell me what this clue means?" Luz asked.

"That you have to add the digits," Miguel replied.

"You have to add the first two digits," Jessica clarified.

"When you add the first two digits together, the answer will be the last number," Daniel added.

"For example, if you had four hundred thirty-seven you would add the four and the three and they would equal seven," Luis said.

"You are all correct," Luz affirmed. "You will have a few minutes to solve the secret number puzzle."

> Both the mathematical and linguistic support Luz provided was essential for the participation and comprehension of her English learners, but it was also beneficial to other students in the class.

Students worked at their tables discussing possible numbers. Luz heard students talking about their thinking and using the academic language presented in the clues. Both the mathematical and linguistic support Luz provided was essential for the participation and comprehension of her ELs, but it was also beneficial to other students in the class.

As Luz monitored the students working, she noticed that many of them had narrowed down the response to the correct answer. With that information, she decided to call the class back together.

Luz said, "Raise your hand if you think you know the secret number." All the students in the classroom put a hand up in the air.

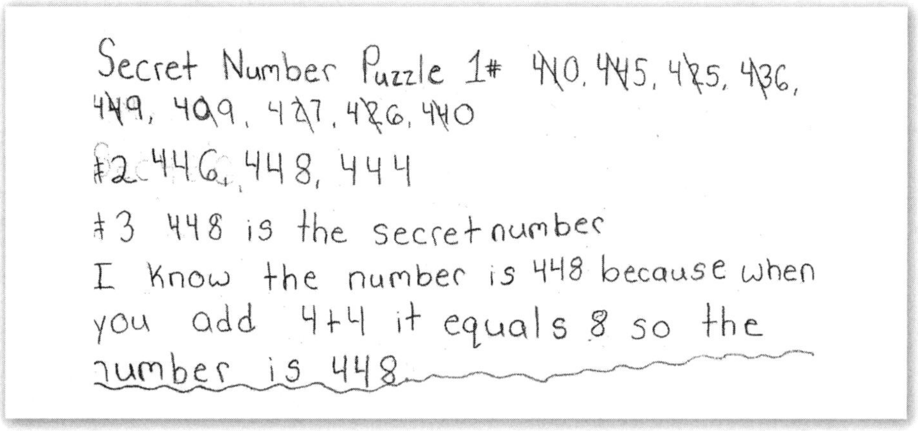

Secret Number Puzzle 1# 410, 445, 415, 436,
449, 409, 417, 486, 440
#2 446, 448, 444
#3 448 is the secret number
I know the number is 448 because when
you add 4+4 it equals 8 so the
number is 448.

FIGURE 2-3. Su explained that the secret number fits Clue 3: four plus four equals eight so the secret number is 448.

"On the count of three, we will all say the number together. One, two, three."

"Four hundred forty-eight!" the class exclaimed.

"How would you explain this?" Luz asked. "Use a sentence frame and the clues to help you."

"I know that four plus four equals eight, so the number is four hundred forty-eight," Su said. (See Figure 2–3.)

"The secret number is four hundred forty-eight because all of the digits are even and they are greater than two," Francine added. (See Figure 2–4.)

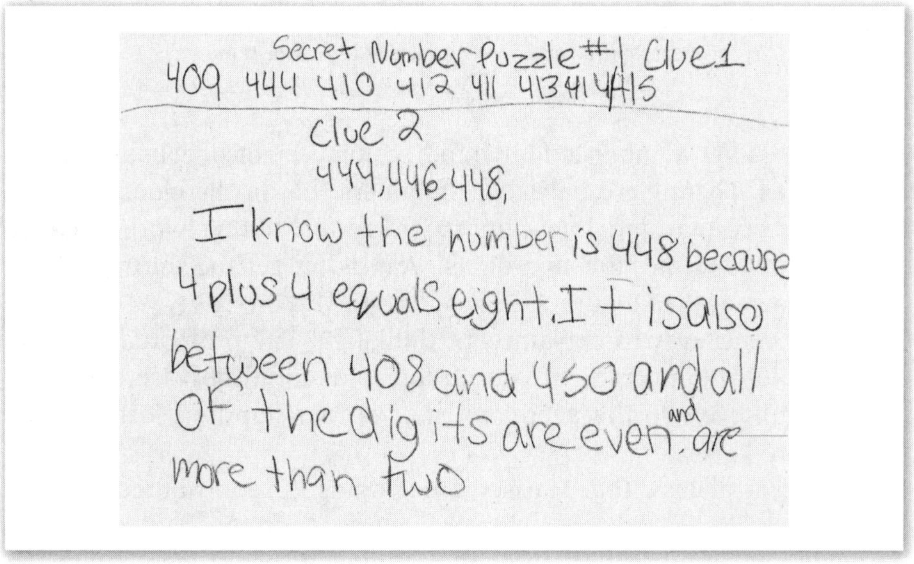

Secret Number Puzzle #1 Clue 1
409 444 410 412 411 413 414 415
Clue 2
444, 446, 448,
I know the number is 448 because
4 plus 4 equals eight. I t is also
between 408 and 450 and all
of the digits are even and are
more than two

FIGURE 2-4. Francine pointed out that the secret number fits Clue 2: all of the digits are even and they are greater than two.

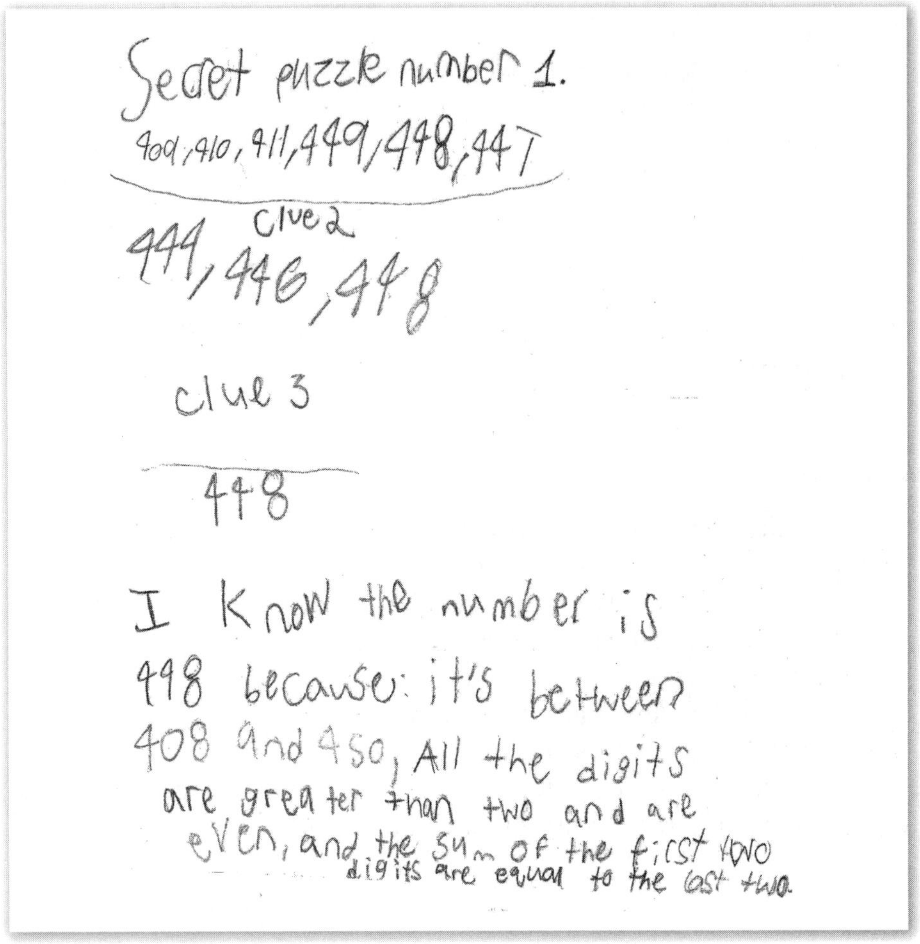

Secret puzzle number 1.

409,410,411,449,448,447

Clue 2

444,446,448

clue 3

448

I know the number is
448 because: it's between
408 and 450, All the digits
are greater than two and are
even, and the sum of the first two
digits are equal to the last two.

FIGURE 2-5. Kristopher explained how the secret number fits all the clues.

"The secret number is four hundred forty-eight because it fits all of the clues. There were only three numbers that fit the clue, and four hundred forty-two and four hundred forty-four didn't work because when you added the first two digits, you didn't get the third," Kristopher explained. (See Figure 2-5.)

"Any other way to explain your thinking?" Luz prompted.

Marisol volunteered, "If you do four plus four, they are eight and they are all even so the secret number is four hundred forty-eight." (See Figure 2-6.)

Luz was pleased that Marisol, a beginning EL, contributed her idea to the class discussion.

Luz felt confident that she had provided all her students with the support they needed to participate fully in the lesson. She concluded

Supporting English Language Learners in Math Class, Grades 6–8

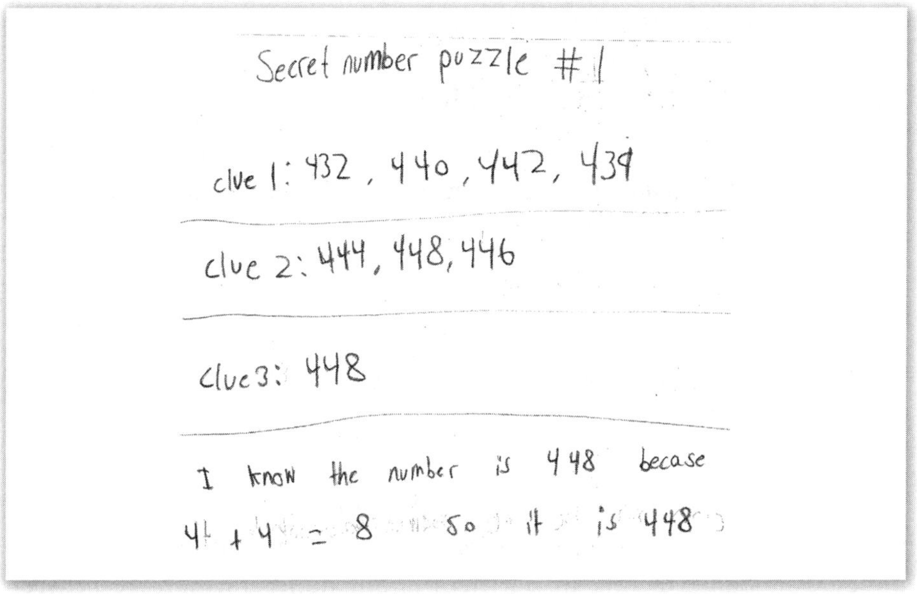

FIGURE 2-6. *The teacher was pleased that Marisol, a beginning English learner, contributed her idea to the class discussion.*

the lesson with a preview for the next day, "I hope you learned more about solving number puzzles today. Tomorrow we will solve another number puzzle, but that one will be even trickier."

Summarizing ✦ Part 1

The first part of this lesson on number puzzles was designed to frontload the language students would need to engage fully in similar types of number problems. It provided the students the vocabulary and language structures they needed to explain how they solved a number puzzle based on clues. Although the math content of Part 1 might seem too simple for grades 6 through 8, Luz recognized that by simplifying the math content, she was allowing her students a chance to be introduced to the mathematical reasoning and language required of the lesson through a less demanding math problem. In addition, students practiced the language throughout the lesson so that they might internalize and transfer the language to other math lessons.

> Although the math content of Part 1 might seem too simple for grades 6 through 8, Luz recognized that by simplifying the math content, she was allowing her students a chance to be introduced to the mathematical reasoning and language required of the lesson through a less demanding math problem.

Secret Number Puzzles

Secret Number Puzzles: Part 2

Solving a More Challenging Problem

"Ready for your first clue to solving the second secret number puzzle?" Luz asked. "Here it is." Luz revealed the first clue, written on a piece of chart paper.

> Clue 1: The number is between 400 and 410.

After reading the clue aloud to the students, Luz referenced the word *between* on the vocabulary bank she had created in Part 1. She directed students to talk in partners about numbers that are *between* 400 and 410. This step was intentionally planned to remind students of the academic vocabulary that had been previously introduced. After about 30 seconds, Luz asked the class to give her some possible answers to the puzzle based on the first clue.

"It could be four hundred one, four hundred two, four hundred three," Kristopher suggested.

"It's greater than four hundred and less than four hundred ten," Jessica replied.

"Can someone use one of our sentence frames to guess the secret number?" Luz prompted, while pointing out the sentence frames on a piece of chart paper.

> *I think the number could be* _____ *because* _____.
>
> *I know that* _____ *so the number could be* _____.

Jazmin volunteered, "I know that four hundred eight is between four hundred and four hundred ten so the number could be four hundred eight."

"I think the secret number could be four hundred two because it is between four hundred and four hundred ten," Mohammad, a beginning EL, added.

Luz was pleased that Mohammad contributed to the class discussion. ELs have more confidence in expressing their ideas orally when they have the support of vocabulary banks and sentence frames.

A few more students volunteered numbers that fit the criteria of the first clue. Luz recorded the students' guesses where everyone could see. Some students used the sentence frames to express their rationale whereas others used additional language. Luz recognizes that not all students need to use the frames to express their thinking, nor should they be required to do so. The frames are meant to be scaffolds to help students express themselves.

Luz recognizes that not all students need to use the frames to express their thinking, nor should they be required to do so. The frames are meant to be scaffolds to help students express themselves.

The students were ready for more information about the secret number.

Luz said, "You have made some good guesses, but you need more clues to help you solve the number puzzle. Here is the next clue."

Clue 1: The number is between 400 and 410.

Clue 2: The number is between 406 and 407 and has 5 places.

Miguel was curious about the type of number this puzzle asked them to find. He asked, "Do decimal points count?"

Miguel was trying to figure out whether the secret number was a whole number, because he was looking for numbers that exist between 406 and 407 that have five places. Luz was happy to hear that students like Miguel were tapping into their number sense by thinking about decimals as being actual numbers.

"Yes. The secret number could be a decimal number with decimal places. Let's take a minute to review the names of the place values for whole numbers and decimal numbers," Luz said.

Luz then proceeded to draw five short lines with a decimal point in between the third and fourth line to represent a decimal number with the five place values students would need to know to solve the number puzzle, like this:

_____ _____ _____ . _____ _____

She asked for a volunteer to give her numbers that could fit into the places she had drawn.

"Four hundred six and fifty-two hundredths," Jessica suggested.

Luz wrote the number 406.52 on the board in the correct places indicated by the lines she had drawn. As she pointed to each of the digits in the number Luz asked the students to tell her the names of the place values. When pointing at the digit 6, Luz asked the students to tell her what the name of this place value is called. Students replied in choral response, "The ones." Luz then wrote *ones* under the digit 6. She continued to do the same with all the digits, while stressing the difference between tens and tenths, and hundreds and hundredths as a way to provide some explicit instruction for her ELs on the difference in the pronunciation and spelling of the values. After this quick review of place value, Luz asked the class if someone could say aloud the name of the number using the place values.

Genesis volunteered, "Four hundred six point fifty-two."

> Luz noticed that Genesis used the correct place value of the whole number, 406, yet she used the face value of the decimal number, point 52, instead of its place value. She decided to address this common mis-use of everyday language in math class.

Luz noticed that Genesis used the correct place value of the whole number, 406, yet she used the face value of the decimal number, point 52, instead of its place value. She decided to address this common mis-use of everyday language in math class. Using the face value of a number is common, because that is how students often hear decimal numbers referred to in their everyday lives. For example, radio stations call out their channel numbers with the face value, and temperatures are read as their face value. It has become a part of the colloquial language of English to say, "point *x*" instead of using the actual value of the decimal. Luz realized that this was a misunderstanding of language that may be challenging not only for her ELs, but may, in fact, be more difficult for her native English speakers, because *point* is what they hear in their everyday lives.

"Thank you for sharing, Genesis," Luz replied. "I want to remind everyone of the proper way to read decimal numbers. I know that many times we hear people use the word *point* to describe a number with a decimal. However, in math class we want to read decimal numbers with their place value."

Referring to the number written on the board, Luz explained the correct way to read it, "Four hundred six and fifty-two hundredths."

She had the class repeat the number back to her using the correct mathematical language.

"Now that we have reviewed the place values of decimal numbers and how to say them correctly, I want you to talk with a partner and write down some possible answers to our number puzzle."

Luz overheard many students listing numbers that fit the criteria and she asked them to explain why they could be the secret number. She reminded them to use the sentence frames, clues, and vocabulary bank to assist them. After a few minutes, Luz called the class back together to record some of their ideas on the board and to have a class discussion about numbers.

"I think the secret number could be four hundred six and ten hundredths, because it has five digits and is between four hundred six and four hundred seven," Miguel volunteered. (See Figure 2–7.)

"The secret number could be any number starting with four hundred six and one hundredth through four hundred six and ninety-nine hundredths. Those would be all of the numbers between four hundred six and four hundred seven that have five places," Daniel added.

Luz decided to check students' understanding of this idea and wrote a variety of numbers on the board and asked for students to show her a thumbs-up if they fit the clues or a thumbs-down if they didn't.

"How about four hundred six and seventy-seven hundredths? Could that be the secret number?" Luz probed.

"How about four hundred seven and twenty-three hundredths?" Luz asked. "Who can tell me why this number isn't possible?"

"It's not in between four hundred six and four hundred seven," Jazmin replied.

"What about four hundred six and forty-one hundredths?" Luz asked.

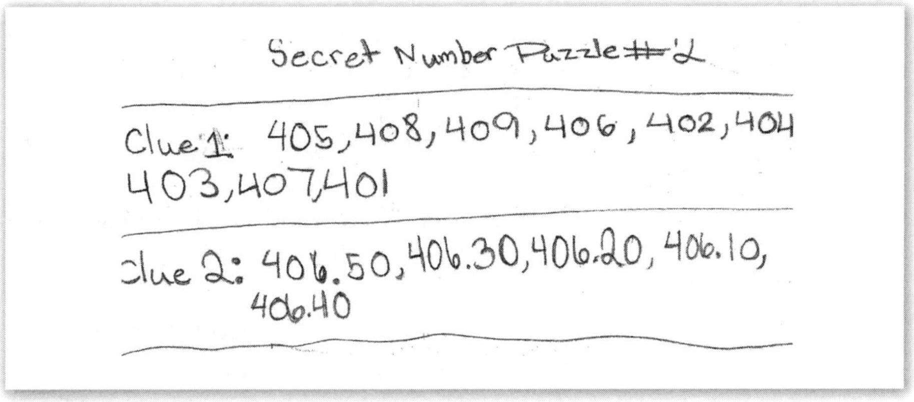
Secret Number Puzzle #2

Clue 1: 405, 408, 409, 406, 402, 404 403, 407, 401

Clue 2: 406.50, 406.30, 406.20, 406.10, 406.40

FIGURE 2-7. Miguel explained that the secret number fits Clue 2: it has five digits and is between 406 and 407.

With each new number that Luz wrote on the board, the students became more confident in understanding the range of numbers between 406 and 407. She then asked for a few more volunteers to share numbers as a final check for understanding.

Lacey suggested the number 406.86.

"I think the secret number could be four hundred six and ninety-nine hundredths," Mohammad guessed.

"Okay. You are ready for your next clue." Luz wrote it on the chart paper.

Clue 1: The number is between 400 and 410.

Clue 2: The number is between 406 and 407 and has 5 places.

Clue 3: The tenths place is bigger than the hundredths place.

"Think about what this clue means and then work with your partner to come up with some numbers that could be our secret number," Luz directed the class.

Students started conversing about the meaning of the clue. Several students generated random lists of numbers whereas others were more systematic in creating lists of numbers in sequential order that met the clue. Jesus and Kristopher made random lists of numbers with five place values; they hadn't yet discovered a systematic way to organize their thinking. Minh and Marisol first determined what digits could fit in the tenths and hundredths places by comparing the numbers to ensure that the digit in the tenths place was in fact greater than the digit in the hundredths place. (See Figure 2–8.)

"Who would like to share a possible secret number?" Luz asked the class after about five minutes of work time. "Remember to use all of the clues and the sentence frames to help you explain your thinking," Luz said. She wanted to remind the class of the language supports to help them express themselves.

"I think the secret number could be four hundred six and seventy-four hundredths because seven is greater than four," Kristopher suggested.

"I know that six is greater than zero, so the secret number could be four hundred six and sixty hundredths," Minh added.

"There are still a lot of possible secret numbers," Francine said.

"Tell me more about that," Luz prompted.

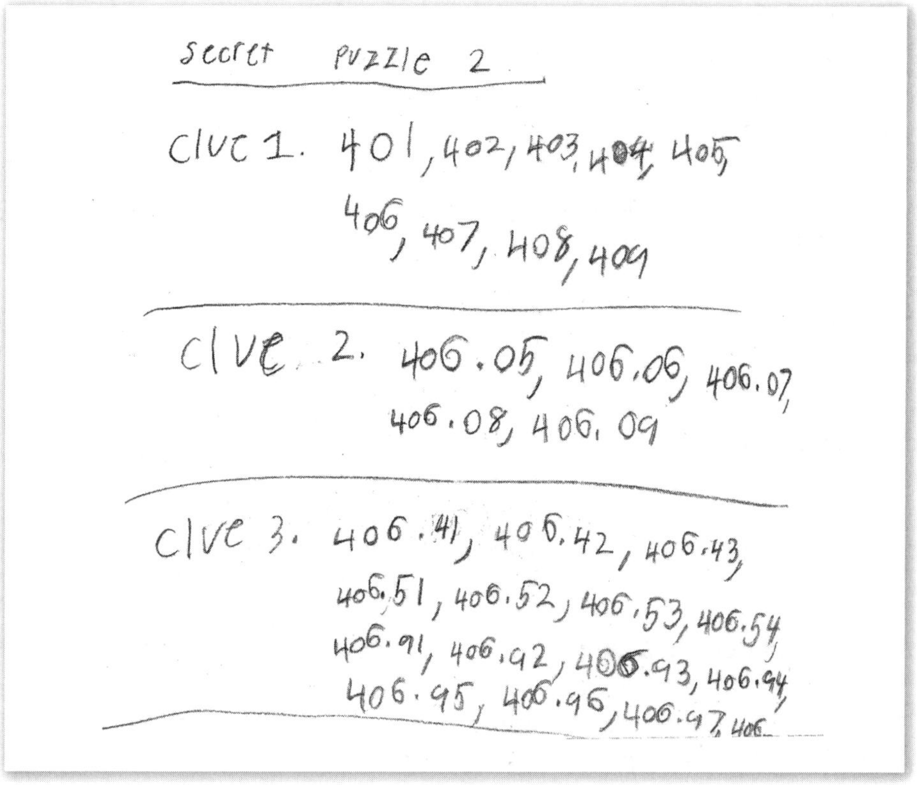

FIGURE 2-8. Minh and Marisol first determined what digits could fit in the tenths and hundredths places by comparing the numbers.

"If you compare all of the numbers from zero to nine you can see that there are a lot of combinations where the tenths digit could be bigger than the hundredths digit," Francine explained.

"Can you give me an example?" Luz probed.

"Sure. Take five," Francine began. "If five is the digit in the tenths place then there are five possible numbers that could be in the hundredths place: four, three, two, one, and zero. It is that way with all of the numbers, so there are still a lot of possible numbers that the secret number could be." As Francine was explaining her thinking, Luz recorded her thoughts on the board as a way to show the different combinations of digits for the tenths and the hundredths place. Her intentions were twofold. One was to illustrate Francine's thinking. Luz knows that ELs often need visuals to access content. In addition, Luz wanted to provide a model for students

Luz knows that English learners often need visuals to access content. In addition, Luz wanted to provide a model for students of how to organize information they were discovering in a more systematic way. The table she created served both purposes.

of how to organize information they were discovering in a more systematic way. The table she created served both purposes.

"I get it," Su said. "If you have eight in the tenths place, then any number from zero to seven could be in the hundredths place."

"Correct," Luz replied. "The next clue is going to help you figure out the numbers in the tenths and hundredths place." As she finished speaking, Luz added Clue 4 to the chart.

Clue 1: The number is between 400 and 410.				
Clue 2: The number is between 406 and 407 and has 5 places.				
Clue 3: The tenths place is bigger than the hundredths place.				
Clue 4: The tenths digit is twice as big as the hundredths digit.				

"What does this clue mean?" Luz asked. "Take some time to think about this before you respond." Luz knows that ELs benefit from additional time to comprehend material presented in their second language as well as to construct a response in that language.

Marisol raised her hand, "It means, like, double."

"Twice as big is when you have to multiply by two," Miguel said.

"It's times two. Like ten is twice as big as five," Genesis added.

"Tell me more about that," Luz probed.

"Five times two is ten, so ten is twice as big as five," Genesis explained.

"Right. Clue three said that the tenths digit was greater than the hundredths digit, and now you know that it is twice as big," Luz reminded the class. "Work with your partner to come up with some possible secret numbers."

Giving students time to work with a partner allows them to work through mathematical ideas and practice using academic language. Luz works diligently with her students throughout the year to ensure that partner talk is used as a strategy for learning and not as a time for socializing, as is all too common in middle school.

"Let's hear some of your ideas," Luz redirected the class after some partner time.

"I think the secret number could be four hundred six and sixty-three hundredths because the tenths digit is twice as big as the hundredths

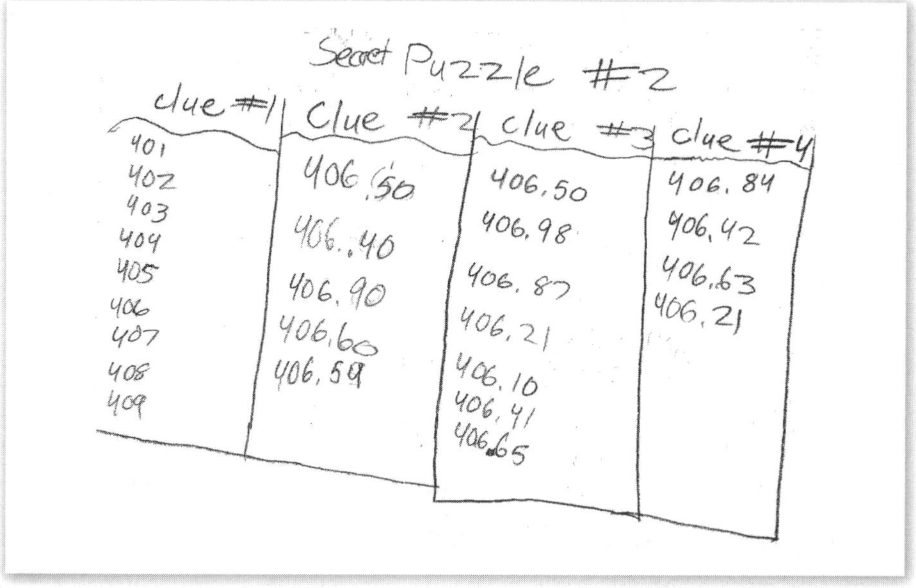

FIGURE 2-9. Bryan pointed out that the secret number fits Clue 4: the tenths digit is twice as big as the hundredths digit.

digit. I know that three times two is six, so sixty-three hundredths works," Bryan explained. (See Figure 2–9.)

"There are only four numbers that could be the secret number. They are four hundred six and twenty-one hundredths, four hundred six and forty-two hundredths, four hundred six and sixty-three hundredths, and four hundred six and eighty-four hundredths," Katrina replied.

"I agree with Katrina," Luis said. "These are the only numbers that fit the clues."

"Who can remind us of the clues?" Luz asked.

Mohammad read the clues to the class. "The number is between four hundred six and four hundred seven, the tenths is greater than the hundredths, and the tenths digit is twice as big as the hundredths digit." Although Mohammad has beginning English skills, he was able to participate in the class discussion because of the scaffold of the written clues he could refer back to.

Although Mohammad has beginning English skills, he was able to participate in the class discussion because of the scaffold of the written clues he could refer back to.

"Do the numbers Katrina shared fit all of the clues?" Luz prompted as she wrote the numbers Katrina suggested on the board. "Give me a thumbs-up if you agree."

"The numbers all fit the clues because two is double one, four is double two, six is double three, and eight is double four," Minh explained.

"'Double' is another way to say 'twice as big,' so Minh is correct," Luz replied.

"We have four possible numbers that could be our secret number. Let's see if the last clue will help us solve this number puzzle," Luz said.

Luz wrote the last clue on the chart paper.

Clue 1: The number is between 400 and 410.

Clue 2: The number is between 406 and 407 and has 5 places.

Clue 3: The tenths place is bigger than the hundredths place.

Clue 4: The tenths digit is twice as big as the hundredths digit.

Clue 5: All of the digits are different.

"In other words, none of the digits are the same," Luz paraphrased to ensure that all students, including her ELs understood the clue.

The students immediately began to eliminate the numbers that didn't fit the clue, and a buzz of excitement began to stir in the class.

"Just like before, on the count of three, we will all say the secret number together," Luz directed.

"One, two, three."

"Four hundred six and twenty-one hundredths," the class stated chorally.

"Who can explain how you know this?" Luz questioned the class.

"The number is four hundred six and twenty-one hundredths because the clues work with it, so all the digits are different," Daniel explained, using a sentence frame to help him. (See Figure 2–10.)

"I know that the secret number is four hundred six and twenty-one hundredths because it is between four hundred six and four hundred seven, the tenths digit is bigger than the hundredths digit, the tenths is twice as big as the hundredths, and all of the digits are different," Jesus replied. (See Figure 2–11.)

Jessica added, "I know four hundred six and twenty-one hundredths is the answer because they're all different digits, and that clue two said it had five places." (See Figure 2–12.)

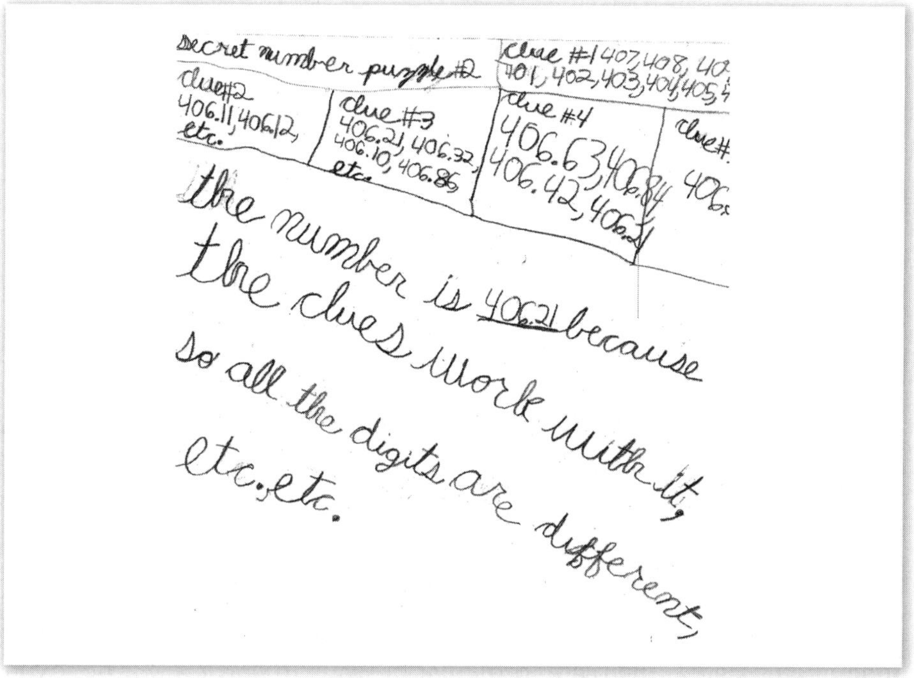

FIGURE 2-10. Daniel justified how all five clues fit the secret number.

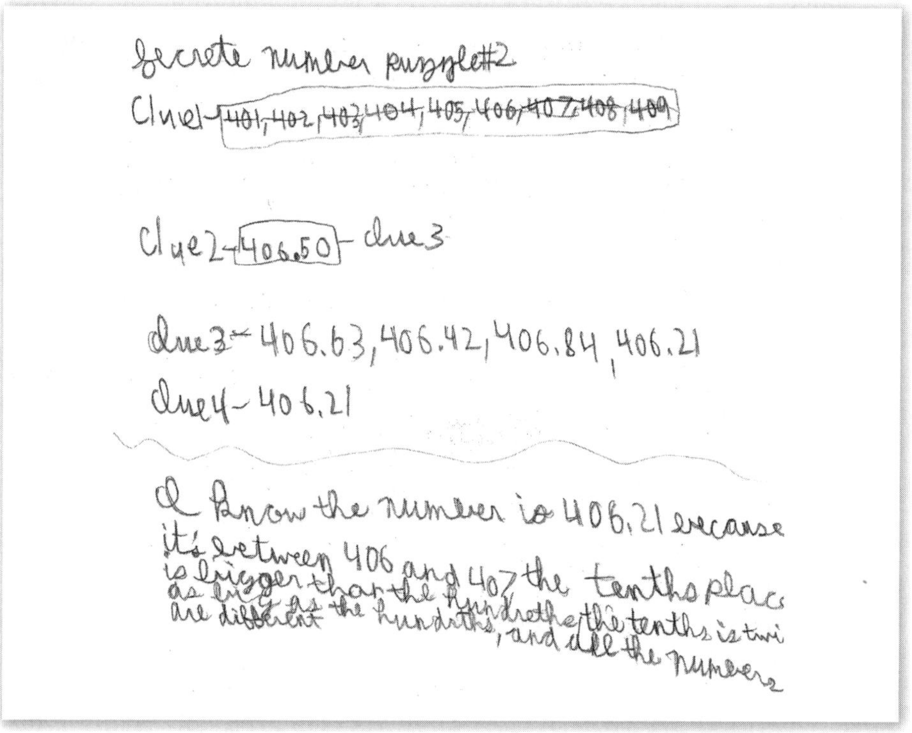

FIGURE 2-11. Jesus summarized how Clues 2, 3, 4, and 5 fit the secret number.

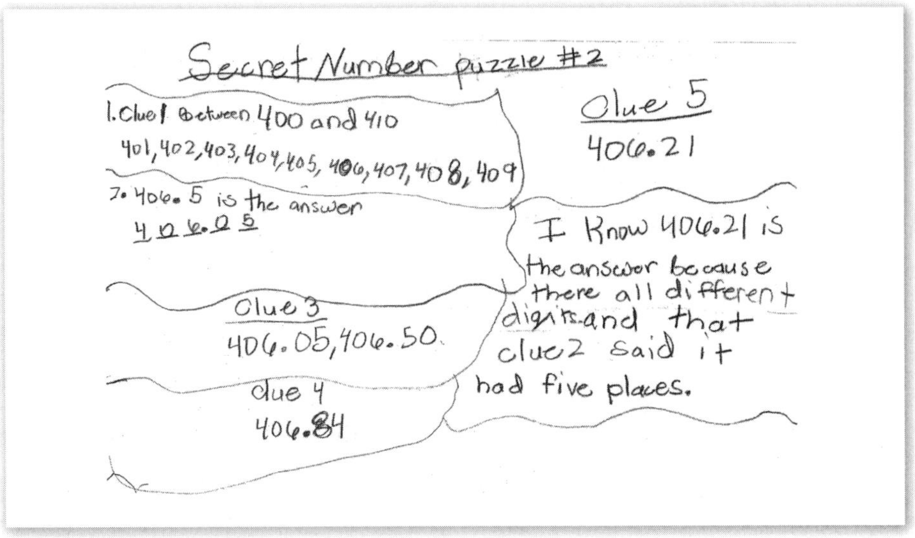

FIGURE 2-12. *Jessica focused on Clues 2 and 5 to verify the secret number.*

"You used a lot of strategies to solve the secret number puzzle today," Luz stated, referring to the list of ways to solve a puzzle. "You used the clues to solve the secret number puzzle correctly and you explained or justified your thinking. We will continue to do more types of these puzzles to help you expand your problem-solving skills in math," Luz said as she concluded the lesson.

Summarizing ✦ **Summarizing the Lesson: Key English Language Learner Strategies**

When students have the chance to engage in problem solving and to talk about their thinking, the result is a deeper understanding of math concepts as well as of English. Luz is optimistic that the problem solving and language her students practiced in this *Secret Number Puzzles* lesson not only transfers to other math lessons, but also assists students in developing their mathematical reasoning skills. During the lesson, Luz implemented a variety of strategies to help students develop number sense and mathematical reasoning.

Strategy 1: Recording Numbers and Language for the Class to Reference

One strategy Luz used was to record numbers and language on the board that students would need to solve the problems. Because the ideas were visible and clearly written, students could refer back to them to help clarify their mathematical thinking or to use a mathematical term.

Strategy 2: Using Partner Talk and Class Discussions

In addition, Luz encouraged an abundance of partner talk and class discussions to help students talk about their thinking. By using partner talk prior to whole-class discussions, Luz created a safe environment in which ELs could practice expressing themselves in English before speaking in front of the class.

Strategy 3: Anticipating Language Demands through Sentence Frames

Last, sentence frames were used as an instrumental strategy to help students partake in discussions. By providing linguistic tools such as sentence frames and vocabulary charts, Luz supported all students in using academic language regardless of their proficiency in English.

Suggestions for Extending the Lesson

Create New Secret Number Puzzle Problems

Beginning (For Lower Grades or Those Students Just Learning Number Puzzles)

+ Use only whole numbers with up to seven place values to help students with thousands, ten thousands, hundred thousands, and millions.
+ Keep the clues more direct to help students determine the correct operation. For example, use terms such as *twice as big, half as big, three times as big, greater than, sum of,* and so forth.
+ Start with only three clues and work your way up to five clues.

Beginning Examples

Secret Number Puzzle #1
Clue 1: It is a whole number with six place values.
Clue 2: It is between 500,000 and 600,000.
Clue 3: All of the digits are odd.
Clue 4: The digits in the hundred thousands and hundreds are the same.
Clue 5: The sum of the remaining digits is four.

The secret number is 511,511.

Secret Number Puzzle #2
Clue 1: The number is between 300 and 600.
Clue 2: All of the digits are greater than two and are even.

Clue 3: The digits in the ones place is the largest.

Clue 4: The digit in the hundreds place is greater than the digit in the tens place.

The secret number is 648.

Intermediate/Advanced (For Higher Grades or More Advanced Students)

✦ Use whole numbers and decimal numbers.

✦ Use a variety of operations in the clues—addition, subtraction, multiplication, and division.

✦ Represent the operations in a variety of ways—such as one-third of, two times greater than—and use them more than once in the number puzzle.

✦ Create puzzles for which there may be more than one answer. Have students write the final clue to identify one single secret number.

Intermediate/Advanced Examples

Secret Number Puzzle #3

Clue 1: The number is between 400 and 410.

Clue 2: The tenths digit is one-third the hundredths digit.

Clue 3: All the digits are different.

Clue 4: The tenths digit is one-half the ones digit.

Clue 5: There are five places in the number.

The secret number is 402.13 or 406.39 (Dacey and Gartland 2009).

Secret Number Puzzle #4

Clue 1: No digit is used more than once.

Clue 2: The number is between 6,600 and 6,800.

Clue 3: When multiplied by four, the result is a whole number.

Clue 4: The digit in the tenths place is one-fourth the digit in the ones place.

Clue 5: The sum of the digit in the hundredths place and the digit in the tens place is even.

Clue 6: There are six places in the number.

The secret number could be 6718.25, 6738.25, or 6798.25 (Dacey and Gartland 2009).

Guess the Function 3

Overview

This lesson demonstrates how to present students with a table of input and output values, then helps them to discover the function rule that works for the given values. Students test their functions on multiple values in the table to determine whether they work for all given values. They also use the function rule to determine either the output or input value, given the other value as a starting quantity.

Math Goal: Students will analyze a variety of number patterns in tables to derive the function rule.

Language Goal: Students will make hypotheses and draw conclusions orally and in writing about the function rule for a given set of variables.

COMMON CORE STATE STANDARDS

Grade 8: Functions

Define, evaluate, and compare functions.

- Understand that a function is a rule that assigns to each input exactly one output.
- Use functions to model relationships between quantities.
- Construct a function to model a linear relationship between two quantities. Determine the rate of change and initial value of the function from a description of a relationship or from two (x, y) values, including reading these from a table or from a graph. Interpret the rate of change and initial value of a linear function in terms of the situation it models, and in terms of its graph or a table of values.

Adapted from *Lessons for Algebraic Thinking* by Ann Lawrence and Charlie Hennessy (2002).

For more on determining
key vocabulary, see
page 180.

For more on creating
sentence frames, see
page 175.

Key Vocabulary: function, function rule, input value,
output value

Materials:

◆ *Guess the Function* Recording Sheets (Reproducible
3–A), 1 copy for each student

Sentence Frames

Beginning

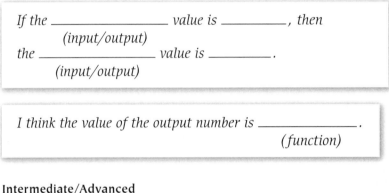

*If the _____ value is _____, then
        (input/output)
the _____ value is _____.*
        (input/output)

I think the value of the output number is _____.
                                    (function)

Intermediate/Advanced

*I know that for every input value n, the value of the
output value is _____.*
                        (function)

*I can conclude that the function is _____,
because _____.*

Guess the Function: Part 1

Luz Chung greeted the students as they entered Ms. Aguilar's eighth-grade
algebra class. Of the 29 students in the class, the majority had Spanish
as their primary language. Although most students had been receiving
instruction in English for the past four to six years, Luz knew that there
would still be the need for linguistic support during the lesson, because
it takes as many as seven years for students to become proficient in
academic language. In addition, the students had a range of proficiency
levels in math. Luz knew that she would have to be very intentional and

strategic in her instruction to ensure that she met the varied needs of the students with whom she would be working.

Introducing Academic Language

As the second-period bell rang, the students each took their assigned seat and chatted quietly with their friends. Ms. Aguilar greeted the students in Spanish, their primary language, and introduced Luz Chung as a guest teacher for the day.

Luz began, "Today we're going to solve an algebra puzzle. We're also going to have conversations about how you solved the puzzle. We're going to use tables to help us solve the algebra puzzle. Do you know what this is?" Luz held up a table with two columns for the whole class to see. One column is headed with the word *Input;* the other column displays *Output:*

Input	Output

Many students nodded in recognition of an input–output table.

"What do you do with this table?" Luz prompted.

"You have to put numbers in it," Bianca answered.

"What do we use this for?" Luz asked, narrowing her question.

"Graphing," Jorge responded.

"Tell me more about that, Jorge," Luz probed.

"You use it to find the difference between the input and the output," Jorge elaborated.

"What do you mean the difference?" Luz asked, continuing with her questioning.

"Like a pattern," Jorge stated.

"Right. You can use the input and output tables to find a pattern of the differences between the input and output values," Luz said, restating Jorge's ideas as one statement. Oftentimes ELs, especially those at the beginning levels of proficiency, find it very helpful to hear ideas restated so they have more than one opportunity to process the information that is presented orally.

> Oftentimes English learners, especially those at the beginning levels of proficiency, find it very helpful to hear ideas restated so they have more than one opportunity to process the information that is presented orally.

"We can also identify a function from an input–output table," Luz added. "Can anyone tell me what a function is?" Luz knows that tapping students' prior knowledge is effective in helping them connect their current understandings of a mathematical idea with the new knowledge that will be presented in a lesson.

Luz used chart paper hung at the front of the room to record the students' ideas. The prompt, *A function is:*, is written on it. She elicited responses to the prompt from the students.

"How it works so you can get the numbers," Hector volunteered.

"The steps so that you can get the *output* number," Denise suggested.

"Both of your ideas are correct," Luz commented. "Here is the definition from a math book." Luz showed the following piece of paper with the definition of a function from an algebra text.

A **function** is a <u>rule</u> that establishes a <u>relationship</u> between two quantities, called the <u>input</u> and the <u>output</u>.

She asked students to follow along as she read, "A **function** is a <u>rule</u> that establishes a <u>relationship</u> between two quantities, called the <u>input</u> and the <u>output</u>." Luz intentionally bolded and underlined the key academic terms she wanted students to start using during the lesson.

Luz intentionally bolded and underlined the key academic terms she wanted students to start using during the lesson.

"What is a *rule*?" Luz asked the class. She wanted to be sure that students were familiar with the meaning of *rule* in mathematics, rather than the everyday meaning of *rule*.

"Like a pattern or something you do to get the answer," Yessenia replied.

"Patterns are an important part of finding a function," Luz said, building on Yessenia's idea. She wrote the word *pattern* after the prompt, along with other ideas about functions.

"Our goal today is to guess the function, the patterns, and the relationships between numbers," Luz said, summing up the ideas that students had expressed and that she recorded. By clearly stating her objective, Luz was preparing students for their upcoming tasks.

Luz then displayed and distributed to each student a three-column table, which was a recording sheet (see Reproducible 3–1; see excerpt that follows).

Guess the Function		
Input		Output

"As I put numbers in the Input column and the Output column on my recording sheet, I want you to start thinking about a pattern, a rule, or a relationship you see. In other words, what's happening to the input and output numbers? What math operations do you think I am using to get such numbers?" (See Figure 3–1.) Luz gave the students many ways to approach the task she was asking them to complete. By using the ideas they shared at the beginning of the lesson, she was reinforcing their knowledge and encouraging connections to it.

Luz gave the students many ways to approach the task she was asking them to complete. By using the ideas they shared at the beginning of the lesson, she was reinforcing their knowledge and encouraging connections to it.

Guess the Function: Puzzle #1		
Input		Output
2		4
12		24
125		250
210		420
25		50
14		28
23		46
22		44
30		60
n		$2n$

FIGURE 3-1. As the teacher wrote the numbers in the Input and the Output columns, the teacher asked the students to start thinking about what patterns or rules they saw.

Luz added, "During the lesson, I want you to take notes on your recording sheet. When you figure out the answer, keep it to yourself. We will share our answers later in the lesson."

Luz began entering the first four input and output values on her recording sheet hung at the front of the room, using causal language to show the relationship between the input and output values (refer to Figure 3–1).

✦ *If the input value is 2, then the output value is 4.*
✦ *If the input value is 12, then the output value is 24.*
✦ *If the input value is 125, then the output value is 250.*
✦ *If the input value is 210, then the output value is 420.*

She stopped intermittently to assess students' understanding and asked them to give her a nod if they had found the pattern.

Feeling confident that students were seeing the relationships between the two values, Luz said, "Now, I will reverse the values. See if you can find the input value when I give you the output value. If you have the correct function, your answers should match mine." She recorded the following values on her chart in this order:

✦ *If the output value is 50, then the input value is 25.*
✦ *If the output value is 28, then the input value is 14.*

"Do you know the pattern?" Luz asked. Most of the students responded with a "yes."

As a final check for understanding, Luz decided to present the students with an input value and elicit the output value from them. Luz recorded 23 in the Input column of the table and asked the students for the output number.

The majority of the students responded chorally, "Forty-six."

She then placed the following sentence frame on the whiteboard:

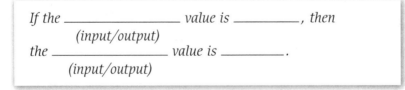

Pointing to each word and blank space in the frame, Luz modeled using the students' response. "A mathematician might say: If the input value is twenty-three, then the output value is forty-six."

To provide students, especially ELs, with more practice with academic language, Luz asked another question regarding the output values. "If the input value is twenty-two, then the output value is?"

She directed the students to check with a partner to confirm their answer using the sentence frame.

Ricardo and Denise were working as partners. Denise shared her idea, "If the input value is twenty-two, then the output value is forty-four."

Ricardo nodded in agreement.

Luz presented another problem. "If the output value is sixty, then the input value is?"

This time Ricardo told Denise, "If the output value is sixty, then the input value is one hundred twenty."

Denise disagreed. "Ricardo, Ms. Chung said that the *output* value is sixty. That means that sixty goes over here." Denise indicated the Output column on their paper.

"Oh, I get it!" Ricardo replies. "If the output value is sixty, then the input value is thirty. You have to reverse the order." Ricardo demonstrated how he used division to determine the input value when given the output value first:

Input		Output
15	30 ÷ 2	30

The partner talk served as formative assessment for both the mathematical concepts and the academic language.

As she concluded this part of the lesson, Luz felt the students had sufficient practice determining the input and output values and were now ready to discuss the function.

> The partner talk served as formative assessment for both the mathematical concepts and the academic language.

Introducing Functions

"Let's talk about how we got the input and output numbers," Luz told the class. "How did you figure out the pattern? Talk with a partner and explain what you did to get the output number. Did you add, subtract, multiply or divide?" Luz directed the students to look at the first set of values. "Talk with your partner about how using an input value of two, I got an output value of four. After you find the rule for the first row, I want you to see if your rule works for all of the different sets of values. Make sense?" Luz asked, checking for understanding.

The students indicated their understanding with a nod and Luz directed them to begin to work. While Luz circulated throughout the room, she heard a few different ideas for the rule. She knew the various ideas would provide for a rich class discussion.

After a few minutes, Luz called the class back together to share their ideas. "Let's start with the first row on the table. How did I get an output value of four?"

Monica originally thought the pattern was adding two to the input value. She volunteered, "Adding two to the input value." (After listening to her peers, however, she changed her idea.) Her paper looked like this:

Input		Output
2	2̶+̶2̶ $2 \cdot 2$	4
12	$12 \cdot 2$	24
125		250
210		420
25	$25 + 25$	50
14	$14 \cdot 2$	28
23		46

"Let's try it. If we add two to two, then it's four," Luz replied. "That rule works. Does it work with twelve?"

"No," a few students replied.

"Two plus twelve equals fourteen," Denise stated.

"That was good thinking, Monica, but the rule doesn't work for all of the input and output values," Luz replied. "Does anyone else have a rule they think works for *all* of the input and output values?" Luz asked.

David suggested, "What if we multiply by two? It works for the two and four and for the twelve and twenty-four."

"So far, so good. Take a minute and see if that rule works for the other values," Luz directed.

After a few minutes of quiet work time, Luz called the class back together to see what they had discovered.

"It works for all of them," Valeria reported.

"Correct." Luz felt confident that the students had discovered the rule for the input and output values she had provided. Her next step was to determine whether students could describe their rule using a variable.

"What if I gave you the letter n to act as our variable?" Luz asked.

Luz felt confident that the students had discovered the rule for the input and output values she had provided. Her next step was to determine whether students could describe their rule using a variable.

Luz recorded the word *variable* on the board and wrote the letter *n* next to it. She then placed another sentence frame on the board.

> *I know that for every input value* n, *the value of the output value is* _____ .

Luz went on to describe how to use the academic language presented in the frame. "For any input value *n*, I want you to find the output value for the letter *n*. Talk to your partners about how to use the variable, *n*, to write a function to match your rule. In other words, what did you do to the input value, *n*, to make the output value? Did you multiply, divide, or add? Use the sentence frame to help you describe the function."

Luz gave the students a few minutes to talk with their partner and identify the function. She also encouraged them to practice using the sentence frame in preparation for sharing with the class.

After a few minutes, Luz brought them back together and asked, "Who would like to share with us the function they identified?"

"*N* times two," Yessenia shared.

"How do you state that as a function?" Luz probed.

Valeria, Yessenia's partner, volunteered, "Two *n*."

Luz recorded Valeria's response on the board.

"Can you use the sentence frame to say that in a complete sentence, Valeria?" Luz prompted. Valeria is a very bright student at the intermediate level of English proficiency. By pushing her to use complete sentences in academic discussions, she will increase her fluency with academic discourse and vocabulary.

"I know that for every input value *n*, the value of the output value is . . . ," Valeria paused.

"I know that for every input value *n*, the value of the output value is two *n*," Luz modeled. "Does everyone see how to use the frame? You place your function in the final space of the frame. Let's try out the function two *n*. Does it work for fifteen?" Luz asked.

"Yes. I multiplied fifteen times two and it's thirty," Yessenia explained.

Luz placed the final sentence frame on the board:

> *I can conclude that the function is* _____
> *because* _____ .

"Yessenia, would you like to use the sentence frame to tell us the function you found and why?" Luz asked.

"I can conclude that the function is two n because it makes sence (sic) in the problem and because the input is times by two," Yessenia responded while she read the answers from her paper. (See Figure 3–2.)

Input		Output
2	2 + 2	4
12	12 · 2	24
125		200
210		420
25	25 + 25	50
14	14 × 2	28
23		46
56		112
32		61
15	30 ÷ 2	30
n	n + n	2n

If the _____ input _____ value is __ 15 __ , then
    (input/output)

the _____ output _____ value is __ 30 __ .
    (input/output)

I know that for every input value n, the value of the output value is _____ 2n _____ .
    (function)

I can conclude that the function is __ 2n __ because it makes sence in the problem . . . and because the input is times by 2 . . .

FIGURE 3-2. Yessenia's chart and her answers.

Having a written response prior to sharing aloud gives ELs a chance to rehearse their language before sharing in front of the class.

Other students also participated in the discussion using the sentence frames as support.

"I can conclude that the function is two *n* because two times two is four," Jorge added as he read from his paper. (See Figure 3–3.)

Input		Output
2	2 · 2	4
12	12 · 2	24
125	125 · 2	250
210	210 · 2	420
25	25 · 2	50
14	14 × 2	28
23		46
11		22
100		200
200		400
600		1200
n		2n

If the ___input___ value is ___23___, then
    (input/output)
the ___output___ value is ___46___.
    (input/output)

I know that for every input value n, the value of the output value is ___2n___.
                (function)

I can conclude that the function is ___2n___
because ___2 · 2n is 2 · 2 and it's 4___.

FIGURE 3-3. Jorge's chart and his conclusions.

"I can conclude that the function is two *n* because one *n* plus one *n* equals two *n*. That is the same as *n* plus *n*, and twelve plus twelve equals twenty-four," David explained. He wrote it this way:

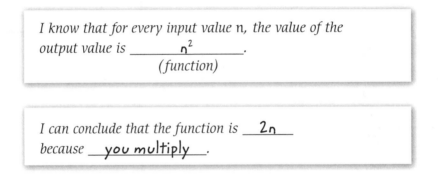

I can conclude that the function is __2n__ *because*
__$1n + 1n = 2n$__ .

"Did anyone get something different?" Luz searched the group for other ideas.

"I got *n* squared," Hector said. Hector had some misconceptions about the difference between mathematical notations, so he used both *n* squared and 2*n* to define the function:

I know that for every input value n, *the value of the*
output value is __n^2__ .
(function)

I can conclude that the function is __2n__
because __you multiply__ .

Luz recorded Hector's idea next to Denise's on the board. "We have two different functions here. Let's test them out."

The two similar-looking notations have very different meanings in mathematics, yet it is not uncommon for students to confuse the two operations. Students can become very proficient at memorizing the symbols for the operations without having a deep understanding of the concepts they represent. Luz directed the students to talk at their tables about the two different functions. After a few minutes, she called them back together to hear their ideas.

> Students can become very proficient at memorizing the symbols for the operations without having a deep understanding of the concepts they represent.

"First, let's talk about two *n*," Luz stated.

David volunteered, "Two *n* is multiplying *n* times two. If the input is twelve then we do twelve times two, which equals twenty-four."

"Correct," Luz affirmed. "How about *n* squared?"

Hector raised his hand tentatively. "I think you would have to multiply twelve times twelve, which is one hundred forty-four. *N* squared is the number multiplied by itself. That is not the same as the output value."

Luz was pleased that Hector solved the problem on his own, because this demonstrated his new understanding. However, she recognized that he needed to have many more experiences with the difference between 2*n* and *n* squared before he would internalize the concepts.

"It is easy to confuse two *n* with *n* squared," Luz reassured the class. "With practice, you will better understand the difference between the two."

Summarizing ✦ Part 1

Luz intentionally chose an easy function for this first part of her lesson. Her plan was to introduce the mathematical concepts and academic language students need to talk about functions. By initially lowering the lesson's cognitive demands, Luz allowed the students to focus their mental energy on learning the academic language. In the next part of the lesson, she posed a more rigorous problem for them to solve.

Guess the Function: Part 2

Identifying Functions

"Ready for your next problem?" Luz asked the class. "Now that you've had practice with the first function, we're going to move on to another one. We'll start with the input and output values just like the first problem. See if you can figure out what is happening to the input and output numbers. What math operations do you think I am using to get such numbers?"

Luz distributed a recording sheet to the students that was the same as that used during the first lesson (Reproducible 3-A). This table would provide the students with a written record of the input and output values, and space to try out the functions to solve the problem. Recording work on paper is helpful for all students, because they can refer back to and check their work. However, it is especially beneficial for ELs that they have a visual to connect with the oral language. In this case, as students copied the values Luz stated aloud, it helped them with the names of numbers in English.

> Recording work on paper is helpful for all students, because they can refer back to and check their work. However, it is especially beneficial for English learners that they have a visual to connect with the oral language.

At the bottom of the recording sheet, Luz had typed the sentence frames she expected students to use when discussing their work.

"Before I begin giving you the input and output values, I want you to look at the sentence frames at the bottom of your paper," Luz started. "We will be using the first sentence frame to talk about the values we discover. We will use the other two later in the problem when we talk about the pattern or function we discover." The students looked at the following sentence frames:

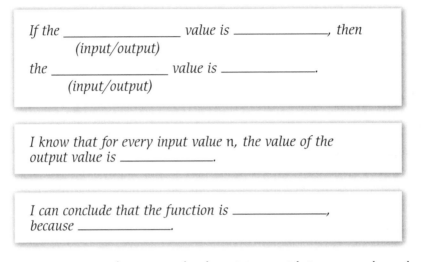

> If the _____ value is _____, then
>   *(input/output)*
> the _____ value is _____.
>   *(input/output)*

> I know that for every input value n, the value of the output value is _____.

> I can conclude that the function is _____, because _____.

"Here are your first sets of values," Luz said. Luz stated out loud the values for the Input and Output columns while she recorded them on her chart at the front of the classroom.

✦ If the input value is 3, then the output value is 7.
✦ If the input value is 5, then the output value is 13.

Input		Output
3		7
5		13

"If you see a pattern, or if you think you know what the function is, just nod your head. Don't say what it is yet," Luz reminded the class.

About half the students nodded their head in response. Luz knew that this function was more complex and that it might take more time for students to discover the pattern.

"Talk with your partner about what you know about the function from these first two sets of values," Luz directed.

Students turned to their partners and began discussing what they had figured out from the two sets of values Luz had given them.

"In the first one, three plus three is six plus one is seven," Samuel told his partner.

"In the second one, five plus five is ten plus three is thirteen," Jorge responded. "Those aren't the same patterns."

"What else could we do? How about multiply?" Samuel suggested.

"How about three times one plus four? That works for the three and seven," Jorge said.

Samuel discovered that multiplication didn't work for all the numbers and replied, "But it doesn't work for the five and thirteen." He looked at his chart:

Input		Output
3		7
5		13

The conversation between Samuel and Jorge was representative of the other discussions happening between partners. Many students had quickly figured out that this function wasn't a one-step process, but only some had it figured out after only two sets of values.

Bianca and Nadia approached the problem differently.

Bianca began, "It's not going to be two *n* like the last one."

"It seems like we need to do more than one thing to find the output value," Nadia added. "What about two *n* plus one?"

"That works for the first set of numbers, but doesn't for the next set," Bianca replied. "How about three *n*? Three times three is nine. How do we get to seven from there?"

"Subtract two!" Nadia responded. "Does it work for five and thirteen? Five times three is fifteen minus two is thirteen. I think we've got it!" Their work looked like this:

Input		Output
3	$3 \cdot 3 = 9 - 2$	7
5	$5 \cdot 3 - 2$	13

Luz called the class back together. "How many of you think you've discovered the pattern? Give me a thumbs-up if you have."

Using nonverbal responses is a way for all students to participate. Luz used the thumbs-up as a way to check in with all students to see where they were in the process of solving for the function.

Not all students affirmed that they had determined the function. Luz gave two more sets of input and output values with these directions, "I am going to give you two more sets of values. If you've figured out the function, I want you to confirm that your function works for these values as well as the others, and if you haven't figured out the function, that's okay; you can use these values to help you."

These were the two sets of values Luz provided to the class:

+ *If the input value is 20, then the output value is 58.*
+ *If the input value is 10, then the output value is 28.*

"Take a few minutes to work with your partner to test your function or to try out a new one," Luz stated.

Luz intentionally incorporates time for partner talk during her lessons, because she knows that discussions are a way to help students deepen their understanding of content and build language skills. Without this planned activity, it is easy for students to work independently and to have minimum practice with language during math class. ELs need many opportunities to communicate in their second language if they are to develop proficiency.

After a few minutes of partner talk, Luz called the class back together.

"What do you know about the function now that you have seen four sets of values?" Luz asked. "Don't tell me the function, but just tell me what you know about it. Tell me if you are adding or multiplying or other steps like that."

"We have figured out that there are two steps to this function," Elias shared.

"You have to multiply and subtract," Monica added.

"You multiply by three," Ricardo elaborated.

"You all have some good ideas," Luz said. "Anything else?"

David suggested, "You subtract by two."

"Give me a thumbs-up if you think you know the function," Luz prompted.

This time almost all the students indicated they knew the function by giving Luz a thumbs-up.

"Now I am going to give you the input value, and I want you to determine the output value. Remember to use the first sentence frame at the bottom of your paper to share your answer," Luz directed.

"The input value is ten," Luz said.

The students worked for about a minute and then Luz told them to raise their hand if they knew the answer.

Yessenia volunteered, "It's twenty-eight."

"Correct, Yessenia," Luz affirmed. "Can you use the sentence frame to say that in mathematical language?"

"If the input value is ten, then the output value is twenty-eight," Yessenia replied.

"Well said," Luz noted. "Did anyone get a different answer?"

When no one volunteered, Luz went on to the next problem. "Your next input value is nine. What is the output value?"

The students worked collaboratively to determine the output value using the rule or function they had determined. After about a minute, Luz brought the class back together.

"Who would like to share with us the output value?" Luz asked. "Remember to use the sentence frame to express your thinking." Luz knows that she needs to be consistent in her expectation for language use during math class and shares her expectation with her students.

Valeria raised her hand. "If the input value is nine, then the output value is twenty-five."

"That's correct, Valeria," Luz responded.

Based on her formative assessment, Luz felt the students were ready to talk about the function they had discovered. "You're doing a good job finding the output values for the input values. Now, let's go back to the first set of values and talk about the function. What do you think the pattern or function is for this problem? What do you think is going on with the numbers?" Luz asked the question in two ways, being sure to model academic language and everyday language, with which some of her students may be more familiar.

> "What do you think the pattern or function is for this problem? What do you think is going on with the numbers?" Luz asked the question in two ways, being sure to model academic language and everyday language, with which some of her students may be more familiar.

Denise volunteered, "It is three times three equals nine, minus two." She showed Luz her paper.

Input		Output
3	$3 \cdot 3 - 2 = 7$	7
5	$5 \cdot 3 - 2 = 13$	13
20	$20 \cdot 3 - 2 = 58$	58
10	$10 \cdot 3 - 2 = 28$	28
9	$9 \cdot 3 - 2 = 25$	25
n		$3n - 2$

Luz recorded Denise's idea on the chart at the front of the class-room in the second column between the input and output values. She wrote, $3 \times 3 = 9 - 2$.

"Does this equation equal seven?" Luz inquired.

"Yes," several students replied.

"Help me with twenty," Luz prompted the class.

Hector suggested, "It's twenty times three equals sixty, minus two is fifty-eight."

Luz recorded Hector's equation in the second column next to the twenty. She wrote, $20 \times 3 = 60 - 2$.

"Does this equal our output value?" Luz asked.

"Yes," Hector answered.

"You seem to have discovered the pattern. How do we write this as a function?" Luz continued with her questioning. "Take a few min-utes to talk with your partner to determine the function using the vari-able n to stand for the input value. Be sure to use the second sentence frame to write your function and then use the third frame to explain how you know."

Luz built in activities for both oral and written language practice in her lesson. The sentence frames supported students in using math-ematical discourse and vocabulary to talk about their understanding.

Luz gave the students about five minutes to work on this task. She was confident that all the students knew the mathematical operations to solve the problems, but she was looking to help them write the alge-braic expression. She called for the attention of the class.

"Let's see what you've come up with," Luz said. "What is the func-tion for this problem?"

Monica volunteered, "Do I use the sentence frame?"

Luz nodded in agreement.

"I know that for every input value *n*, the value of the output number is three *n* minus two."

"Do you agree?" Luz asked the class.

Several students nodded in agreement.

"Can someone who agrees tell me why that is the function? You can use the third sentence frame," Luz prompted.

Elias said, "I can conclude that the function is three *n* minus two, because you replace the *n* with the input value and you get an output." Elias read from his paper. (See Figure 3–4.)

By allowing students to construct a written response prior to sharing, it gives them a chance to collect their thoughts and craft an answer using the appropriate language.

Input		Output
3	$3 \cdot 3 - 2$	7
5	$5 \cdot 3 - 2$	13
20	$20 \cdot 3 - 2$	58
10	$10 \cdot 3 - 2$	28
9	$9 \cdot 3 - 2$	25
n		$3n - 2$

If the _____**input**_____ value is _____**3**_____, then
     (input/output)
the _____**output**_____ value is _____**7**_____.
     (input/output)

I know that for every input value n, the value of the output value is _____**3n - 2**_____.

I can conclude that the function is ___**3n - 2**___,
because ___**you replace the n with the input and**___
___**you get an output**___.

FIGURE 3-4. Elias's chart and his responses.

Input		Output
3	$3 \cdot 3 = 9 - 2 =$	7
5	$5 \cdot 3 = 15 - 2 =$	13
20	$20 \cdot 3 = 60 - 2 =$	58
10	$10 \cdot 3 = 30 - 2 =$	28
9		25
n		$3n - 2$

If the _____**input**_____ value is _____**20**_____, then
    (input/output)
the _____**output**_____ value is _____**58**_____.
    (input/output)

I know that for every input value n, the value of the
output value is _____**3n - 2**_____.

I can conclude that the function is _____**3n - 2**_____,
because ___**you first have to multiply the input**___
by 3 and then subtract 2___.

FIGURE 3–5. Nadia's chart and her responses.

"Thank you, Elias. Does anyone else have an idea?" Luz asked, encouraging others to share their rationale.

"I can conclude that the function is three *n* minus two, because you first have to multiply the input by three and then subtract two," Nadia shared. (See Figure 3–5.)

"Right. Anyone else?" Luz prompted.

Ricardo raised his hand. "I can conclude that the function is three *n* minus two, because the input is times three minus two."

"Those are all correct reasons to explain how you got the function," Luz stated. "We will continue to work on writing functions and finding the input and output values next week. I hope that today you were able to start seeing the patterns or rules between the input and output values, and make a connection to writing an algebraic expression. These

Supporting English Language Learners in Math Class, Grades 6–8

concepts are very important in algebra, so we will continue to work on this type of activity this year."

Luz collected the students' papers for review and concluded the lesson as the bell rings, indicating the end of the period.

✦ **Summarizing the Lesson: Key English Language Learner Strategies**

Luz incorporated many strategies to help her ELs fully participate in the lesson: *Guess the Function*.

Strategy 1: Creating a Table

One key strategy Luz used was creating a table to help students see the patterns in the numbers. Having their own recording sheet along with the class chart gave students different ways to access the content without relying solely on language to understand the material that was presented. The tables provided the visual support for the values in the chart and helped to show how they were changing.

Strategy 2: Using Partner Talk and Class Discussions

In addition, the use of partner talk at predetermined places in the lesson was another way to help students grasp the concepts being presented. Communication and thought were connected. By building in opportunities to discuss their evolving thoughts, students developed a deeper understanding of content. As students grappled with finding the correct equation, even in the first problem, it was through their discussions with one another and with the teacher that they were able to solve for the function. Moreover, in the class discussion, Luz was able to address a common misconception about mathematical notations. Failing to address students' misconceptions can have a profound impact on their success in mathematics.

Strategy 3: Anticipating Language Demands through Sentence Frames

Last, anticipating the language demands, both receptive and expressive, helped Luz design and implement a lesson that supported her

ELs' growing proficiency in mathematics, and also aided all learners in developing academic language in the area of mathematics. By intentionally inserting sentence frames in the lesson, students had the linguistic support to express themselves and participate in the conversations regarding the lesson. When used consistently, the sentence frames will eventually become internalized and will help students gain a stronger grasp on the language of mathematics.

Suggestions for Extending the Lesson

Expand Input and Output Values

+ Use real numbers to encourage students to think about how and why their function applies to all the numbers on the number line.
+ In addition, use negative integers as input and output values to help students review operations using positive and negative numbers.

Graphing

+ After determining the input and output values and the function, have students graph the functions. This activity extends students' understanding of functions and how they are represented in different ways. Graphing functions is a common core standard in eighth grade.
+ Use these graphs to explore *slope* and *intercept*.
+ Explore the equation of a line: $y = mx + b$

By graphing various functions, students will also review/acquire important vocabulary: *ordered pair, scale, domain, range, quadrant, axes, slope,* and *intercept*.

Create New *Guess My Function* Problems

+ Have teams of students create their own *Guess My Function* problems for other classmates or other classrooms to use.
+ As a class, or as a team, students can determine the rules for designing these problems. For example, which real numbers can be included as input and output values?

Discover Linear Functions in "Real Life"

+ Give students an example of why functions can be useful in real contexts. For example: If you pay $10 per month for your cell phone plan, and five cents per minute of usage of the monthly cost of your cell phone, how would you represent this in a linear function?
    + Let c = total monthly cost.
    + Let m = minutes used.

- Then, $c = 0.05m + 10$
- Have students come up with their own "real-life" examples of linear functions.
- Have students graph these functions, and then lead a discussion on the types of information one can infer from these graphs.

Explore Nonlinear Functions

- Use *Guess My Rule* to explore nonlinear functions (for example, quadratic, cubic).
- Lead a discussion on the differences between linear and nonlinear functions.

4 Cats and Birds

COMMON CORE STATE STANDARDS

Authors' Note: This lesson was implemented in an eighth-grade algebra class. As with all the lessons included in this book, *Cats and Birds* can be implemented in grades 6 through 8. Because this lesson focuses on problem-solving strategies that lead to algebraic reasoning, we have included the Common Core State Standards across grades 6 through 8. These are the standards that students address while working to decipher the clues for *Cats and Birds*.

Grade 6: Expressions and Equations

Apply and extend previous understandings of arithmetic to algebraic expressions. Write, read, and evaluate expressions in which letters stand for numbers.

Grade 7: Expressions and Equations

Use variables to represent quantities in a real-world or mathematical problem, and construct simple equations to solve problems by reasoning about the quantities.

Grade 8: Expressions and Equations

Analyze and solve pairs of simultaneous linear equations. Solve real-world and mathematical problems leading to two linear equations in two variables.

Overview

Cats and Birds is a problem-solving lesson that involves using clues and algebraic reasoning to find the solution to a problem. Students are initially given only one clue out of many to solve a problem. After working together for a while, students eventually realize that they have limited information and can only guess at the solution. After sharing their possible solutions, each group then receives all the clues and works collaboratively to solve the problem.

Math Goal: Students will be able to apply a variety of strategies to solve mathematical problems. They will reflect on their process of solving the problems and monitor their progress toward solving them.

Adapted from *Family Math: The Middle School Years, Algebraic Reasoning and Number Sense* by Virginia Thompson and Karen Mayfield-Ingram (1998).

Language Goal: Students will make inferences orally and in writing about the possible solutions to the math problems. They will describe their process for discovering the final solution in their small groups and with the whole class.

Key Vocabulary: altogether, clues, divisible, expression, factor, multiple, possible, solution, times

Materials:
✦ Math Vocabulary Review sheet (Reproducible 4–1A), 1 copy per student
✦ A Quick Review of Some Algebraic Expressions (Reproducible 4–1B), 1 copy per student
✦ Cats and Birds: Clues (Reproducible 4–2), 1 set of clues per group of 4 students
✦ Poster paper, 1 per group of 4 students
✦ Markers for each group of students

For more on determining key vocabulary, see page 180.

Note: For Reproducibles 4–1A and 4–1B, consider photocopying them so the recording sheet is double sided, with 4–1B falling on the back of 4–1A. For Reproducible 4–2, photocopy for each group of students and cut apart the clues in preparation for the lesson (see Part 1). Make an additional photocopy and cut apart the clues for Part 2 of the lesson. Consider mounting the clues on cardstock.

Sentence Frames

For more on creating sentence frames, see page 175.

Intermediate/Advanced

> *Our guess is that the possible number of cats is _____ and that the possible number of birds is _____.*

> *We think so because _____.*

> *The number of cats is _____. The number of birds is _____.*

> *We know this is the right solution because _____.*

Cats and Birds: Part 1

Luz Chung, the guest teacher for the day, greeted each of the eighth graders as they settled into their assigned seats in algebra class. The class was comprised of a diverse mix of native English speakers and ELs. The students were seated in tables of four, designed to promote cooperative learning and discussions. (In this particular lesson, it's ideal to have six groups—in the case of this particular classroom, we were able to place students into six groups of four—because the lesson deals with six clues. Given the complexity of the language in all the clues, consider partnering beginning and intermediate ELs with advanced ELs or native English speakers who can help facilitate receptive tasks and model language production tasks.)

The chairs at each table faced each other, with a workspace in the middle. This seating arrangement helps facilitate the collaborative work that Luz wants the students to engage in during the lesson. In addition, by facing each other, students can talk with one another more easily as they work. During her math lessons, Luz always encourages talk as a way to develop students' mathematical understanding and their use of academic language.

Introducing Academic Language

Luz first explained her objective for the lesson. "Good morning! Today we're going to be using clue cards to solve a problem. Each clue card will give us important information to find out the solution to the problem."

Before diving into the problem-solving activity, Luz knew that it would be beneficial to review the mathematical concepts students would be using to solve the problems and their corresponding algebraic expressions. In addition, Luz wanted to be sure that language wouldn't serve as a barrier to engaging in the math lesson, so she planned to spend time reviewing key mathematical terms as well. Luz saw this time as an upfront investment in preparing students for success. This step was especially important for the ELs in the class.

"There are many vocabulary words and algebraic expressions that we need to review to be able to find the solution to the problems. So, before I hand out the clues, let's review some of these important math vocabulary words and algebraic expressions."

Luz distributed a recording sheet to each student. On the front side it read "Math Vocabulary Review"; on the back side it read "A Quick Review of Some Algebraic Expressions" (see Reproducibles 4–1A and 4–1B).

Math Vocabulary Review	
Times	
Divisible	
Factor	
Multiple	
Altogether	
Expression	
Solution	

FIGURE 4-1. Math Vocabulary Review Sheet.

"Let's start with some vocabulary words," Luz said, referring students to the side of the recording sheet titled "Math Vocabulary Review."

"Go ahead and explain your understanding of these words. You may use words, pictures, or any other way to represent your thinking. Talk at your tables to come up with your ideas," Luz directed.

Prompted by Luz's instructions, students began to chat with one another about the words listed on the recording sheet. (See Figure 4–1.)

"*Times* means multiplication," Javier shared at his table.

"*Divide* is parts of a number," Araceli said.

"*Factor* is . . . I don't know that one," Eden confessed.

"Let's skip *multiple*. *Altogether* means putting things together or adding," Navid stated.

"I know the *solution* is the answer," Bethany added.

Luz listened to her students discuss their ideas about the vocabulary. She noticed that some words were easier for students to define than others. To ensure that everyone understood the meanings of the words (critical for solving the problem later in the lesson), Luz decided to have students share their definitions as a whole class. Creating shared definitions helps ELs develop their academic language.

> Creating shared definitions helps English learners develop their academic language.

As students volunteered ideas for the definitions, Luz paraphrased or synthesized their ideas, then recorded one definition on a class chart. (See Figure 4–2.) Students would be able to copy or refer to this chart during the problem-solving part of the lesson.

Math Vocabulary Review	
Times	*Multiplication*
Divisible	*Division* *Parts of a number*
Factor	*Numbers you can pull out*
Multiple	*Something times something equals* _____
Altogether	*Adding*
Expression	*Equation w/ or w/out = sign*
Solution	*Answer*

FIGURE 4-2. Teacher's Completed Whole-Class Chart.

"Now that we have reviewed some of the key words that will be part of the math problems you will solve, we also need to review some algebraic expressions," Luz explained. "As with the vocabulary words, you can use your own words or drawings to represent the expressions on the sheet."

Luz asked the students to turn over their recording sheets to the side titled "A Quick Review of Some Algebraic Expressions." (See Figure 4–3.)

Although the review of key vocabulary and expressions takes time from instruction of new content, this step is essential in providing comprehensible instruction for ELs. Without dedicating time to go over phrases and academic vocabulary, ELs may have trouble understanding the teacher's instruction.

A Quick Review of Some Algebraic Expressions	
Use your own words, draw diagrams, or give examples to explain what you know.	
Expression	This is my explanation:
There are 3 times as many apples as there are oranges.	
The total number of apples and oranges share common factors.	
The total number of oranges is a multiple of 4.	
The total number of apples is divisible by 3.	

FIGURE 4-3. A Quick Review of Some Algebraic Expressions Sheet.

Students began collaborating to create explanations of the algebraic expressions listed on their papers. Each group of students came up with different, yet correct, ways of explaining the expressions. Luz wanted the class to hear the various ways students described each mathematical expression. She called the class together for a whole-group discussion.

"As I walked around the classroom, I heard you talking about, and I saw, many different ideas for representing the expressions on your papers. I'd like for you to share your ideas so we can all see the many different ways to approach and solve similar mathematical problems."

Luz read the first expression aloud, "There are three times as many apples as there are oranges. Who can explain what this expression is telling us?" Luz looks for opportunities to encourage students to express and demonstrate their ideas in a variety of ways to promote and model flexible thinking.

"It's saying that the apples is more than the oranges," Gloria, an intermediate-level EL, read from her paper. (See Figure 4–4.)

A Quick Review of Some Algebraic Expressions	
Use your own words, draw diagrams, or give examples to explain what you know.	
Expression	This is my explanation:
There are 3 times as many apples as there are oranges.	It is saying that the apples is more than the oranges.
The total number of apples and oranges share common factors.	That the total of numbers are shared factors. 12 6 → 3 common factor 8 4 → 2 common factor 4 2 → 2 common factor
The total number of oranges is a multiple of 4.	It will help us solve the equation and get a right answer. $2 \cdot 2 = 4$ 8, 12, 16 are multiples of 4 ↑ ↑ ↑ 2 (4), 3 (4), 4 (4)
The total number of apples is divisible by 3.	Because if you times 2 into 6 you get an equal number. But if you times 2 into 5 you get an remainder, we are not trying to get a remainder.

FIGURE 4-4. Gloria is an intermediate English learner who has not yet mastered English grammar. She is inconsistent in her use of language though not shy in expressing her explanations.

Luz is always pleased when students who are not yet fluent in English participate in class discussions. She knows that ELs make progress toward language proficiency by using the English language, and by receiving feedback and instruction in how the language works.

"Correct, Gloria," Luz replied. "I'm going to write down another way of saying that in English that would be more commonly heard. I'm going to write: *There are more apples than oranges*," Luz explained. "I'd like for all of you to write this idea on your paper."

The students copied onto their papers the sentence Luz had written on her paper, which was on display for the whole class to see.

Luz makes sure that she doesn't just repeat back to students the correct way to phrase an idea in English; she intentionally demonstrates the proper English form. She doesn't want to leave it to chance that her ELs will automatically acquire the correct forms of English.

Farah, another intermediate EL in the class, volunteered to read from her paper. (See Figure 4–5.) She said, "If theres [sic] 5 oranges their [sic] is 15 apples."

"Does that make sense?" Luz asked the class, checking for understanding. The students responded with nods. She then asked, "Who would like to give us an example for the first expression?"

| **A Quick Review of Some Algebraic Expressions** ||
| *Use your own words, draw diagrams, or give examples to explain what you know.* ||
Expression	This is my explanation:
There are 3 times as many apples as there are oranges.	If theres 5 oranges there is 15 apples. $0 = 5$ $3 \cdot 5$ $a = 15$
The total number of apples and oranges share common factors.	Share some factors 4 6 They share 2
The total number of oranges is a multiple of 4.	This shows how theres 4 oranges and you multiply by 4 you get 16.
The total number of apples is divisible by 3.	10 is not divisible by 3 because there is a remainder of 1.

FIGURE 4-5. Farah is an intermediate English learner who has not yet mastered English grammar. She is inconsistent in her use of English though able to convey her mathematical reasoning.

Scott volunteered, "*y* equals three *x*. *y* equals apples and *x* equals oranges."

Luz recorded Scott's idea onto her copy of the recording sheet. She then asked the class for a thumbs-up or -down to see if they agreed with Scott. Asking students to show a "thumbs-up" is a way for students to signal their thinking and provides a safe learning environment for ELs who otherwise may not feel comfortable sharing their thinking orally with the class.

Luz noticed that Jay showed a thumbs-down. When asked to explain why he disagreed, Jay stated: "I think it's *y* equals three *x*; *x* is the number of apples and *y* is the number of oranges. There are three times as many apples as oranges, so you have to multiply *x* times three."

Luz saw this as an opportunity to clarify a possible misconception about setting up variables to write a linear equation. To help students think in concrete terms, Luz asked students to use substitution as a way to test Scott's and Jay's hypotheses.

"Both Scott and Jay have shared two very different equations, and both equations seem to satisfy the expression 'There are three times as many apples as there are oranges,'" Luz stated. "OK, let's test both equations and see which one fits the expression," Luz continued. "Let's forget the equations for now; let's just look at the expression. So, for example, if I have five oranges, how many apples do I have?"

Luz gave students a few minutes to think, then asked them to respond chorally. All students responded, "Fifteen!"

"OK," Luz continued, "if we use Scott's equation *y* equals three *x*, where *y* equals apples and *x* equals oranges, and we have five oranges, how can we use this information to find the number of apples and oranges?"

Angelique responded, "We can use substitution."

"Can you explain how to do that?" Luz inquired.

"You said that we have five oranges, that's *x*, so we plug in five into *x* and then we solve the equation," Angelique answered.

"So you are saying that in this case *x* equals five and that we must find the value of *y*," Luz confirmed. Luz then addressed the entire class, "Give me a thumbs-up if you all agree." Seeing that all students gave a thumbs-up, Luz added, "Work with a partner and use substitution to find the number of apples." After a few minutes, Luz asked the students to share chorally what they got for *y*.

"Fifteen!" all the students responded enthusiastically.

There are 3 times as many apples as there are oranges.

> *y = 3x*
>
> *y = apples*
>
> *x = oranges*

We have 5 oranges $\longrightarrow$ *x = 5*

How many apples do we have? $\longrightarrow$ *y = ?*

> *y = 3x*
>
> *y = 3(5)*
>
> *y = 15*

15 apples

5 oranges

FIGURE 4-6. Teacher's recording of math procedure.

"Let me do what Angelique suggested so everyone can see it. I will use substitution to find the value of *y*," Luz replied. Luz then proceeded to show the math for students to follow along. (See Figure 4–6.)

"It looks like Scott's equation satisfies the expression," Luz stated. "Let's try Jay's equation using substitution. Again, work with a partner to see what you get for *y*. In other words, you have to find the number of apples. Remember that the number of oranges, or *x*, equals five."

After a few minutes, Luz asked the students to share what they got for *y*.

"Five-thirds," some students responded.

"One and sixty-six one hundredths," other students responded.

"Five-thirds is the same as one and sixty-six one hundredths," responded another student.

Jay also added, "The answer is not fifteen."

Luz proceeded to show the math on the board for students to follow along. (See Figure 4–7.)

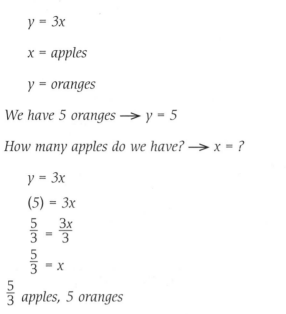

There are 3 times as many apples as there are oranges.

$y = 3x$

$x = apples$

$y = oranges$

We have 5 oranges $\longrightarrow$ $y = 5$

How many apples do we have? $\longrightarrow$ $x = ?$

$y = 3x$

$(5) = 3x$

$\dfrac{5}{3} = \dfrac{3x}{3}$

$\dfrac{5}{3} = x$

$\dfrac{5}{3}$ *apples, 5 oranges*

FIGURE 4-7. Teacher's recording of math procedure.

After seeing the solutions, Jay immediately states, "Oh! I see what I did wrong. I get it! I flipped the *x* and the *y*!"

"Sometimes we get confused when setting up the variables," Luz shared. "I do that, too, because sometimes the language is tricky. So, a good lesson that I learned is to test our equations to see if they work. Actually, Jay, I'm glad you shared your equation and your variables because it made us think about different ways in which expressions can be written in algebra."

Luz is mindful of middle school students' misconceptions in math, especially as they progress through more abstract concepts in algebra. At the same time, Luz is also aware of middle school students' self-efficacy regarding their math ability and knowledge after they engage with concepts that require algebraic thinking. Therefore, Luz constantly works toward reassuring and encouraging students as they navigate "abstract waters" in algebra.

Luz moved on to the other expressions on the recording sheet. As with the first problem, students offered a variety of explanations for the other expressions. (See Figures 4–8 to 4–10.)

Cats and Birds

A Quick Review of Some Algebraic Expressions

Use your own words, draw diagrams, or give examples to explain what you know.

Expression	This is my explanation:
There are 3 times as many apples as there are oranges.	$3a + o$ $x = oranges$ $y = 3x$ $y = apples$
The total number of apples and oranges share common factors.	Both of them share one number in common. Like 6 and 12 their number is 3.
The total number of oranges is a multiple of 4.	Oranges has [sic]: 8, 12, 16, 20 $2 \cdot 2 = 4$
The total number of apples is divisible by 3.	Any number can be divide [sic] by 3. $\frac{a}{3} = $ no remainder

FIGURE 4-8. *Antonio describes all the expressions with simple explanations.*

A Quick Review of Some Algebraic Expressions

Use your own words, draw diagrams, or give examples to explain what you know.

Expression	This is my explanation:

There are 3 times as many apples as there are oranges.	$3x + O$ If we have 5 oranges, we then have 15 apples
	
	 $y = 3x$
	     $x = oranges$
	     $y = apples$

The total number of apples and oranges share common factors.	Ex: 4 & 8 Ex: 12 & 6 CF: 2 CF: 3
The total number of oranges is a multiple of 4.	$\underline{\quad} \cdot \underline{\quad} = 4$ $2 \cdot 2 = 4$ 8, 12, 16 are multiples of 4 ↑ ↑ ↑ 2(4) 3(4) 4(4)
The total number of apples is divisible by 3.	Its saying that the total number of apples is divisible by 3 like, that 10 is not divisible by 3. $\frac{2}{3}$ *10 is not divisible by 3 because there is a remainder of 1.

FIGURE 4-9. *Laura provides examples to illustrate her understanding of each expression.*

A Quick Review of Some Algebraic Expressions	
Use your own words, draw diagrams, or give examples to explain what you know.	
Expression	This is my explanation:
There are 3 times as many apples as there are oranges.	$y = 3x$ $x = oranges$ $y = apples$ If we have 5 oranges then we have 15 apples
The total number of apples and oranges share common factors.	$2a \cdot 4a = 8$ $12 \quad 6 \rightarrow 3$ $\quad 4 \quad 8 \rightarrow 2$ $8, 12, 16$ are multiples of 4
The total number of oranges is a multiple of 4.	$4 \times 4x = 16x \qquad 2 \cdot 2 = 4$ multiple of 16 oranges $\qquad$ total # of oranges $x = oranges$
The total number of apples is divisible by 3.	$A \div 3$ The # can't have a decimal because it will have a remainder in it. And 10 is not divisible by 3. $\frac{a}{3}$

FIGURE 4-10. *Jade shows understanding of the basic premise behind* multiple, factor, *and* divisible, *even if some of the algebra used is incorrect.*

At the conclusion of this part of the lesson, Luz felt confident that the students had a solid foundation with the concepts and academic language they need to use in the upcoming problem-solving activity.

Summarizing ✦ **Part 1**

Frontloading key vocabulary words, as well as key algebraic concepts, was extremely important to tap into students' prior knowledge and to develop students' awareness of vocabulary words in mathematical contexts. During this part of the lesson, students demonstrated a basic understanding of arithmetic and algebraic reasoning, and were able to provide examples to illustrate algebraic expressions. ELs were active participants, because they were encouraged to talk in their groups about the definitions behind each key vocabulary word and each algebraic expression. Luz also acknowledged each of the students' contributions during whole-class discussions, hence validating all students' prior knowledge about the academic language. However, misconceptions still arose, especially in how some of the students had set up the first algebraic expression ("there are three times as many apples as there are oranges"). Rather than immediately correcting such a misconception, Luz, using appropriate scaffolds, allowed for students to think through the arithmetic operations behind the expression before algebraically "testing" the validity of the two different versions of the equation the students provided. By making algebraic expressions more concrete (e.g., "If we have five oranges, how many apples do we have?"), ELs in particular are able to make sense of the complex syntax present in many algebraic exercises and problems.

Cats and Birds: Part 2

Solving the Problem with One Clue

"You are ready to move on to solving a problem about some cats and birds," Luz explained to her students. "You will use the vocabulary and algebraic expressions we just reviewed to solve the problems. Feel free to keep those papers out and refer back to them if you need help with any part of your clues."

Cats and Birds is a puzzle that prompts students to solve a series of problems to find the exact number of cats and birds. The puzzle consists of six clues. (See Figure 4–11; the full-sized version is available at the end of the book as Reproducible 4–2.)

"Before we begin, I want to explain a few more words that can be confusing sometimes," Luz emphasized. She knew that there was some vocabulary that needed clarification, especially for her ELs. However, she also knew that her other students would benefit from the quick review.

"One word that you may see in your clues is the word *pet*," she explained. "Pet can be either a noun, as in, 'The dog is my *pet*' or it can be used as a verb, as in, 'I *pet* my dog when he is happy.' It is important to read the clues carefully to make sure you know how *pet* is being used."

Cats and Birds: Clues

Cats and Birds

Clue Card 1

Ms. Lang keeps cats and birds.
She has 25 heads to pet.
How many cats and birds does she have?

Cats and Birds

Clue Card 4

Ms. Lang keeps cats and birds.
The total number of cat paws is a multiple of 5.
How many cats and birds does she have?

Cats and Birds

Clue Card 2

Ms. Lang keeps cats and birds.
She counted 3 times as many cat paws as bird feet.
How many cats and birds does she have?

Cats and Birds

Clue Card 5

Ms. Lang keeps cats and birds.
The total of the number of cat paws and bird feet is divisible by 2, 4, 8, 10, 20, 40, and 80.
How many cats and birds does she have?

Cats and Birds

Clue Card 3

Ms. Lang keeps cats and birds.
The number of cat paws and the number of bird feet share common factors.
How many cats and birds does she have?

Cats and Birds

Clue Card 6

Ms. Lang keeps cats and birds.
The total number of bird feet is a multiple of 5.
How many cats and birds does she have?

FIGURE 4-11. *Cats and Birds: Clues*

Step 1: Write down as much as the clue tells you.

Step 2: Write down key mathematical concepts and ideas to help you solve the clue.

Step 3: Find out the number of cats, and the number of birds (it's OK to GUESS because you only have one clue).

Step 4: Be prepared to present your poster to the class.

FIGURE 4-12. Cats and Birds Directions

"Another word that may be tricky is *paw*. An animal's foot is called a *paw*," Luz explained, providing a synonym for the word *paw*. Vocabulary words can often be explained with a brief description or synonym, especially if students are already familiar with the concept the word represents.

"Using a clue that I will give you, you will work at your table groups to solve the problem of cats and birds," Luz directed. "Here are the directions."

As Luz stated each direction, she recorded it where the entire class could see it. (See Figure 4–12.)

"It is important that you realize that you will be guessing the answer based on your clues," Luz clarified. "You will have about fifteen minutes to read your clue, write an algebraic expression, and write your guess to the question of how many cats and birds."

With the final set of instructions, Luz distributed a different clue to each table along with a piece of poster paper and markers. (See Reproducible 4–2, *Cats and Birds*: Clues.) Note that there were six table groups to match the six clues. All clues have similar levels of complexity and require students to use key vocabulary, as well as arithmetic and algebraic reasoning, to understand what each clue is asking them to find. On the surface, it would appear that Clue 1 is the "simplest" one. However, during the implementation of this portion of the lesson, the group in charge of this clue discussed the many possible combinations for the number of cats and birds, and how their clue could fit into the other groups' clues as they overheard other groups talking about what their clues required.

Students excitedly read their clues and began to discuss what they knew about their clue and how they could determine the number of cats and birds.

The students with Clue 1 immediately began to work. Their clue read:

Ms. Lang keeps cats and birds.
She has 25 heads to pet.
How many cats and birds does she have?

"The first step says we have to write down as much as the clue tells us," Angelique said, getting the group started. "What do we know about our clue?"

"It says that she has twenty-five heads to pet. I remember that Ms. Chung said something about the word *pet*," Estevan, a student with early-intermediate English proficiency, added.

"Right. That means she has twenty-five pets or twenty-five cats and birds," Angelique replied, helping Estevan discern the meaning of *pet*.

Eden asked, "Should I write that down on our paper?"

"Yeah," Angelique responded.

Eden recorded the information that the group had deduced from Clue 1 and continued to make a series of guesses that showed the possible number of cats and birds. (See Figure 4–13.)

The group of students with Clue 5 had a bit more of a struggle making sense of their clue. It read:

Ms. Lang keeps cats and birds.
She counted 3 times as many cat paws as bird feet.
How many cats and birds does she have?

"Does anyone know what we are supposed to do?" Javier asked his group.

"Well, we know that the total number is divisible by all of those numbers," Araceli replied.

"I still don't know how we are supposed to figure out the number of cats and birds," Bethany said.

Luz noticed that this group was struggling. She decided to provide a few guiding questions to help them.

"The clue says that the total number of paws and feet is divisible by two, four, eight, ten, twenty, forty, and eighty. What is a number that is divisible by all of those numbers?" Luz asked, prompting the group. "In other words, what number can be divided by all of those numbers?"

"One hundred?" Navid suggested.

"Let's try it out," Luz replied. "Can you divide one hundred by two?"

"Yes," the group responded.

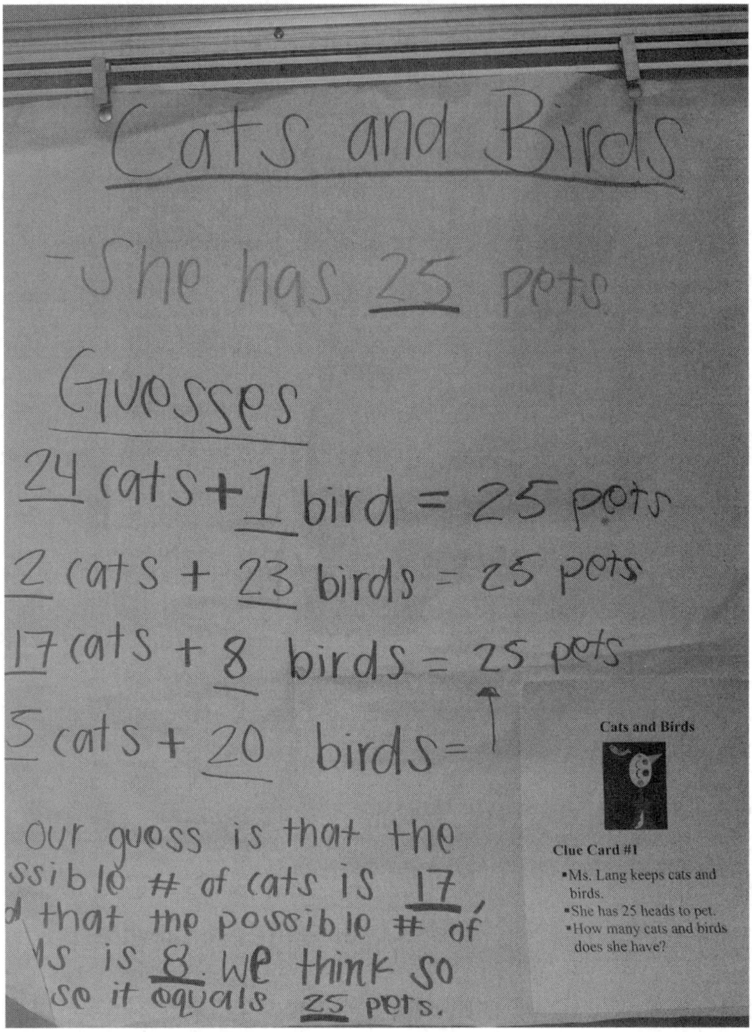

FIGURE 4-13. *The students recorded their guesses for Clue 1, which resulted in different combinations for the number of cats and birds.*

"How about one hundred divided by four?" Luz asked.

"Yes!" the group said enthusiastically, sounding as if they were onto something.

"Can you divide one hundred by eight?" Luz asked.

"Not evenly," Bethany said.

"So is one hundred divisible by all the numbers?" Luz asked.

"I get it now," Bethany said. "We have to choose a number that we can divide all of the other numbers by."

Navid added, "How about eighty? Would that work?"

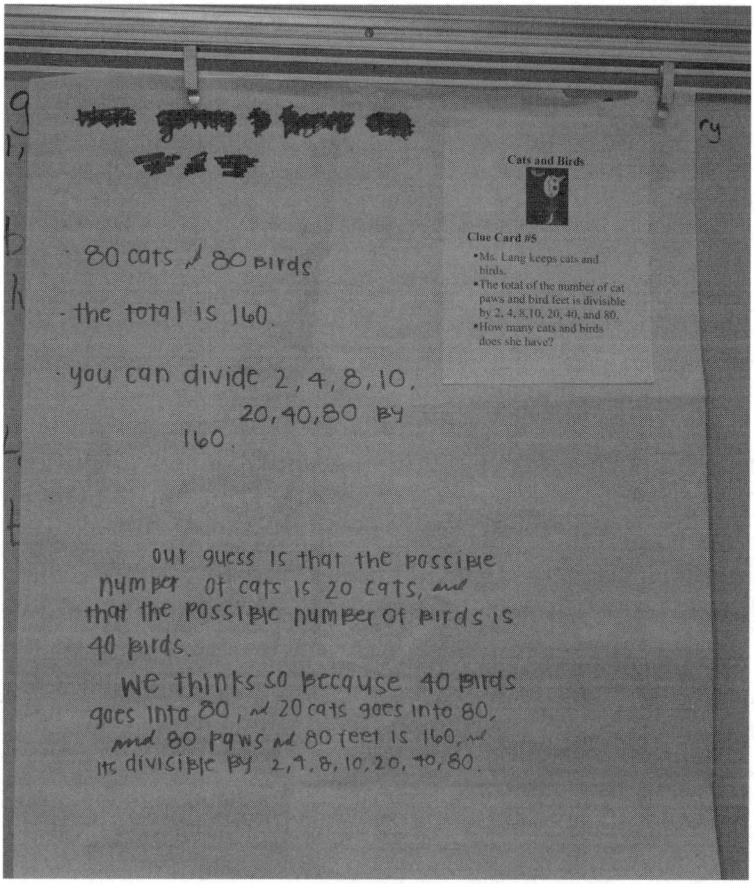

FIGURE 4-14. *The students recorded their guesses about the number of cats and birds based on their understanding of divisibility properties.*

Luz decided it was time to pull away from the group to let them continue to grapple with the clue. She felt confident that she had provided enough scaffolding and that the group was headed in the right direction. She also knew that their poster would provide her with some kind of formative assessment regarding their understanding. (See Figure 4-14.)

Luz noticed that many groups were close to finishing their work. She called for students' attention. "Many of you are almost done with your posters. Remember that you will present them to the class," Luz reminded. "I would like for you to use sentence frames to explain your guess to your clue. Make sure you write your explanation on your poster. You may also read it when you present your posters."

Luz then placed the following sentence frames where everyone could see them and read them aloud:

> *Our guess is that the possible number of cats is _____ and the possible number of birds is _____. We think so because _____.*

"Notice the word *possible*," Luz noted. "You will use that word because you don't have all of the clues yet, so it means that you are making a guess about the number of cats and birds. Be sure to explain *why* your group thinks that those numbers are *possible* based on the clue and the math that you've done. Be sure you record that on your poster as well."

The groups wrote their final guesses using the sentence frames. As students presented their clue and "guess" to the class orally, many relied on their written explanation to describe how they came to their conclusions. The use of sentence frames is central in providing ELs access to opportunities to share their knowledge and their thinking orally (and in writing) as they make sense of what the clues are asking them to analyze. We suggest having all students in each group write their own guesses using the sentence frames. It is also important to ask each group to have each member share his or her guess, and then to come to a consensus so that the group's final statement is based on the collective contributions of all group members. In this way, by having students work as a group to prepare statements that summarize and explain the rationale for their guesses, ELs are able to practice the use of academic language orally as they discuss and share their own ideas. This can also build confidence among ELs, as their group members validate their ideas, even if their final sentences may contain grammatical or syntactical errors. Also, by having a collective statement from each group, ELs can be part of the production of the academic language required by this task.

> The use of sentence frames is central in providing English learners access to opportunities to share their knowledge and their thinking orally (and in writing) as they make sense of what the clues are asking them to analyze.

Solving the Problem with All the Clues

"Now that you have made your guess as to how many cats and birds Ms. Lang has based on one clue, I am going to give each of your groups all of the clues to solve the problem," Luz stated.

Students gave a sigh of relief. They realized the first part of the problem-solving activity was not enough to help them find the solution. However, Luz knew that attempting to solve the problem with just one clue was an important step; it primed the students for working with algebraic expressions. It also gave them a chance to be introduced to and to practice academic language.

Luz distributed all six clues to each table. Students worked collaboratively to read and make sense of the information. (See Figure 4–11 for all six clues, which is also available in Reproducible 4–2.)

"Remember that some of the clues involve algebraic expressions. You may use the sheets we completed at the beginning of the lesson to help you out," Luz reminded them.

Students began reading the clues and working to solve each step of the problem. Luz circulated and listened in as the students worked. Araceli, Navid, Gloria, and Estevan began in earnest.

"How about if we make the number of cats equal c and the number of birds equal b?" Araceli suggested.

"Based on the first clue, we could say that c plus b equals twenty-five," Navid chimed in.

"Right. The clue says that the number of cats and birds is twenty-five, so that makes sense," Gloria added. "What's the next clue?"

"Ms. Lang keeps cats and birds. She counted three times as many cat paws as bird feet. How many cats and birds does she have?" Estevan read. "I'm not sure what that means."

"It means that if she has—. Wait. I need to think about this," Araceli replied. "Cats have four feet and birds have two feet. So if there are four cat feet we have to divide by three to get the number of bird feet. We can't do four divided by three."

Upon hearing this conversation, Luz joined the group. Whenever possible, Luz encourages and reminds students to use academic terms and phrases to express their mathematical thinking. She asked the students if there is another way to say "we can't do four divided by three." Luz referred them to the vocabulary sheet they filled out at the beginning of class. This is especially important for ELs, because they are not only building English language vocabulary, but also content-based vocabulary necessary to access text, to understand tasks,

> By modeling academic language use in math, English learners benefit in developing both content-area knowledge and the ways in which syntax is constructed to talk about ideas and concepts in math.

and to produce correct academic language. By modeling academic language use in math, ELs benefit in developing both content-area knowledge and the ways in which syntax is constructed to talk about ideas and concepts in math.

After examining the sheet, Estevan responded, "Four is not divisible by three."

"What if we start with the number of bird feet and multiply that by three?" Navid suggested.

Araceli added, "So two bird feet means that there are six cat paws."

"But that can't be right because cats have four paws so it has to be a number that is divisible by four," Araceli continued. "What about four bird feet, and then there would be twelve cat feet?"

"That works!" Estevan exclaimed, happy that his group had made progress with the second clue.

At another table, Luz noticed similar discussions taking place. Bethany, Javier, Eden, and Angelique were working on Clue 3.

"It says that the number of cat paws and bird feet share common factors," Bethany read.

Angelique asked, "Common factors are what? I don't remember."

"Remember, Ms. Chung explained that they are numbers that we can pull out, like twelve and six have the common factor of three, and four and eight both have the common factor two," Eden explained, referring to the paper with algebraic expressions that the class had completed earlier in the lesson.

"Oh, yeah! Now I remember. So, if we decided that the number of bird feet was four and the number of cat feet was twelve, they both have the common factor four. Right?" Angelique looked for confirmation from her peers.

"Right," confirmed Bethany.

Small-group discussions help students explain and verify their thinking processes. Luz positively reinforced each group whenever she overheard them using academic language, and whenever they referred to the vocabulary review that took place at the beginning of the lesson. Luz was particularly pleased when a group of students would help each other remember key vocabulary as well as key mathematical concepts, as illustrated in the previous conversation. Through talking, students share their mathematical understandings and receive feedback about their thinking. It is through this process that academic language and mathematical concepts are deepened and solidified.

> Through talking, students share their mathematical understandings and receive feedback about their thinking. It is through this process that academic language and mathematical concepts are deepened and solidified.

Students continued working in their small groups and wrestled with the clues until they came up with a solution to the question, *How many cats and birds does Ms. Lang have?*

All the groups were successful in determining the solution to the problem, and documented their process on poster paper. Luz wanted to ensure that all groups had the opportunity to share their work with the rest of the class.

"In preparation for sharing, I want you to use more sentence frames to explain how you came to your answer." Luz displayed the following sentence frames for everyone to see:

> *The number of cats is _____. The number of birds is _____.*
>
> *We know this is the right solution because _____*

"Talk with your group to determine how you will explain your solution or answer," Luz directed. "Then, write down how you solved the problem. Remember, you will be sharing your steps with the class. You may use the papers we completed at the beginning of the class to explain your thinking."

Luz frequently reminds students of the linguistic supports they have been given to help them in discussing their mathematical thinking. ELs often refer to these supports, because it helps them remember the vocabulary they need to use during discussions.

Students talked at their tables, determining how they would explain how they came up with their solution. After about five minutes, Luz called the class back together.

"Who would like to share first?" Luz asked.

Javier raised his hand. "We will!" His group made their way to the front of the room with their poster. (See Figure 4–15.)

"The number of cats is fifteen and the number of birds is ten. We know this is the right solution, because we read all the clues and made sure our answers worked with all of them."

"Can you give an example of a clue that you know helped you?" Luz probed, looking for Javier or his group to explain their mathematical thinking in depth.

Eden stepped forward and replied, "For example, we knew we're still kinda making up guesses 'til clue three, but then clue four said that

Luz frequently reminds students of the linguistic supports they have been given to help them in discussing their mathematical thinking. English learners often refer to these supports, because it helps them remember the vocabulary they need to use during discussions.

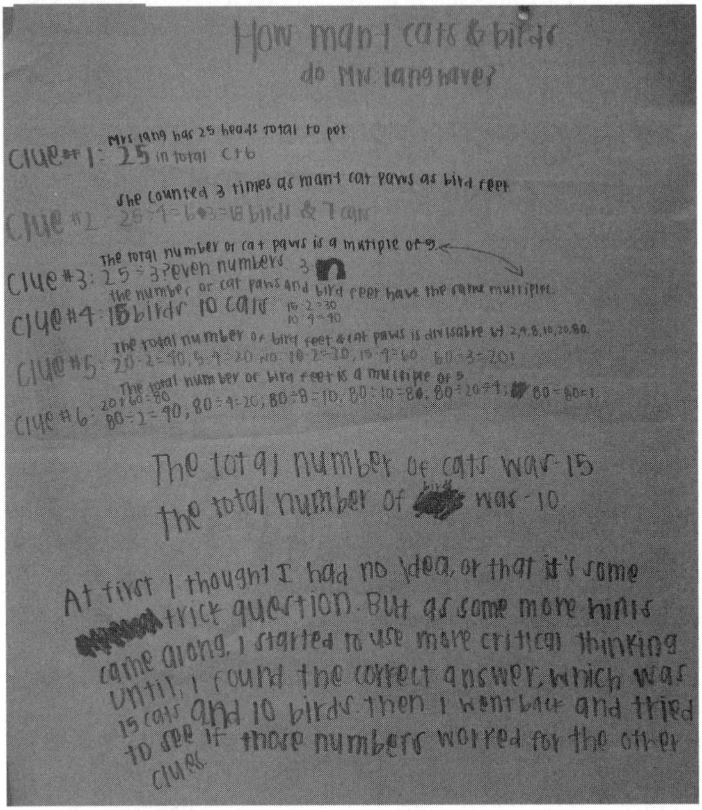

FIGURE 4-15. These students listed all the clues and used different explanations and examples to illustrate how each clue led them to the number of cats and birds.

the number of cat paws was a multiple of five, so that helped us know that twelve wasn't the right guess, but fifteen or twenty could be."

"Thank you, Eden and group," Luz said. "Is there another group that is ready to share?"

Groups took turns presenting their posters and, with each one, Luz asked questions to help the students explain their thinking about the algebraic expressions they had created and the clues that led them to their solutions.

One group shared that they knew they had found the right solution because in clue five they created the expression $4c + 2b = 80$, because the total number of cat paws and bird feet had to be divisible by all the numbers in the clue. They figured out that the answer to that clue had to be 80, so they could figure out the solution to the problem from there.

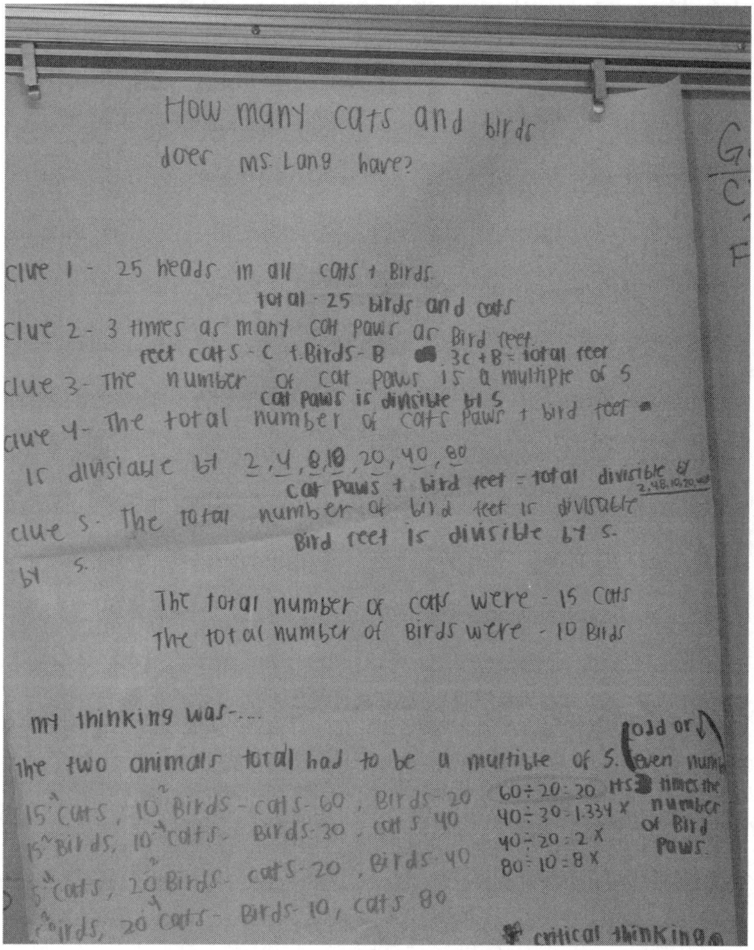

FIGURE 4-16. This group of students solved the puzzle by testing different combinations for the sum of cats and birds while listing each clue's key requirements.

The clues in *Cats and Birds* provided a terrific vehicle for students to tap into their prior knowledge about problem solving, arithmetic, and algebraic reasoning to discover the mathematics behind each clue. Students solved the puzzle of *Cats and Birds* using a variety of strategies, as illustrated in the following student samples.

One of the groups solved the puzzle by testing out different possibilities for the number of cats and birds, while keeping in mind the key requirements that each clue demanded. For example, Clue 6 required students to keep in mind that the total number of bird feet is a multiple of five. They tested out various possibilities until they found a combination that satisfied each of the clues and their key requirements. (See Figure 4–16.)

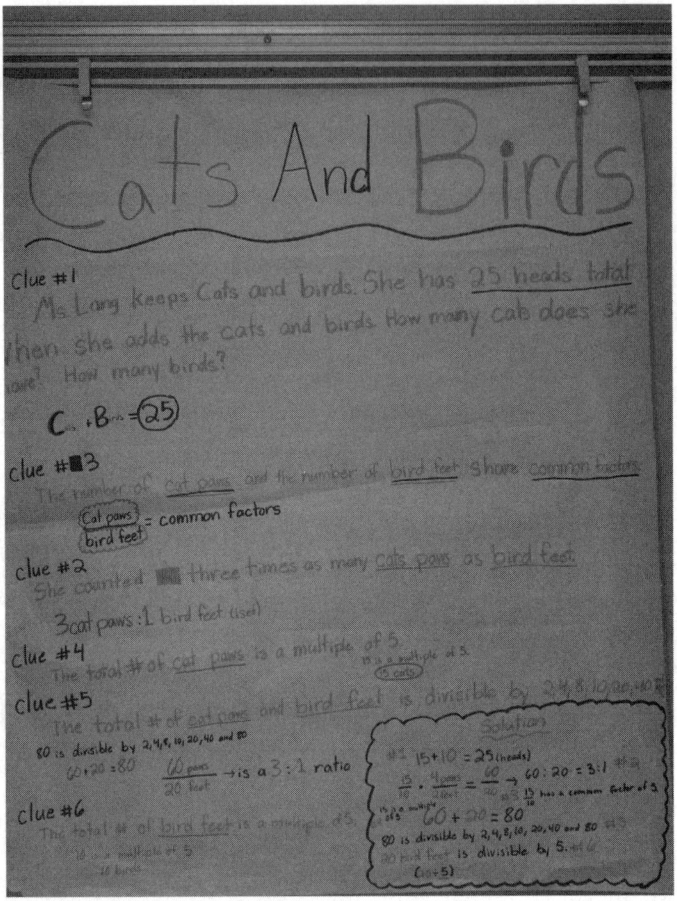

FIGURE 4-17. *This group solved the puzzle by focusing on the ratio of cat feet to bird feet, and listed each clue's key requirements.*

Another group used the idea of ratios as the focus of their calculations. (See Figure 4–17.) For example, for Clue 2, "She counted 3 times as many cats as bird feet," this group wrote "3 *cat paws: 1 bird feet (1 set)*" to explain their use of ratios. This group used their understanding of *multiples, divisibility,* and *common factors* along with the 3:1 ratio to see which numbers would satisfy the ratio of three cat paws to one set of bird feet, and each of the key requirements of all the clues.

Another group used their knowledge of solving linear equations and solving systems of two linear equations to solve the puzzle. (See Figure 4–18.) This group set up variables for the number of cats (C) and the number of birds (B). They used Clue 1, "She has 25 heads to pet," to set up the first linear equation: $C + B = 25$. This group also figured out that the

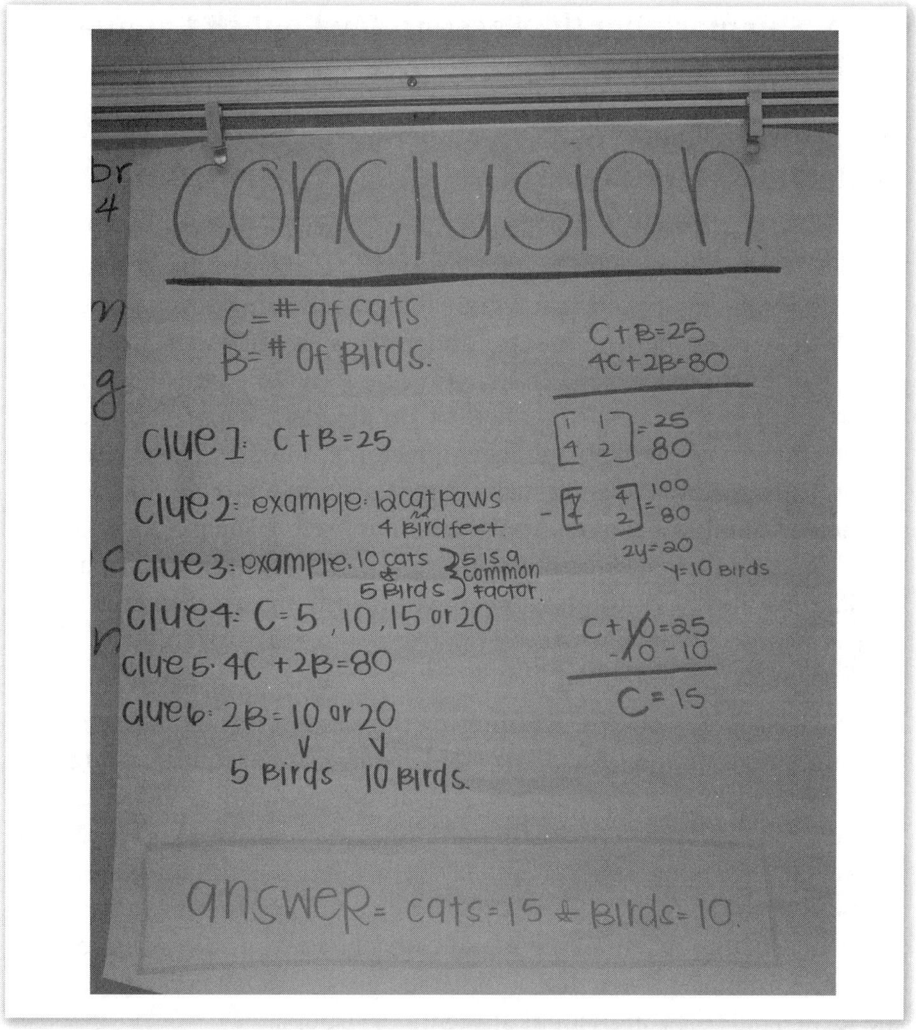

FIGURE 4-18. *This group solved the puzzle by solving a system of two linear equations.*

total number of feet is 80. (Clue 5: The total of the number of cat paws and bird feet is divisible by 2, 4, 8, 10, 20, 40, and 80.) They also figured out that each cat has four feet, and each bird has two feet; therefore, they set up their second linear equation as $4C + 2B = 80$. They solved this system of equations by linear combination to arrive at the answer.

After each group shared their posters with the class, Luz brought the lesson to a close. "Today you solved a problem using lots of information about numbers and algebra. You had to work together to solve the clues to get to the final solution. By discussing your thinking with each other, all of the groups were able to find the solution to the problem."

Cats and Birds

Strategy 1: Reviewing and Learning Vocabulary to Set up Algebraic Expressions

Frontloading a whole-class discussion of key vocabulary words provided ELs with immediate access to new and developing concepts in algebra. By eliciting their prior knowledge of words that may be used differently in nonmath contexts, and by having a discussion of how these words are used in math, ELs are able to build academic language as well as content knowledge. Setting up algebraic expressions can be daunting, even for English speakers, given the nuances of the syntax of many of these expressions (such as that seen in Clue 2, "She counted 3 times as many cat paws as bird feet"). Therefore, helping ELs understand and use algebra-based vocabulary and syntax can aid their thinking as they start to "translate" words into algebraic expressions.

Strategy 2: Creating Scaffolds

As mentioned earlier, the wording of the clues in *Cats and Birds* can cause extra confusion, especially for ELs. Luz knew that this might be the case in her lesson, so she was strategic in planning her lesson to create scaffolds in order for students to be successful. These scaffolds included previewing key vocabulary terms and algebraic expressions by brainstorming within groups, providing sentence frames to help students articulate their thinking while problem solving, providing opportunities for small-group work, and having whole-class discussions on the ideas shared by individual students or groups.

Strategy 3: Using Collaborative Group Work

Using collaborative group work, during which native English speakers work together with ELs, allowed English speakers to serve as peer models during receptive and productive tasks when accessing text, holding group discussions, and generating text via the sentence frames. At the same time, because Luz required that all students share their ideas in their small groups, ELs were able to make meaningful contributions, regardless of their English proficiency level. When designed with the purpose of inclusion, collaborative work can also contribute to reducing affective filters. It is important to note that besides providing scaffolds to ensure that all students are able to access and produce academic language as well as content, setting up collaborative group work requires purposeful and careful monitoring on the part of the teacher. For example, Luz walked around the room while students were working in their groups and made sure that the language being produced was academically and mathematically appropriate (for example, prompting students to use terms such as *divisible by* and *the sum of*). Not only did Luz check for students' understanding of the text, and the content, but also for the ways in which students were constructing their language.

Suggestions for Extending the Lesson

Use Multistep Problems

Provide students with many opportunities to solve multistep problems. Here is a list of four more problems that are similar to *Cats and Birds* (adapted from Thompson and Mayfield-Ingram [1998]). A reproducible of the clue cards for each of the following problems is included at the end of the book:

1. Octopi and Sea Star (Reproducible 4–3)
2. Farmer Eddie (Reproducible 4–4)
3. The Tran Family (Reproducible 4–5)
4. Cycles (Reproducible 4–6)

5 The Game of *SKUNK*: An Investigation into Probability

COMMON CORE STATE STANDARDS

Grade 7: Statistics and Probability

Investigate chance processes and develop, use, and evaluate probability models.

- Develop a probability model and use it to find probabilities of events. Compare probabilities from a model to observed frequencies; if the agreement is not good, explain possible sources of the discrepancy.

- Develop a uniform probability model by assigning equal probability to all outcomes, and use the model to determine probabilities of events. *For example, if a student is selected at random from a class, find the probability that Jane will be selected and the probability that a girl will be selected.*

Overview

SKUNK is a game created by Dan Brutlag. *SKUNK* involves five rounds (thus the letters S, K, U, N, K) during which a pair of dice is rolled. The sum of the numbers on the dice determines how many points students can accumulate (or lose) during the game. Students play this game of probability using dice. They use their understanding of the words *choice* and *chance* to decide whether they should continue playing the game based on the chance that a certain roll of the dice (a one on either or both dice) will occur. Students are engaged in problem solving, including making choices to decide when to stop playing the game, as well as investigating strategies for winning games.

Adapted from *"Choice and Chance in Life: The Game of SKUNK"* by Dan Brutlag (1994).

Math Goal: Students will use an understanding of probability to make and test conjectures about strategies that will help them win a game.

Language Goal: Students will orally describe the strategies they use during the game of *SKUNK*. Students will write a description of two different strategies they used during the game.

Key Vocabulary: chance, choice, likely, "play it safe," probability, probable, strategy, "take a risk," unlikely

Materials:
✦ Directions for Playing the Game *SKUNK* (Reproducible 5–1), 1 per student
✦ Dice, 1 pair per group of 4 students

For more on determining key vocabulary, see page 180.

Note: Dice are to be used by the teacher to demonstrate the game and to model the math and the academic language needed for this lesson. As students are ready to try this game on their own, hand out one pair of dice per group of four students.

Sentence Frames

Beginning

> *I am going to* _____.

For more on creating sentence frames, see page 175.

Intermediate/Advanced

> *I am going to* _____ *, because* _____.

> *A* _____ *strategy is* _____.

The Game of *SKUNK*: Part 1

Kathy Melanese greeted each of her sixth-grade students as they walked into her classroom. The 24 energetic middle school students, a diverse mix of native English speakers and ELs, were excited about the

chance	*probable*
choice	*strategy*
likely	*"take a risk"*
"play it safe"	*unlikely*
probability	

FIGURE 5-1. Key Vocabulary Words Posted for the Entire Class.

end of the school year and moving up to the seventh grade. With this in mind, Kathy knew that a game context would be motivating and help students focus on and engage in learning about probability.

Introducing Academic Language

Because the game of *SKUNK* requires students to reason strategically and consider how *choice* and *chance* figure into the decisions they make, Kathy first decided to post key vocabulary words for everyone to see. (See Figure 5–1.)

Kathy began by tapping into students' prior knowledge about four of the key terms: *choice, chance, likely,* and *unlikely.* She read each word aloud, then asked the class to indicate whether they knew the word and its meaning, and whether they could provide examples. The following are some of the students' ideas:

"On *American Idol,* it is *likely* the girl will win, because everybody thinks she has a good voice."

"I made the *choice* to wear a red blouse today."

"I found this quarter on the floor by *chance.*"

"It is *likely* that we will have fun today with this game!"

"It is *unlikely* that it will rain today. It's been sunny all day."

Next, Kathy set the tone for the game by asking students to answer the hypothetical question: "If I gave you math homework tonight, but I told you that I *might* collect the homework tomorrow, would you do the homework?"

Kathy's purpose in asking this question was to probe students' thinking about the choices we make based on the idea of *chance.* By asking students to relate their own experiences and prior knowledge about the possible consequences of not doing their homework, or the possibility that their teacher might not collect the homework, Kathy immediately established a relevant connection between the math concepts to be reviewed and the students' real-life experiences with the concept of probability. Furthermore, by providing such relevancy, Kathy helped students think about the importance of making informed decisions based on predictions and past experiences. Familiar contexts or situations help all students, particularly ELs, make sense of math concepts.

Kathy asked the students to think about the question and how they might answer it. She gave them about a minute to think, and then asked them to give her a "thumbs-up" if they were ready to share their answer. By providing students with time to think on their own, Kathy allowed them to make sense of the question. Furthermore, asking students to show a "thumbs-up" is a way for students to signal that they have thought of an answer, and provides a safe learning environment for ELs who otherwise may not feel comfortable sharing their thinking orally with the class. After everyone showed Kathy a "thumbs-up," she then asked students to turn to a partner and share with him or her whether they would do the homework and explain why.

Asking students to show a "thumbs-up" is a way for students to signal that they have thought of an answer, and provides a safe learning environment for English learners who otherwise may not feel comfortable sharing their thinking orally with the class.

Students immediately took this opportunity to talk to each other about their experiences with homework in their math class. For example, at Yolanda's table she said to her partner, "Sometimes we turn in our homework packet on Fridays, so the teacher might collect it tomorrow, because tomorrow is Friday."

At another table, Louise said that she would not do the homework because "the teacher said that she might or might not collect it."

In response, her partner Alex said that he "would do half of it just in case the teacher collects the homework." Alex added that if the teacher does collect the homework, he would tell her that he would finish it later, in the hope of not losing any credit.

When they were finished sharing, Kathy elicited students' ideas.

Griselda said, "I would do my homework!"

Kathy asked Griselda, "Does that mean that you don't want to take a chance?" Griselda nodded in agreement.

Ray said, "I would not do my homework because you [referring to the teacher] might not collect it."

Kathy followed up by asking Ray, "Does that mean that you are going to take the chance?" Ray smiled and nodded in agreement.

Kathy proceeded to explain, "The idea behind this question is that you have a choice. If I said, 'I am going to collect your homework,' would you then do your homework?" Students nodded in affirmation. Kathy responded, "As you get older, you have to make choices based on the idea of chance. Today we are going to be playing a game of chance. You will have to make some choices to win. Are you ready?"

The students enthusiastically responded, "Yes!"

Summarizing ✦ **Part 1**

Introducing academic language early on during the lesson provided all students with access to key mathematical concepts to be addressed during the game. By using a common experience that students can relate to (for example, the consequences of not turning in homework), Kathy tapped into students' prior knowledge and understanding of words such as *chance* and *choice*. All students, regardless of their English language level or their prior experiences with probability problems, were able to connect probability ideas immediately to a "real-life" topic. At the same time, students were able to practice using key vocabulary words as they conversed with their partners within the context of probability.

The Game of *SKUNK*: Part 2

Playing the Game

Kathy explained to her students, "We're going to play a game called *SKUNK*. How many of you have played *SKUNK* before?"

About half the students raised their hands. Playing games multiple times is important for several reasons: knowing the game's procedure allows students to focus on the mathematics, and the repetition gives them further opportunities to try out developing strategies.

Kathy continued, "This is a game in which we will be reviewing our knowledge of *probability*. All we need is some paper and a pencil. All of us will play, and I will be rolling a pair of dice during the game."

Next, Kathy went over the rules of the game. She also posted the rules where everyone could see them. Posting rules for everyone to see is a helpful reminder for all students, especially for ELs, because they can refer to the written rules instead of relying solely on auditory

Directions for Playing the Game *SKUNK* with the Entire Class

Objective: *The object of* SKUNK *is to accumulate the greatest possible point total over five rounds. The rules for play are the same for each of the five rounds.*

Overview: SKUNK *is a game created by Dan Brutlag. The game of* SKUNK *involves five rounds (thus the letters S, K, U, N, K) during which a pair of dice is rolled. The sum of the numbers on the dice determines how many points students can accumulate (or lose) during the game.*

1. To start the game, all students must make a score sheet like the one presented here.

S	K	U	N	K

2. Each letter of *SKUNK* represents a different round of the game. Play begins with the S column and continues through the K column.
3. At the beginning of each round, every player stands up. The teacher rolls a pair of dice. (*Important:* Everyone playing uses that roll of the dice.)
4. All students figure the total (sum) of the dice and record it in the appropriate column on their score sheets, using the following guidelines:
   - If a 1 comes up, play is over for that round and all the player's points in that column are wiped out.
   - If double 1s come up, all points accumulated in prior columns are wiped out as well.
   - If a 1 does not come up, students consider the sum as points and may choose either to try for more points on the next roll (by continuing to stand up) or to stop and keep what they have accumulated (by sitting down).

Note: If a 1, or double 1s, occurs on the very first roll of a round, then that round is over and the game starts again. Students should record their scores in the next column.

FIGURE 5-2. Directions for Playing the Game SKUNK with the Entire Class.

delivery. (The rules of the game are presented in Figure 5–2 and are also available in Reproducible 5–1 at the end of the book.) We suggest playing the game with the entire class, because this will model the math and language objectives of this lesson.

Kathy then handed out a *SKUNK* score sheet to each student. (See Figure 5–3.) She also displayed a *SKUNK* score sheet to the class, so that she could play along with her students while discussing the mathematics and the academic language involved. Kathy started by rolling the dice. She rolled a 3 and a 4.

Posting rules for everyone to see is a helpful reminder for all students, especially for English learners, because they can refer to the written rules instead of relying solely on auditory delivery.

The Game of *SKUNK*: An Investigation into Probability

S	K	U	N	K

FIGURE 5-3. *SKUNK* Score Sheet.

She then asked students to find the sum of the two dice to get the number they would need to record in the S column. Chorally, students answered, "Seven!" Kathy indicated where to record the number seven on the *SKUNK* score sheet. (See Figure 5–4.) The students followed Kathy's lead and also recorded that number on the first column of their own *SKUNK* score sheet.

Before rolling the dice a second time, Kathy emphasized, "You will use *chance* to figure out whether you want to keep playing. Remember that this is a game of *chance*. Now it's time for you to make your decision. If you want to continue playing, stay standing; otherwise, sit down."

All students remained standing. Seeing that her students had made their decision, Kathy continued, "It looks like you have made the *choice* to take a *chance*. Can some of you tell me why you decided to remain standing?"

S	K	U	N	K
7				

FIGURE 5-4. *The game of SKUNK score sheet: Kathy rolled a 3 and a 4, totaling seven.*

S	K	U	N	K
7				
8	.			

FIGURE 5–5. *The game of* SKUNK *score sheet: Kathy rolled a total of eight.*

Jorge said, "It's only been one round. I don't think two ones are going to come up."

"So, are you taking a *chance?*" Kathy asked.

"Yes, I'm taking a *chance,*" Jorge confirmed.

For the second round, Kathy rolled a total of 8. Kathy modeled the next step by recording the number eight under the number seven in the S column. (See Figure 5–5.) Modeling helps English learners understand and "see" the directions without necessarily having to attend to oral instructions.

> Modeling helps English learners understand and "see" the directions without necessarily having to attend to oral instructions.

Before rolling the dice a third time, Kathy reminded her students, "You will use *chance* to figure out whether you want to keep playing. Remember that this is a game of *chance.* Now it's time for your decision. If you want to continue playing, stay standing; otherwise, sit down."

About half the students stayed standing. Seeing that all students had made their decision, Kathy said, "For those of you who stayed standing, it looks like you have made the *choice* to take a *chance.*"

For the third round, Kathy rolled a 3 and a 1, then referred the students to the rules, reminding them of what happens if a 1 is rolled.

Jaime exclaimed, "We lose all our points!"

All the students who were standing jokingly complained, whereas the students who sat down celebrated for making the right choice.

"For those of you who sat down, please add the numbers together that are in the S column on your score sheets," Kathy directed. "The total is your score for that column. So, if we add seven and eight, we get. . . ."

Students chorally responded, "Fifteen!"

The Game of SKUNK: An Investigation into Probability

S	K	U	N	K
7 + 8 15				

FIGURE 5-6. *The game of SKUNK score sheet: the score for those students who sat down.*

Those students who earned the 15 points were elated. Kathy modeled what students needed to write on their *SKUNK* score sheet to indicate they earned 15 points. (See Figure 5–6.)

Kathy added, "For those of you who remained standing, please cross out the seven and eight on your score sheets and write a zero under those numbers." Kathy modeled what students needed to do to indicate that they had lost their points. (See Figure 5–7.) These students were disappointed, but not discouraged, and certainly ready to play the second round.

Kathy now focused students' attention on the second column (K) and asked everyone to stand up. She rolled a 3 and a 2, and then recorded the sum (five) in the K column. She continued rolling the dice, each time reminding the students beforehand that they would use *chance*

S	K	U	N	K
7 8 0				

FIGURE 5-7. *The game of SKUNK score sheet: the score for those students still standing.*

Supporting English Language Learners in Math Class, Grades 6–8

to make their *choice* of whether to remain standing or to sit down. The next numbers she rolled were a 5 and a 4 (sum of nine), a 6 and a 5 (sum of 11), a 4 and a 2 (sum of six), and finally a 4 and a 1 (sum of five). Before each of these rolls, students made decisions as to whether to stay standing or to sit down. Again, students who sat down before the last roll (a 4 and a 1) celebrated, whereas the students who remained standing realized that they lost all their accumulated points for this column.

After round 2 came to a close, Kathy moved to the third column: U. She asked everyone to stand up. She then rolled a double 1, to which all the students responded in disappointment, because they all got a zero in their U column.

Summarizing ✦ Part 2

During the first three rounds, Kathy not only modeled how the game is played, she also modeled how to use the correct academic language. Kathy consistently used the terms *chance* and *choice* while playing. This is an important strategy, because one may have multiple interpretations of "chance"—an opportunity, an act of luck, a risk, a prospect, and so forth. By consistently repeating "you will use *chance* to figure out whether you want to keep playing," as well as "remember that this is a game of *chance*" throughout the game, Kathy emphasizes how this particular word is being used, and for what purpose. This allows ELs not only to gain a new meaning for the word but also to understand its possible applicability in a variety of settings.

The Game of *SKUNK*: Part 3

Discussing Strategy

After modeling the third round of the game, Kathy took the opportunity to lead a class discussion exploring students' ideas and thinking behind their choices. "It seems to me that you're using *strategy* to play the game," she observed. "When you play other games, such as dodgeball for example, what is your strategy?"

Tomás responded, "My strategy is not to get hit."

By starting with a topic such as dodgeball, ELs have greater access to the discussion, because it is based on a familiar concept—game-playing strategies.

The Game of SKUNK: An Investigation into Probability

Class Strategies for SKUNK

Play It Safe	Take a Risk
"You sit down"	*"You stay standing"*
A 1 is <u>likely</u> to come up	*"Take a <u>chance</u> that a 1 will be rolled"*
	"There is a <u>possibility</u> that there might be more points"
	"It is <u>unlikely</u> we will roll a 1"

FIGURE 5–8. Examples of class strategies for playing the game SKUNK.

"Now, let's think of some strategies to play the game of SKUNK," Kathy said. She pointed to a two-column chart she had placed for everyone in the classroom to see. The chart had the headings "Play It Safe" and "Take a Risk." To activate their background knowledge, Kathy asked students to give her examples of strategies that may go under each of the headings. As she recorded students' ideas, Kathy underlined key vocabulary words on the chart. (See Figure 5–8.)

> English learners especially benefit from hearing and seeing key vocabulary words recorded on a chart. This practice is an additional layer of support when writing is requested as part of the lesson.

By eliciting students' input, Kathy helps students build their knowledge base about strategy use. In addition, by underlining key words, Kathy emphasizes important vocabulary words to be used when expressing one's thinking and rationale behind choices made to gain advantage in a game of chance. Although this strategy is helpful for all students, ELs especially benefit from hearing and seeing key vocabulary words recorded on a chart. This practice is an additional layer of support when writing is requested as part of the lesson. These words are central to the mathematical vocabulary development of all middle school students, especially in the area of probability. Words such as *likely* and *unlikely* can help students express their ideas about the likelihood of a particular event taking place, whether in the context of math or in a real-life setting. For ELs, this is of particular importance, because words can have different meanings across contexts and content areas, and therefore it becomes crucial to help them build relevance and applicability with words they might find challenging or out of context. For example, as mentioned earlier, the word *chance* conveys multiple meanings.

After filling out the "Class Strategies for *SKUNK*" chart with her students, Kathy moved on to the fourth round of the game—the N column. She rolled a 5 and a 2 (sum of seven). Students wrote 7 in their N column.

Before rolling the dice a second time, Kathy again reminded her students, "You will use *chance* to figure out whether you want to keep playing. Remember that this is a game of *chance*. Before you play, tell your partner whether you are going to 'play it safe' and stop playing the game or whether you are going to 'take a risk' and continue to play the game. Remember to explain why."

Expecting students to explain their strategy to their partner provides all students, including ELs, with an opportunity and an authentic reason to communicate their mathematical thinking in English. Without this expectation, students might play *SKUNK* without ever sharing their thinking.

Kathy knows that without structured support, some ELs may not have the language to explain or describe their strategies. Before Kathy had students share their thinking in partners, Kathy directed them to the following sentence frame that was posted where everyone could see it.

> Expecting students to explain their strategy to their partner provides all students, including English learners, with an opportunity and an authentic reason to communicate their mathematical thinking in English.

I am going to _____, because _____.

She modeled how this sentence frame might be used. "I am going to take a risk, because I think it is unlikely that a one will be rolled."

Kathy gave students a few minutes to think of their own response before sharing it with their partner. When they had finished, Kathy asked a few students to volunteer their answers using the sentence frame as a guideline.

Sara said, "I am going to stay standing, because there's a possibility that there might be a higher number." Sara referred to one of the

Take a Risk strategies from the chart to explain her choice. (Refer back to Figure 5–8.)

Having accumulated a significant number of points, Bao referred to the Play It Safe strategies from the chart to explain his decision. "I am going to sit, because I don't want to lose my points."

Jorge said, "I am going to take a risk, because there's not going to be a one."

Kathy viewed Jorge's response as an opportunity to revisit some of the key vocabulary words underlined on the strategies chart. She explained to the class that she was going to rephrase Jorge's idea using one of the underlined key words on the chart. She said, "I am going to take a risk, because I think it is *unlikely* that a one will be rolled."

The sentence frame helped students use the key vocabulary in complete and grammatically correct sentences. After complimenting the students on their use of the sentence frame to explain their strategy, Kathy proceeded to the N round of the game.

After the first roll, Kathy asked the students again to use the sentence frame to explain to their partner their Take a Risk or Play It Safe strategy. Kathy knows that offering students multiple opportunities for talk during math lessons can help them develop their English language skills. Providing support for talk in the form of sentence frames is crucial.

Kathy quickly made her way around the room, listening in on students' ideas. As she circulated, she noted a variety of ideas from students: "I am going to take a risk, because I want to get more points." "I am going to take a risk, because I want to beat my record." "I am going to play it safe, because I lost the last game."

When partners were finished, Kathy continued rolling the dice for the N column until a 1 was rolled. She then moved on to the last round: K. After the first roll of this round, Kathy asked students again to use the sentence frame. "What strategy are you going to use for the K round? Use the sentence frame and tell your partner whether you are going to 'play it safe' and stop playing the game or whether you are going to 'take a risk' and continue playing the game. Remember to explain why."

Before rolling the dice for the second time, and as students acted on the decision they had made by either sitting down or remaining standing, Kathy asked those students sitting down why they had made their decision.

Alicia responded, "I think we are going to get a zero. I mean, we are going to get a double one."

Kathy then asked a clarifying question by inserting one of the key vocabulary words, "So you are saying that is *likely* that I will roll a double one?" Alicia nodded in agreement.

Kathy asked students if they would change their strategy after hearing Alicia's comment. "Yes," said Omar. When asked why, Omar responded, "I'm going to do what Ileana is doing." (Ileana was sitting next to Omar and had accumulated a large number of points.)

Alfonso, one of the students who remained standing, said, "It's *unlikely* that a one is going to show up." Kathy was pleased that Alfonso used one of the key vocabulary words for this game.

Kathy continued playing the last round on column K until a 1 was rolled on one of the dice. Kathy then had students add all their points across the columns. "This will be your total score for the game," she instructed.

As students enthusiastically added their scores and shared them with each other, Kathy reminded the class that winning was not the goal of this game, but rather the goal was to make informed decisions based on their observations and their understanding of how probability works in a game of chance.

To finish up the game, Kathy directed students' attention to the strategy chart again. She asked students if they had other strategies to add after having played the game and having discussed some of their strategies with their classmates. Students came up with additional ideas after playing an entire round of *SKUNK* and they were added to the chart. (See Figure 5–9.)

Intrigued by Esneida's strategy, "There is a one in six chance that you will roll a one," Kathy prompted Esneida to explain her strategy to the class. Esneida described her strategy by stating that "there are two dices [sic], each dice [sic] has six faces, and there's a one in each dice [sic], so there's [sic] two out of twelve chances."

Kathy asked students if there were other ways to illustrate Esneida's explanation. Tomás raised his hand and said, "A die has six faces, each face has dots, from one to six dots, so if you roll one die, you can get a one, or a two, or a three, or a four, or a five, or a six, in one roll."

To help students visualize Tomás's and Esenida's thinking, Kathy used a die to show the class the idea that there is one out of six chances of getting a 1 when rolling one die. To connect the words with the numbers, she wrote, "*1/6*" and "*one out of six*" on the board. Kathy followed up by asking the class if they thought this probability would change when rolling two dice. She asked them to think about this question, letting them know that they would come back to this discussion

Class Strategies for SKUNK

Play It Safe	Take a Risk
"You sit down"	"Stay standing"
"A one is <u>likely</u> to come up"	"Take a <u>chance</u> that a one will be rolled"
"A lot of rolls have a 1"	"There is a <u>possibility</u> that there might be more points"
"A lot of rolls are likely to have a 1"	"It is <u>unlikely</u> we will roll a 1"
"So you don't lose your points"	"There is a one in six <u>chance</u> that you will roll a 1"

FIGURE 5-9. The list of class strategies after students played an entire round of the game SKUNK.

at another time (see "Authors' Note: The Mathematics of Rolling Two Dice" later in the chapter).

Summarizing ✦ Part 3

While playing the game with her students, Kathy continued to model the use of the lesson's key vocabulary words and provided ample opportunities for students to practice using these words while making predictions during the game. Also, as illustrated by the discussion based on Esneida's observation—"There is a one in six chance that you will roll a one"—the conversations were also focused on how the mathematics behind rolling a pair of dice can help make predictions in probability games. Capitalizing on her students' conversations about the decisions they made during the game, Kathy coconstructed the "Class Strategies for *SKUNK*" chart (Figures 5–8 and 5–9) with her students. By asking students to use a sentence frame to explain their next move, all students, including ELs, were able to participate and contribute to the "Class Strategies for *SKUNK*" chart, and therefore collectively build a resource for the entire class to use during this game of probability.

The Game of *SKUNK*: Part 4

Writing to Learn

Capitalizing on students' enthusiasm in discovering strategies to play the game *SKUNK*, Kathy asked students to write a "Play It Safe" and a "Take a Risk" strategy. To help students describe their strategies in writing, Kathy provided them with a second sentence frame.

A _____ *strategy is* _____.

Kathy gave the students a few minutes to write their strategies, reminding them to use the key vocabulary words they learned during the game, as well as the strategies listed on the strategies chart. When all students were finished, Kathy asked them to share their writing with a partner. Some of the strategies that students shared are presented in Figures 5–10 through 5–13.

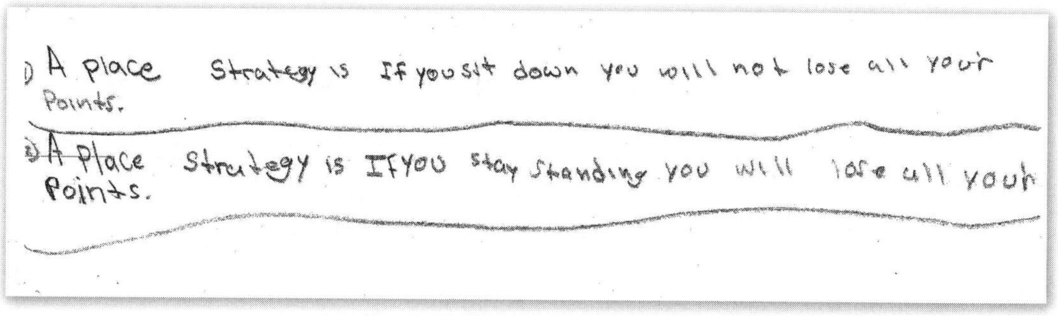

> 1) A place Strategy is If you sit down you will not lose all your Points.
>
> 2) A place Strategy is IF You stay Standing you will lose all your Points.

FIGURE 5-10. Juan explains a strategy to retain points. He is at an intermediate level of English language proficiency.

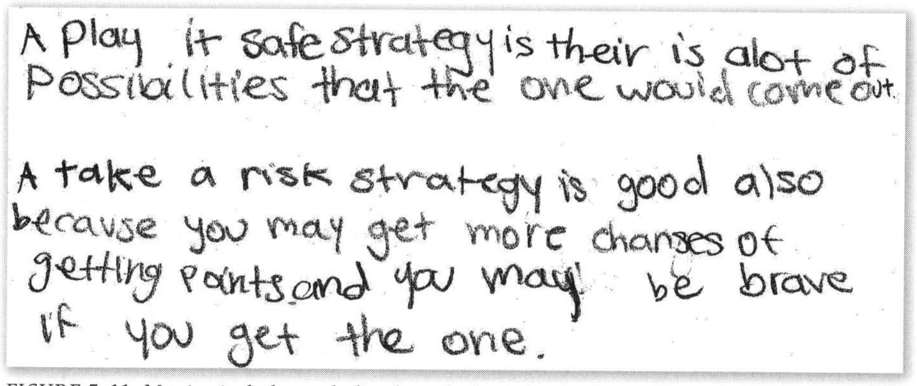

> A Play it safe strategy is their is alot of Possibilities that the one would come out.
>
> A take a risk strategy is good also because you may get more chanses of getting points and you may be brave if you get the one.

FIGURE 5-11. Monica includes underlined words from the class's strategy chart. She is at an advanced level of English language proficiency.

The Game of SKUNK: An Investigation into Probability

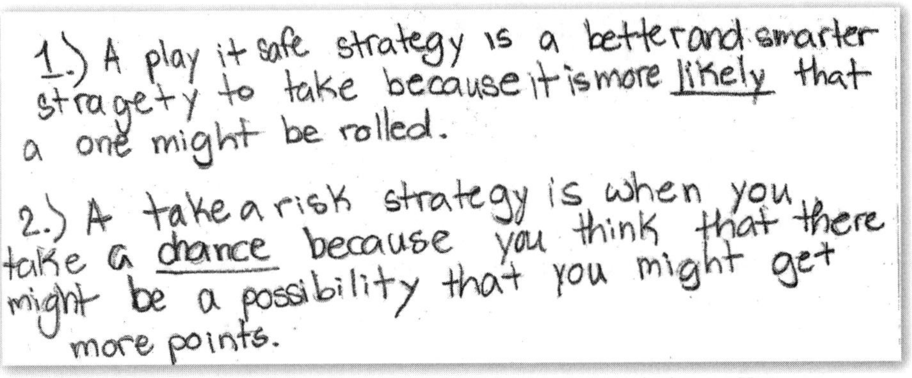

1.) A play it safe strategy is a better and smarter stragety to take because it is more likely that a one might be rolled.

2.) A take a risk strategy is when you take a chance because you think that there might be a possibility that you might get more points.

FIGURE 5-12. Pham includes one of the key vocabulary words from the lesson. He is at an advanced level of English language proficiency.

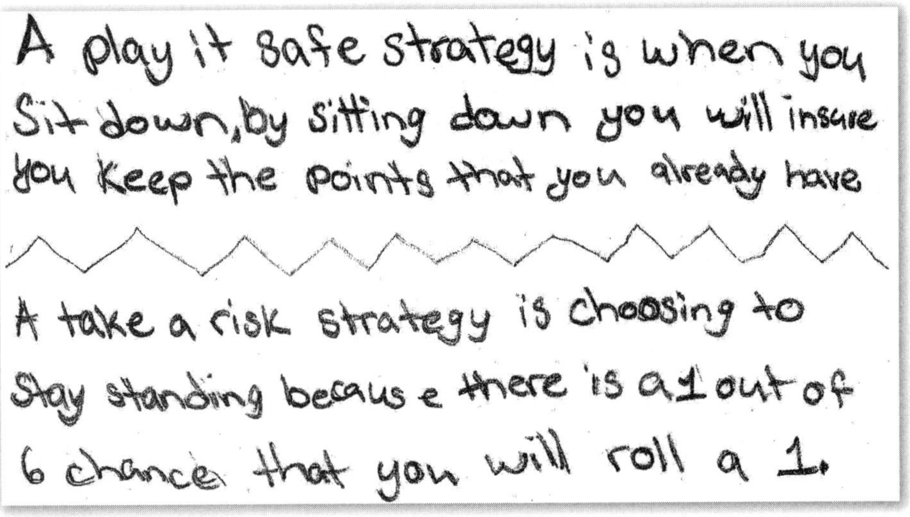

A play it safe strategy is when you Sit down, by sitting down you will insure you keep the points that you already have

A take a risk strategy is choosing to Stay standing becaus e there is a 1 out of 6 chance that you will roll a 1.

FIGURE 5-13. Esneida uses key vocabulary words from the lesson as well as ideas from the class's strategy chart. She is at an advanced level of English language proficiency.

Summarizing ✦ Part 4

Throughout the lesson, Kathy provided plenty of opportunities for students to interact with each other and to have conversations about their predictions and strategies, all while using key academic language. By having all students write a Play It Safe and a Take a Risk strategy using a sentence frame, Kathy added an extra layer of support for ELs (and for all students in general). Kathy used writing as a vehicle for students to share their ideas and to expand their understanding of the concepts covered in this lesson. Writing to learn provides ELs with additional venues to express themselves in a safe, collaborative environment, all while helping them develop important academic writing skills that can be used across curricular areas.

The Game of *SKUNK*: Part 5

Closing

Kathy thanked the students for their participation and for their thoughtful ideas on how to strategize for the game of *SKUNK*. She reminded students that they were not just playing a game; they were actually doing math. Some students seemed to be surprised that this was a math lesson, so Kathy asked the students why this game is also about math (see Authors' Note: "The Mathematics of Rolling Two Dice" later in the chapter).

Esneida said, "Because we know that there's a one in six chances to get a one when rolling a dice [sic], and that's probability!"

"I agree," Samantha concurred. "Because one in six is like one over six [one-sixth] and that's a fraction."

Sonya added, "Yes, and that's like ten percent."

"What do you mean?" Kathy probed.

Sonya responded, "That's, like, a ten percent chance that you will get a one."

"Good observation!" Kathy inquired further, "Is one-sixth exactly ten percent?"

"Not exactly, but it's an estimate," Sonia replied.

"Let's do the math to see how close your estimate is to the actual answer. What's one way to turn a fraction to a percent?"

Sonia replied, "We need to convert one-sixth to a decimal, by dividing one by six."

"Okay, that's one way, Kathy said. "Let's take a minute and try Sonia's suggestion and divide one by six." Kathy was aware that there are other ways to convert a fraction to a percent, but she did not want to lose the students' focus on the probability lesson. Kathy decided that reviewing the relationship between fractions, percents, and decimals could be scheduled at a later time.

After a minute or so, Kathy asked the students for their results. She called on Jorge.

"We get one hundred sixty-six thousandths, with a repeating six," Jorge said.

"And how do we convert one hundred sixty-six thousandths to a percent?" Kathy asked.

"We multiply times one hundred," said Sonya, "and we get sixteen and sixty-six hundredths percent."

"Is that the same as ten percent?" Kathy asked.

"No!" responded the students chorally.

Sonia rephrased her estimate, "Then it's not a ten percent chance that you will get a one, it's a little more than sixteen percent chance that you will get a one; but it's still not a very high chance, like eighty percent or something like that, so maybe you can take more risks when playing the game."

"Interesting point. Any other ideas?" Kathy asked the class.

Bao shared, "But maybe there's a pattern."

"Tell us more, Bao."

Bao continued, "So maybe after five rolls you should sit down because there's a one in six chance that you will get a one, so you have to take five chances."

"Maybe, but sometimes we got a one on the first roll," Ileana interrupted.

"Very good observations!" Kathy exclaimed, impressed with her students' conjectures.

Kathy took note of students' different responses regarding the mathematics of the game. In particular, Kathy was pleased to hear their different ways of looking at the likelihood of rolling a 1, because this was a central piece in the game rules, as well as in students' various strategies for determining whether to take a risk or to play it safe. She also realized that further teaching in examining the relationship between probability ratios, percentages, and charting or diagramming data would be useful in helping students see the interconnectedness between their fundamental understanding of math and everyday applications of probability.

Summarizing ◆ Key English Language Learner Strategies

Kathy incorporated many strategies to help her ELs participate fully in the lesson: The Game of *SKUNK*.

Strategy 1: Tapping into Prior Knowledge

As Kathy stated at the beginning of her lesson, although not always evident, probability is in our everyday lives as we make decisions and strategize based on prior experiences or knowledge. In this lesson, students had the opportunity to revisit basic notions of probability by generating a discussion about a "real-life" question: Should one take a chance in not turning in homework if the teacher says she might or might not collect it?

Strategy 2: Modeling and Encouraging the Use of Academic Language

Kathy purposefully integrated partner talk throughout the lesson. Kathy modeled the use of sentence frames to describe strategies to play the game of *SKUNK*, which helped students understand the usefulness of such frames in constructing their own oral and written descriptions about strategy, prediction, and the mathematical reasoning behind their choices. Moreover, because all students were encouraged to explain their strategies, both orally and in writing, first with a partner, and then with the entire class, students were given ample opportunities to engage in conversations about math using key academic vocabulary.

Strategy 3: Building a Classroom Community

Throughout the lesson, ELs were provided with linguistic supports to receive information and to produce academic language pertaining to the topic of this lesson. Such scaffolds are central to creating a safe environment in which students at all language levels are able to participate. Kathy acknowledged all students' contributions and ideas, and helped them make connections to the academic content of the lesson. Therefore, these students were not only active participants and contributors to the building of knowledge in the classroom, but they were also developing content-based as well as linguistic strategies to access complex ideas in mathematics for themselves.

Authors' Note: The Mathematics of Rolling Two Dice

There are 36 different possibilities when rolling two dice. (See Figure 5–14.) To get a sum of five for example, we need to roll a 3 and a 2. But there are other possibilities to get a sum of five, as Figure 5–14 confirms.

Using the values in Figure 5–14, we can also build a frequency distribution table to figure out the probability of rolling different numbers and sums. (See Figure 5–15.)

The frequency distribution table helps us visualize that when we roll one die, there is a one-in-six chance of rolling a 1. Also, when rolling two dice, there's a one-in-thirty-six chance of rolling snake eyes (meaning, when rolling a pair of dice, each die comes up with a 1).

The odds of a specified outcome are always the same on every throw of the dice. You could roll double 1s 10 times in a row, and the chances of the next roll being a double 1 will still be the same: 35 to 1.

The Game of *SKUNK*: An Investigation into Probability

Dice #1

Dice #2	⚀	⚁	⚂	⚃	⚄	⚅
⚀	2	3	4	5	6	7
⚁	3	4	5	6	7	8
⚂	4	5	6	7	8	9
⚃	5	6	7	8	9	10
⚄	6	7	8	9	10	11
⚅	7	8	9	10	11	12

FIGURE 5-14. The game of SKUNK: There are 36 different possibilities when rolling two dice.

The odds for any outcome are the same for every roll. It is a common misconception by gamblers that this is not true. Odds work out over a period of time and over a number of random results. A casino that takes thousands of bets an hour knows this. The *law of averages* works

Frequency Distribution Table

Values	Probability
2	1/36
3	2/36
4	3/36
5	4/36
6	5/36
7	6/36
8	5/36
9	4/36
10	3/36
11	2/36
12	1/36

FIGURE 5-15. Building a frequency distribution table to figure out the probability of rolling different numbers and sums.

over the long term. If you throw a die an infinite number of times, the results will match the true odds; but, the lower the number of rolls, the more the results *can* differ. Some gamblers lose a lot of money waiting for the law of averages to work for them, with no chance of recouping it.

Suggestions for Extending the Lesson

Keep Track

✦ Students roll a die and keep track of the number of rolls before rolling a 1.

✦ The teacher keeps track of students' totals on a class chart numbered 1 through 30 so the students can see how many times they roll before a 1 comes up.

✦ This activity can be repeated with rolling two dice as well.

Use Write-to-Learn Activities (adapted from Illuminations, n.d.)

I. In life, many things happen. Some are the result mostly of chance or "luck," and others mostly result from the choices and decisions you make. Think about some things that happened recently in your life.
    a. List two things that happened to you mainly because of chance.
    b. List two things that happened to you mostly because you made a choice.

II. Rolling a 1 in *SKUNK* is a disaster. To get a better score, it would be useful to know, on average, how many good rolls happen before a 1 or double 1s come up. (Give students two dice so that they can experiment and keep track. To guide your students, ask them to roll the dice and to note the points they receive each time until a 1 is rolled. Then, the points could be totaled and the average value per time calculated.)
    a. Decide on a way to find out.
    b. Carry out your plan and describe the results.

III. In *SKUNK*, when a 1 isn't rolled, what is the average score on a single roll of the dice? (Give students two dice so that they can experiment and keep track. To guide your students, you could ask them to roll the dice and to note the points they receive each time until a 1 is rolled. Then, the points could be totaled and the average value per time calculated.)
    a. Decide on a way to find out.
    b. Carry out your plan and describe the results.

IV. Write about the strategies one could use to play *SKUNK*.
   a. Describe your Play It Safe strategy.
   b. Describe your Take a Risk strategy.
   c. Estimate the kind of scores each strategy would be likely to produce.
   d. Play *SKUNK* using each of your strategies and keep a record of your scores.
   e. How well do your results agree with what you expected?

Use a Rating Chart (adapted from Illuminations, n.d.)

✦ In groups, students create a "rating chart." For example:
   ✦ 0 to 20: needs improvement
   ✦ 21 to 40: you might do better
   ✦ 41 to 60: average
   ✦ 61 to 80: good
   ✦ More than 80: outstanding
✦ This rating chart was devised by assuming that, on average, a 1 comes up on about the third dice roll and the average score per good roll is eight. Therefore, with a strategy of "roll twice then stop" on each round, a person might get about 16 points on perhaps four out of five rounds, for a total score of about 64. The 20-point intervals used for each category are arbitrary. Whichever rating scale students create, they should justify their reasoning for the intervals.

Create Your Own Game (adapted from Illuminations, n.d.)

✦ Have teams of students devise their own game involving *choice* and *chance*.
✦ Tell students to write up consistent, clear rules for their game, so that it involves mathematical logic.
✦ Have teams present their game to the rest of the class and to other classrooms as well.
✦ Let the teacher and the students decide when to play each of the games designed by each team.

Scaling Up!

6

Overview

In this lesson students work on multiple measurement concepts, including measuring length, scale, ratio, and proportion. Students apply all the concepts in an activity that involves enlarging a picture to scale so that it fits on a piece of graph paper. Students must take measurements, determine the ratio they will need to enlarge the picture, and, finally, ensure that the drawing is proportional. At the end of the lesson, students discuss and write about the steps they took to create their scaled-up drawing. For more on how this lesson was designed, see page 186.

Math Goal: Students will be able to solve problems involving scale factors, using ratio and proportion as measured by a scaled-up drawing of a figure.

COMMON CORE STATE STANDARDS

Grade 7: Ratios and Proportional Relationships

Analyze proportional relationships and use them to solve real-world and mathematical problems.

- Compute unit rates associated with ratios of fractions, including ratios of lengths, areas, and other quantities measured in like or different units.

- Recognize and represent proportional relationships between quantities.

- Decide whether two quantities are in a proportional relationship.

- Identify the constant of proportionality (unit rate) in tables, graphs, equations, diagrams, and verbal descriptions of proportional relationships.

Adapted from the lesson "Scaling Up and Down" (145) in *Sizing Up Measurement: Activities for Grades 6–8 Classrooms* by Ann Lawrence and Charlie Hennessy (2007).

Language Goal: Students will sequence the steps they used to solve the problem of creating a scale drawing using math vocabulary and sequence words.

For more on determining key vocabulary, see page 180.

Key Vocabulary: proportion, proportional, ratio, scale, scale factor, similar figures

Materials:
✦ Scaling Up! Recording Sheet (Reproducible 6–1A), 1 per student
✦ Scaling Up! Directions (Reproducible 6–1B), 1 per pair of students
✦ Sample scaled-up drawing and directions (for display; a cartoon character works well)
✦ Pictures for students' scaled up drawings, 1 per pair of students
✦ Scaling Up! Table for Converting Measurements (Reproducible 6–1C), 1 per pair of students (optional)
✦ Grid paper, 34 × 27 inches (or any other large-size grid paper) with 1-inch squares, 1 piece per pair of students
✦ Paper ruler, 2 × 27 inches, cut from the grid paper, 1 per pair of students

Pictures Note: For students at earlier grades or when beginning the concept of scale factors, begin with pictures of simple figures. More complex drawings of cartoon characters or pictures of real-life objects can be used with older students or those who have had more experience with scale.

Sentence Starters (Sequence Words)
First
In the beginning
At first
Then
Next
After that
Following (previous subject)
Finally
At the end
Lastly

Paper Ruler Note: To create paper rulers, cut strips from the grid paper that are 2" (2 squares) high and 27" (27 squares) long.

Scaling Up!: Part 1

Luz Chung, the guest teacher for the day, greeted each of the 33 seventh graders as they filed into class. The class was comprised of a diverse mix of native English speakers and ELs. In addition, students also brought different prior experiences in mathematics and were at a variety of math proficiency levels. Luz knew that the varying levels of proficiency in English and in math could present her with many challenges, and that she would have to be very intentional and strategic in her instruction to ensure that she met the varied needs of the students with whom she would be working. She wanted to make a personal connection with every student before beginning her math lesson on ratio and proportion.

The seventh-grade class was a typical middle school group, with peers socializing in, primarily, same-gender groups. Luz made note of their interactions; she was planning for a lot of partner and group work in her lesson and wanted to ensure that meaningful discussions occurred. Luz knows that there are many things to take into account when planning for talk in the middle school classroom, including attitudinal and behavioral issues related to adolescent identity development, as well as socialization patterns and perception factors between peers and between gender groups. In respecting such, Luz modified the seating chart for the day to foster student talk strategically. She created heterogeneous groups of students based on academic and English language levels. Luz also ensured that the groups had same-sex pairs, because she knows students tend to work better in such partnerships.

The lesson Luz had prepared for the day included a review of some of the measurement standards the students had previously been taught. She knew that the students had received direct instruction on the concepts of ratio and proportion, and was looking forward to seeing how they would apply the concepts in a drawing activity while also developing their use of academic language.

Introducing Academic Language

"Today we are going to work on some drawings during class," Luz began. "Before we start, I want to review a few of the important concepts and vocabulary that you'll need to know to make your drawing. You've probably heard these words before. I want you to answer the question: What do you know about *scale* or *ratio, scale drawing, similar figures,* and *proportions*?"

Luz recorded the words using a blue marker on chart paper. Later in the lesson, Luz planned to introduce sentence starters (sequence words) as part of the academic language, and she intended to use a different-color marker to identify these words.

Luz distributed a recording sheet to each student. (See Figure 6–1, which is also available as Reproducible 6–1A at the end of the book.) She asked students to log their ideas on the sheet.

Scaling Up! Recording Sheet

The following recording sheet can be reproduced for use during Part 1: Introducing Academic Language, of the lesson.

Scale (think ratio):
Scale drawing:
Similar figures:
Proportions:

(See Figure 6-2 for an example of how a student filled out a section.)

FIGURE 6-1. Scaling Up! Recording Sheet.

Luz instructed the class, "You may work with the person sitting next to you to talk about these ideas. You can use words, pictures, examples, or any other way to show everything you know about these four concepts."

ELs don't always have the words in English to express their understanding, so allowing them to use visuals, such as pictures and numbers, gives everyone a chance to participate.

The students began chatting with one another about the terms on their recording sheets. As Luz circulated, she noticed that some students were having a hard time using words to define the terms. She encouraged them to give numerical examples or to use drawings as an alternative. After about five minutes, Luz called the class back together to review the four key vocabulary words.

"Who can tell me what *scale* or *ratio* is?" Luz asked.

Viviana volunteered, "Whenever the bottom number is a one."

"Can you tell me more about that?" Luz probed.

"Like ten to one or three to one. When you write out the ratio the one is on the bottom," Viviana answered.

Although Viviana's ideas serve as a good example for the upcoming lesson, she seemed to think that all ratios included a number compared with one. Luz wanted her to see that a ratio can tell how *any* two numbers are related. Luz called on Eric to see if he could shed some more light on the concept.

"A comparison of two numbers," Eric explained.

"Tell me a little bit more about what you mean by a comparison of two numbers," Luz probed. Luz looks for opportunities to help students explain their thinking in more detail and asks probing questions to facilitate this process.

"Like, there are two girls to five boys is a comparison," Eric added.

Luz wrote the words that Eric volunteered on chart paper, plus the numerical or symbolic representation of 2:5 and 2/5 that students shared. She recorded Viviana's examples as well: 1:3, 1/3 and 1:10, 1/10, like this:

Scale or ratio: Two girls to five boys—2:5 and 2/5
1:3 and 1/3, and 1:10 and 1/10

When ideas are presented orally, writing them down so the whole class can see the ideas gives ELs a chance to read the words at their own pace, make sense of them, and revisit the ideas throughout the lesson.

"So a ratio is a comparison of any two numbers," Luz clarified. "How about another example of *ratio* or *scale?*"

George raised his hand, "It is a comparison of two different numbers like two teachers to thirty-three students." (See Figure 6–2.)

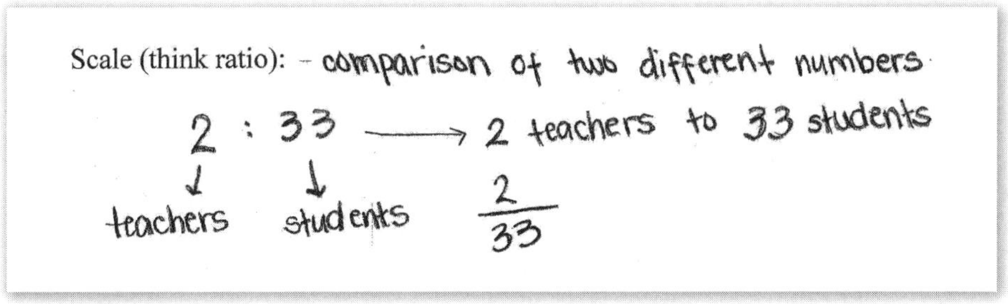

When ideas are presented orally, writing them down so the whole class can see the ideas gives English learners a chance to read the words at their own pace, make sense of them, and revisit the ideas throughout the lesson.

Scale (think ratio): – comparison of two different numbers

$2 : 33 \longrightarrow$ 2 teachers to 33 students

teachers   students $\dfrac{2}{33}$

FIGURE 6-2. *George demonstrates his understanding of scale using words and numerical representations.*

"How is this *ratio* or *scale*?" Luz probed.

"It's a ratio of the number of teachers compared with the number of students," George explained.

Luz recorded George's example on the chart paper for *ratio* or *scale* and moved on to the next concept.

"What is a *scale drawing*? As some of you found out, it is not a drawing of a scale," Luz stated lightheartedly. It is not uncommon for ELs to use what they know of everyday English vocabulary and apply it to academic English. Multiple-meaning words, such as *scale*, have a different meaning in everyday use from their use in mathematics. In this case, some students knew the word *scale* as an item used to measure the weight of something; however, this wasn't the correct definition of the mathematical term *scale drawings*.

> It is not uncommon for English learners to use what they know of everyday English vocabulary and apply it to academic English.

Luz used wait time to determine whether any students had an idea for the definition of *scale drawing*. Eventually, a few students raised their hand. Luz called on Kim.

"A drawing of the ratio," Kim stated.

"Right," Luz responded and recorded Kim's idea on the chart paper next to the word. Luz had noticed that many students struggled with the term *scale drawing* during their partner discussions; she realized that this was a very abstract concept for students to grasp. In addition, she knew that the main concept of her lesson was to teach scale drawings. Therefore, she told students that after they moved on to the actual drawing part of the lesson, this concept would become clearer.

"Okay, let's move on to *similar figures*," Luz said. "What are *similar figures*?"

"Figures," José answered.

"They are the same things but not the same size," Jacob clarified.

"Who can give me an example of *similar figures*?" Luz asked the class.

Christina volunteered. Following Christina's directions, Luz drew a triangle on the chart paper and then drew the same triangle but in a smaller size next to the first one. (See Figure 6–3.)

"Those are equilateral triangles," Christina explained.

"Correct. They are equilateral triangles that are *similar*," Luz replied with an emphasis on the term *similar*. Luz then reminded students of the basic properties of similar triangles, which indicate

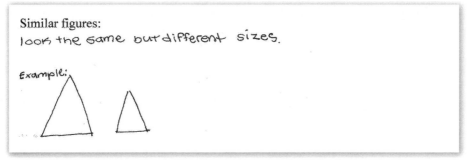

FIGURE 6-3. *Christina illustrates her understanding of similar figures with a drawing of two triangles.*

that for triangles to be similar, their corresponding angles must be the same and their corresponding sides must be proportional in size.

Not all students were willing to share their ideas orally, so Luz also looked at their work to assess their understanding as she circulated in the classroom. Luz noticed that Simone had written on her paper, "They look the same, but they have different sizes. They are compare to each ather [sic]." Luz was pleased that Simone, a beginning EL, attempted to write about her mathematical understanding using the English that she did have. Luz made a mental note to help Simone with her grammar when appropriate and to give her some corrective feedback that would help her make progress in English. Luz knows this step is essential to help ELs reach full English proficiency.

"On to the last word on our paper. Who can give me an example of a *proportion*?" Luz prompted the class.

"Twenty over five and four over one," Andres said.

Luz recorded the fractions on the chart paper. "What goes between the two numbers? Why are they *proportions*?" she probed.

"You can put an equal sign between them. If you simplify twenty over five, you get four over one," Andres clarified.

"You're right. These are proportional numbers," Luz replied. "A *proportion* is when two ratios are equal, as in Andres's example. Ellie, can you tell the class the example you told me about *proportion*? Ellie used a story problem to explain the term."

"If you write twenty words in five minutes, how many words can you write in one minute?" Ellie stated.

Luz wrote Ellie's word problem on the chart paper and then asked the students how to write the mathematical notation for the problem.

Kim shared, "It's twenty over five equals *x* over one." Luz recorded this on the chart paper as well like this:

> **Proportion:**
> *If you write 20 words in 5 minutes, how many words can you write in 1 minute?*
>
> $$\frac{20}{5} = \frac{x}{1}$$

Kim shared the procedure for finding the value of *x* in a ratio problem, revealing her knowledge of mathematical procedures. It is important for students to have experiences with skills, procedures, concepts, and problem solving as part of their math curriculum. This lesson is designed to help students with all these aspects.

"Right," Luz replied. Students copied the equation and many murmured that they now remembered proportion. Luz is aware that it may take many examples before students have a solid understanding of concepts or for them to recall what they've learned.

While circulating during partner talk, Luz noticed that José, a native Spanish speaker, wrote his definition of proportion in Spanish. He wrote, *Una proporcion es como una fracion* (A proportion is like a fraction). Luz was pleased that José was able to demonstrate what he knew about proportions in his primary language. Her goal now was to help him develop his English skills through targeted support so he could begin to express his understanding of mathematics in English.

"Do you remember *proportion* now?" Luz asked.

"Yes!" several students replied in unison.

"Now that we have reviewed *ratio* or *scale*, *scale drawings*, *similar figures*, and *proportion*, we are ready for the next part of the lesson. We're going to make drawings using *scales* or *ratios*. If I ask you to scale up a drawing, what does that mean?" Luz inquired.

"Draw it bigger," a number of students replied chorally.

"You're going to do scale drawings today," Luz explained. She held up a paper ruler. (See Figure 6–4.) "You are going to use the squares on this strip of paper to make your measurements. These will serve as your rulers. You probably are used to using rulers with centimeters or inches on them, but today you are going to measure in squares using these special rulers."

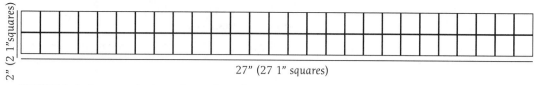

FIGURE 6-4. A paper ruler is used to scale up drawings. The paper rulers should be 2 squares deep and 27 squares long (each square should be 1").

Luz showed the class a strip of grid paper that was two squares high by 27 squares long. The grid paper used to create these nonstandard rulers was the same as the grid paper students would be using to make their scale drawings.

Luz asked the students how they could use these nonstandard rulers to measure.

"By counting the number of squares," the students responded.

Luz intentionally planned for students to use the grid paper squares for measuring their drawings, because it would be easier for them to scale up the measurements instead of having to convert measurements using inches or centimeters.

As a review, Luz questioned the class again, "Scale up means what?"

"Make it bigger!" the class answered.

"I'm not going to tell you what ratio or *scale* to use to make your picture bigger; you'll have to decide that. Your drawing does need to be proportional, however. What does proportional mean?" Luz recognizes that to develop a deep understanding of mathematical concepts and the corresponding academic language, repetition of key ideas presented in multiple contexts is important.

"Similar," Viviana answered.

"Right. The drawings have to be similar," Luz confirmed. "For example, if I make the scale or ratio of the eye one to two and make the scale of the arm one to ten, will my picture be proportional?"

"No. The ratios for each part of the body have to be similar to make similar figures," Ellie explained. Luz was pleased that Ellie was using the academic language to respond to her question.

Next, Luz distributed the written directions to the students to help them with their task. (See Figure 6–5, and Reproducible 6–1B at the end of the book.)

Luz read the directions to the class and then modeled how she made her scale drawing of a picture (in this case, her picture is a cartoon character). While demonstrating, she made reference to the sentence starters (sequence words) and the academic terms that she

Scaling Up! Directions

1. The **goal** is to **scale up** the original picture, and to draw its **larger version (as exact as possible)** on the graphing paper.

2. With your partner, figure out **a scale/ratio** that will make you draw a picture big enough to cover most of the graphing paper.

3. The **scaled up (larger)** picture has to be **proportional** to the original picture.

4. **Measure at least five** parts of the original picture so that you can draw its larger version.

FIGURE 6–5. Scaling Up! Directions.

wanted students to use in their description of how they made their scale drawings later in the lesson. She placed a list of sentence starters (sequence words) and phrases color coded in red on chart paper next to the key academic vocabulary *scale* or *ratio*, *scale drawing*, *similar figures*, and *proportion*, which were written in blue, like this:

Key Vocabulary	Sentence Starters (Sequence Words)
Scale	First, In the beginning, At first
Scale drawing	Then, Next, After that, Following _____,
Similar figures	Finally, At the end, Lastly
Proportions	

She referred to both sets of words as she explained her steps in constructing her scale drawing. Modeling *how* to use the academic language is essential if students are expected to use it.

Luz began, *"First*, I decided which part of the picture I would measure first. *Next*, I measured the diameter of the head to see if it was symmetrical. *Then*, I tried different ratios to see which one would give me the largest drawing possible. *After that*, I realized that the best ratio was one to three."

Luz was careful not to give the students too much direction regarding to how to create the proportions, but wanted to model the steps and academic language she used to begin her scale drawing.

"When I first began, I had to increase the scale or ratio, because my picture wasn't going to be big enough to cover all of my paper. That is a goal you have with your picture. What will you need to do to make the proportions bigger?" Luz inquired.

"Multiply," a few students replied.

"So you multiply the number of squares?" George asked.

"You multiply it by how much you want to make it bigger," Kim clarified.

"Correct. For example, I made my ratio one to three," Luz explained. "For every one square on my original drawing, I had to have three on the scaled drawing. To figure this out, I multiplied the number of squares for a particular measurement by three to get the measurement for the scaled-up drawing."

In some classrooms, students may benefit from using a recording sheet to help them with the conversion of their measurements. Although Luz didn't use one in this class, a sample recording sheet "Scaling Up! Table for Converting Measurements" is included at the end of the book (Reproducible 6–1C).

"Ready? If so, then you may begin. You will work in pairs to scale up your drawing. Remember to think about *scale* or *ratio*, *scale drawing*, *proportions*, and *similar figures*," Luz reminded them, pointing to the key vocabulary words on the chart paper.

Summarizing ✦ Part 1

During the first part of this lesson, Luz spent time revisiting important mathematical concepts and key vocabulary that students would need to understand to make their scale drawings. This time also allowed Luz to do formative assessment and address any common misconceptions that students had. Feeling confident that students had enough background knowledge and academic language to tackle the next part of the task, Luz moved on to Part 2 of the lesson: making scale drawings.

Scaling Up!: Part 2

Making Scale Drawings

Luz distributed a variety of pictures, one per pair of students. She paid particular attention to the complexity of each picture, knowing that to scale up more complex pictures, students need to have more advanced math skills. Luz was intentional in selecting pictures for pairs based on the students' math level (not on their English proficiency) to ensure that all students would be able to complete the task successfully. She also gave each pair of students a large piece of grid paper and a ruler made from the same grid paper to help them figure out ratios and proportions.

Students began working with their partners. As expected, the teams approached the work in a variety of ways. Some partners worked collaboratively to measure the dimensions of certain parts of their picture, whereas others worked in tandem, with one measuring and one converting the measurement for the scaled-up drawing.

Luz observed Andres and Jacob as they worked.

"Where should we start measuring?" Andres asked his partner, Jacob.

"What if we do this way first and then across the body?" Jacob replied.

Jacob and Andres worked to find all the measurements of five parts of the original picture before working to find the correct proportion for their scaled-up drawing.

"How do we figure out what to multiply it by?" Andres asked Luz. He and Jacob had started off the assignment with a clear understanding, but were stuck at the scaling part of the task.

"Can you tell me what you did already so I can understand where you are in making your scaled-up drawing?" Luz asked the boys.

"First, we measured five parts of the cartoon," Jacob explained.

"After that?" Luz guided.

"After that, we need to figure out how big to make the picture, but we don't remember how to do that," Jacob explained.

Luz was pleased that Jacob was using the sequence words in his explanation, but realized that he wasn't using the academic terms she previously introduced. Luz intentionally asked a question using the mathematical vocabulary she expected students to use.

"Remember, you need to try to make the picture as big as you can so it can cover most of the paper. What do you think the scale or ratio will be?" Luz prompted.

"I think it will be one to two," Andres said.

"So we will need to multiply the numbers by two," Jacob added.

Jacob and Andres continued their work by multiplying all their original measurements by two, and then began drawing on the grid paper. Before getting too far along, Andres noticed that their scaled drawing was not going to be big enough to cover much of the paper.

"I think we need to redo the measurements," Andres stated. "Our picture is not going to be big enough."

Through exploration in this lesson, Andres discovered a mistake with his original thinking. Discovering and confronting mistakes, as well as restarting a task, is an important part of problem solving. Having the opportunity to explore and tinker with ideas is key to developing confidence and competence in mathematics.

> Discovering and confronting mistakes, as well as restarting a task, is an important part of problem solving. Having the opportunity to explore and tinker with ideas is key to developing confidence and competence in mathematics.

Jacob and Andres returned to their original calculations and started over with a new ratio of one to four. (See Figure 6–6.)

Simone and Ellie were partnered up for this assignment. Luz intentionally paired the students by gender, because she knows that students in this age group tend to work better in same-sex partnerships. She also considered the students' English proficiency and their math skills. In this case, both Ellie and Simone had strong math skills, but differed in their English proficiency. Ellie is a native English speaker and Simone's first language is French. Simone is still at the early stages of English proficiency and benefits from working with students at the same math level and who have strong communication skills in English (see pages 20–21 for more details on grouping students).

Luz noticed that Simone and Ellie were moving along well with their scaled drawing. The girls were working collaboratively to measure the dimensions of six parts of their original drawing. They had calculated the scale or ratio to be 1:3 to make their picture big enough to cover most of the paper. They spoke quietly while determining where to begin their drawing.

Scaling Up!

FIGURE 6-6. *Jacob and Andres were able to complete the scaled up drawing of a cactus successfully after they determined the ratio to be 4:1.*

"How about if we start with the bottom?" Ellie asked.

"I will draw a line for the feet. How big the line?" Simone conferred with her partner.

"The line is twenty-six squares long," Ellie replied.

"What comes next?" Simone inquired.

Ellie responded, "What if we draw the sides next?"

Luz noted that the girls were using sequence words in their discussion. By planning activities during which students need to talk with one another to complete the task, Luz is being deliberate about academic language development. She knows that without this structured opportunity to work in pairs, many students would complete tasks independently without interacting with others.

"What proportion or ratio are you using to scale up your drawing?" Luz probed, wanting to check for the girls' understanding of the key vocabulary.

"One to three," Simone answered.

"We decided that one to three would be a good ratio for making our scale drawing big enough to cover the paper," Ellie explained.

FIGURE 6-7. *Ellie and Simone created an accurate and proportionate scale drawing of a flower.*

"Is your scale drawing proportionate?" Luz asked. She crafted this yes-or-no answer as a way for Simone to demonstrate her understanding without requiring extensive language production.

"Yes," Simone replied.

"How do you know?" Luz asked.

"We do the same measuring for all the numbers," Simone explained.

Ellie contributed more details, "We multiplied all of our original measurements by three to be sure that all of the measurements would be proportional."

"You are on the right track. Keep going and I will come back to check on your work in a bit," Luz concluded. (See Figure 6–7.)

Luz continued to circulate around the room, checking in on students' work and checking for understanding. She prompted pairs of students to tell her the sequence of their steps using the words and phrases that she had posted. In addition, she promoted the use of academic vocabulary by asking direct questions that included the key vocabulary and eliciting responses from students that used the academic terminology.

After about 35 minutes of work time, the majority of the class had completed their scaled-up drawings. (See Figures 6–8 and 6–9.)

FIGURE 6-8. *Working collaboratively, Christina and Viviana produced an accurate scale drawing of a Christmas tree.*

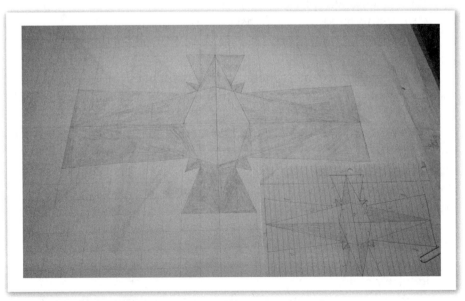

FIGURE 6-9. *José and Eric had a much more elaborate drawing to scale up, yet were successful in doing so with careful measurements and calculations.*

In this part of the lesson, students had demonstrated their skills in computation and problem solving to make their scaled-up drawings, and along the way had engaged in conversations to help them deepen their mathematical understanding. In the next part of the lesson, Luz assesses students' understanding of the process of creating scale drawings, the mathematical concepts of ratio and proportion, and their use of academic language.

Scaling Up!: Part 3

Writing Directions

Luz continued to the next task. "Now that you have completed your scaled-up drawings, I want you to write directions explaining how you did the task. What are the five or six most important steps you used to scale up your original drawing? Here are the steps I used." Luz read her directions. (She had written them on chart paper beforehand, see below.) "*First,* I decided which part of the picture I would measure first. *Next,* I measured the diameter of the head to see if it was symmetrical. *Then,* I tried different ratios to see which one would give me the largest drawing possible. *After that,* I realized that the best ratio was one to three."

> *First,* I decided which part of the picture I would measure first.
>
> *Next,* I measured the diameter of the head to see if it was symmetrical.
>
> *Then,* I tried different ratios to see which one would give me the largest drawing possible.
>
> *After that,* I realized that the best ratio was 1:3.

Luz drew the students' attention to the list of key vocabulary and sentence starters (sequence words) on the chart paper. This was the same chart she had used earlier in the lesson when introducing the academic vocabulary, shown on page 138.

Key Vocabulary	Sentence Starters (Sequence Words)
Scale	First, In the beginning, At first
Scale drawing	Then, Next, After that, Following _____,
Similar figures	Finally, At the end, Lastly
Proportions	

Luz asked the students to read each word or phrase chorally on the list. By taking the time to practice saying the phrases out loud, students get a chance to try out the language with guidance before being expected to use it independently.

Luz directed the students first to work with their partner to talk about the steps and sequence words they would eventually use to write their directions. She also reminded them of the key vocabulary words and encouraged them to use these words as well. Luz knows that it is important for students to practice language orally before writing it. Oral language development is often missing in classrooms, and it is a foundational piece that is key to internalizing academic language.

Christina and Viviana discussed their process together.

Viviana started, "First we measured five different parts of the picture."

Christina added, "After that, we multiplied by three to make the scale big enough to fit onto the paper."

Referring to the chart with the sequence words, Viviana said, "After we finished that, we made our drawing on the graph paper. Then, we had to make sure that our drawing was proportion [sic]."

"Finally, we colored in our picture to match the original," Christina concluded.

Luz noticed that Viviana used the word *proportion* in her explanation, but she used the incorrect form of the word. As is common with academic terms, it is important for teachers to show how a word is changed when used as different parts of speech. In this case, Luz called the class back together and explained the difference between *proportion* and *proportional*.

"As I have been walking around listening to you talk with your partner, I've noticed that many of you are using the word *proportion* in your explanation." Luz wrote the words *proportion* and *proportional* for the class to see. Motioning to the first word, Luz explained, "Proportion is a word we use to describe the relationship between two numbers or things. For example, we can say that my drawing is *in proportion*. Or, the *proportion* of my scaled-up drawing is correct. Pointing to the second word, Luz said, "If you want to describe that you made the right calculations and that your proportion is accurate, you can say that your picture is *proportional*." To check for understanding, Luz asked the class if anyone could restate how to use the word *proportion*.

Andres volunteered, "The *proportions* of my drawing are correct."

"Perfect," Luz replied. "Can anyone give us an example of how to use *proportional*?"

"The parts of my drawing are *proportional*?" Kim ventured.

"That's right, Kim," Luz affirmed.

Although Luz knows that the students will need more practice and examples with the words to be able to use them fluently, she decided that enough time had been spent on these terms and directed the students to continue talking with their partners.

Luz monitored the conversations between students, providing feedback as she went. As students finished describing their sequence of steps, Luz distributed paper and instructed the students to write their directions. Students' writing would provide additional evidence of student learning of both the math content and academic language, as well as serve as Luz's final form of assessment. (See Figures 6–10 through 6–12.)

"You have worked very hard to create scale drawings that are proportional. Give me a thumbs-up if you have a better understanding of the terms *scale* or *ratio*, *scale drawing*, *similar figures*, and *proportion*." With

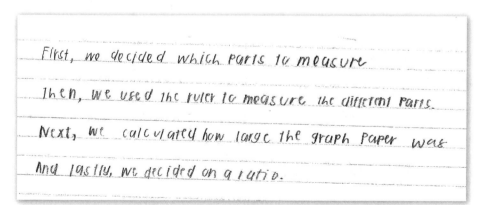

FIGURE 6-10. *José, an intermediate EL, used four sequencing words to describe his process for making a scaled drawing.*

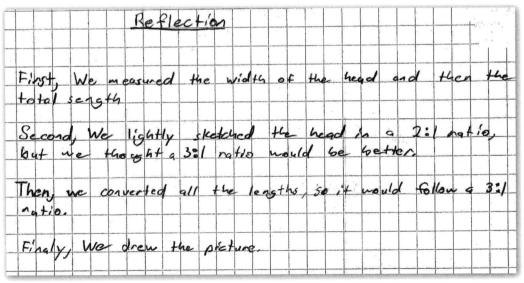

<u>Reflection</u>
This is what I did to draw the scaled up size of the picture:

First I decided on what to measure first.

Next I measured the distance from head to toe for length and width. (same with all the other parts)

Then I played with the numbers to see if it was too big or too small for the larger paper. (same w/ the rest)

Last I ended up multiplying everything by 5 and blowing it up.

FIGURE 6-11. *Viviana is a student at the advanced level of English proficiency. She gives a clear, detailed description of the steps she used for completing a scale drawing.*

<u>Reflection</u>

First, We measured the width of the head and then the total length

Second, We lightly sketched the head in a 2:1 ratio, but we thought a 3:1 ratio would be better.

Then, we converted all the lengths, so it would follow a 3:1 ratio.

Finally, We drew the picture.

FIGURE 6-12. *Eric, a native English speaker, used more precise language to describe the steps he took to complete the task.*

each word, the majority of the students raised their thumb, an indication that most students seemed confident about their learning.

◆ Summarizing the Lesson: Key English Language Learner Strategies

Luz incorporated many strategies to help her ELs fully participate in the lesson *Scaling Up!*

Strategy 1: Partner Work

In the lesson *Scaling Up!*, students worked in pairs to apply their prior knowledge of ratio and proportion in a scale drawing activity. Partner work provides ELs opportunities to develop their academic English language and mathematical understanding when discussing the math content with their partner. During collaboration of the scale drawing, students had an authentic purpose to communicate and to use language—to complete their scaled-up drawing. When there is purposeful and accountable talk with partners, ELs and native English speakers alike accomplish dual tasks: negotiating their understanding of the math content while simultaneously developing their oral language skills.

An important factor to consider when pairing partners is to think about the English proficiency of each student and their disposition toward working together. Luz made sure that students at the earlier proficiency levels of English were paired with students who were strong English models and who also demonstrated patience and tolerance when working with students of diverse backgrounds.

Strategy 2: Promoting Talk with Language Support

Luz is cognizant of the fact that the richness of math discussions can be lost on her ELs if she is not strategic in providing them with the support they need to participate fully in the lesson. Luz provided vocabulary lists to allow all students a chance to participate in math discussions and to demonstrate understanding of the content without the barrier of language. She created and displayed a chart with both the academic vocabulary and the sentence starters (sequence words) that she expected students to use during the lesson. In addition, Luz modeled how to use the language in a grammatically correct way. By providing models of the correct academic English, Luz was making certain that all

Scaling Up!

her students, including her ELs, would be able to participate fully and learn the key concepts she had determined as her objective.

Strategy 3: Differentiating Assessments

Luz used a variety of assessments to measure student learning. To be responsive to ELs at different proficiency levels, Luz crafted specific questions for different students. Some questions for students at the beginning levels of English proficiency required only a yes-or-no answer, whereas other questions for students with advanced language skills required more open-ended responses. By doing this, Luz's questions provided all students with opportunities to demonstrate their understanding. Luz also planned for differentiated demonstrations of learning that were not necessarily language dependent. By encouraging students to draw, use numerical representations, and write with language scaffolds, all students were able to demonstrate their understanding of the math content. Noting how students engaged in reviewing vocabulary, measuring, doing calculations, drawing, and writing helped Luz formatively assess their understanding throughout the lesson.

Suggestions for Extending the Lesson

Scale Down a Drawing

Instead of scaling up a drawing, which involves multiplication, have students scale down a drawing, which involves division. This problem could create some unique problem-solving activities, because the ratios may not divide easily. This task will engage students in determining the measurement they will use to make sure their drawing remains proportional.

Vary the Complexity of the Picture from Simple Shapes to Actual Objects

For students in earlier grades, or when beginning the concept of scale factors, begin with simple figures to reproduce. This activity makes the measurements and drawing simpler. As students become more sophisticated in their understanding, increase the complexity of the drawing to pictures of real-life objects.

Use Standard Measurements to Create Scale Drawings

Another way to increase the complexity of this activity is to have students use standard measurements. Using the nonstandard ruler with the squares similar to the grid paper makes the task easier as the "measurements" students get will easily transfer to the grid paper. By using standard measurements, students rely on their understanding of scale and conversion of units.

7 Archimedes' Puzzle

COMMON CORE STATE STANDARDS

Grade 6: Geometry

Solve real-world and mathematical problems involving area

- Find the area of right triangles, other triangles, special quadrilaterals, and polygons by composing into rectangles or decomposing into triangles and other shapes; apply these techniques in the context of solving real-world and mathematical problems.

Grade 7: Geometry

Solve real-life and mathematical problems involving angle measure and area.

- Solve real-world and mathematical problems involving area of two-dimensional objects composed of triangles, quadrilaterals, and polygons.

Overview

In this lesson, students investigate aspects of geometry including identifying and finding the area of geometric shapes. At the start of the lesson, students name the polygons they can identify in *Archimedes' Puzzle*. After that, they determine the area of regular polygons such as squares, rectangles, and triangles that are inside the puzzle. Finally, they combine two pieces of the puzzle to create an irregular polygon and determine the area of that shape.

Math Goal: Students will calculate the area of regular and irregular polygons.

Language Goal: Students will describe and sequence the steps they used to calculate the area of polygons.

Key Vocabulary: area (base, height, length, side, width), integer, multiple, polygons (triangles, quadrilaterals, pentagons), regular, irregular

Materials:

✦ Archimedes' Puzzle, Description and Picture (Reproducible 7–1), 1 copy for the teacher
✦ Archimedes' Puzzle (Reproducible 7–2), 1 copy per pair of students
✦ Polygon Hunt Recording Sheet: Finding Polygons (Reproducible 7–3A), 1 copy per student
✦ Polygon Hunt Recording Sheet: Combining Polygons (Reproducible 7–3B), 1 copy per student
✦ Writing About Archimedes' Puzzle Recording Sheet (Reproducible 7–4), 1 copy per student

For more on determining key vocabulary, see page 180.

Note: For the preparation of Reproducible 7–2, for each pair of students have two copies of the puzzle: one uncut on a piece of paper and one cut up, placed in a zip-locked baggie.

Note: For the preparation of Reproducibles 7–3A and 7–3B, copy them such that 7–3A is on the front of the handout and 7–3B is on the back.

Sentence Frames

For Sequencing

For more on creating sentence frames, see page 175.

> *First, _____. Then, _____. Finally, _____.*
>
> *At first, _____. Following that, _____. Next, _____.*
> *As a last step, _____.*

For Describing

> *I found the area by _____.*
>
> *In order to find the area, _____.*

Archimedes' Puzzle: Part 1

The bell rang, signaling the start of first period. Luz was ready to begin her lesson. She was looking forward to teaching *Archimedes' Puzzle* to the group of seventh-grade students. She knew that the hands-on element of the lesson combined with the partner work in problem solving would make for a rich, engaging lesson.

The class was comprised of students from a variety of ethnic and linguistic backgrounds. Many of the students were native English speakers or at higher levels of English proficiency, but there were also a few students at the intermediate level and one student who had just arrived from another country with beginning English skills. In addition to the varied English proficiency levels, there was a range of math levels in the class. Given these two critical factors, Luz knew she would have to monitor, adapt, and be strategic in her instruction to make sure all students would have access to the content and also be challenged during the lesson, as well.

Introducing Academic Language

To provide a context, Luz started the lesson by showing students a picture of Archimedes' Puzzle and explaining the history of the puzzle. (See Figure 7–1, and Reproducible 7–1 at the end of the book.)

Luz wanted the students to have some background on the 2,200-year-old puzzle before they worked with it. She also knew that many students had experience working with tangrams in elementary school. By showing them the puzzle, it might tap their prior knowledge

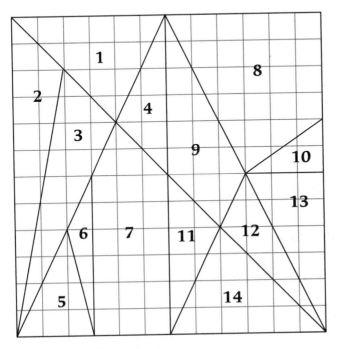

FIGURE 7-1. Archimedes' Puzzle.

of working with geometric puzzles. Creating opportunities for students, especially ELs, to tap into their existing schemas makes new content more accessible.

"As you may have noticed, the puzzle is made up of different shapes or polygons," Luz began. "Who remembers what a polygon is?" Luz asked.

Luz waited for several seconds, then called on Rodrigo.

"It's a shape that has five sides," Rodrigo replied.

"Does it always have to have five sides?" Luz probed.

"No, that's a pentagon. It can have many sides, but the sides have to touch," Julia clarified.

"Can anyone else add on to our definition of a polygon?"

"The sides have to be straight," Nancy added.

"Correct. A polygon is a shape with straight line segments that is closed," Luz summarized. "For the first activity with *Archimedes' Puzzle,* you will complete a Polygon Hunt with your partner. On the recording sheet that I will hand out to you, you'll record each polygon you can find in the puzzle and identify it by number and name." (See Figure 7–2, and Reproducible 7–3A at the end of the book.)

> Creating opportunities for students, especially English learners, to tap into their existing schemas makes new content more accessible.

Polygon Hunt

Polygon #	Type of Polygon
1	
2	
3	
4	
5	

FIGURE 7-2. Excerpt of Polygon Hunt Recording Sheet: Finding Polygons

Luz distributed the following items to each pair of students: an uncut copy of *Archimedes' Puzzle* (Reproducible 7–2, at the end of the book), a plastic zip-top bag with cut-up pieces of *Archimedes' Puzzle* (one for each student; see Reproducible 7–2), and two copies of the *Polygon Hunt* recording sheet. She then called the class to attention.

"Let's do the first puzzle piece together," Luz directed the class. "What kind of polygon is puzzle piece number one?"

"A triangle," several students replied.

"Right. So you would record that on the first line," Luz explained, demonstrating how to record the finding on the *Polygon Hunt* recording sheet.

"You will have about five minutes to record all of the polygons that you can on this sheet. You may work with a partner." (See Figure 7–3.)

> Working with a peer creates a safe environment for acquiring new terms and it provides opportunities for using the words for an authentic purpose.

Luz knows that students benefit from working in pairs, because they can negotiate their understanding of content through their discussions. ELs also benefit when their partner is able to provide the names of certain items or phrases for explaining a concept in English. Working with a peer creates a safe environment for acquiring new terms and it provides opportunities for using the words for an authentic purpose.

After about five minutes, Luz called the class back together to see what they had discovered.

"Who can tell me the name of polygon number ten?" Luz asked.

"A triangle," Jason answered.

"A right triangle," Hanh added.

"Why?" Luz probed.

Hanh replied, "Because it has a ninety-degree angle."

"Correct," Luz affirmed. She then made a gesture with her arms, showing students what a 90-degree angle looks like. She also drew a 90-degree angle on the board and labeled it. These two steps were intentional in providing a visual of a 90-degree angle that would help ELs understand the oral sharing of ideas.

Luz recorded Hanh's idea on a piece of chart paper for all students to see. This step was the beginning of a vocabulary chart that Luz would leave in the classroom as a reference for students during this lesson and throughout the year. The vocabulary chart would contain three important elements—the name of the polygon, a picture of it, and a definition. Vocabulary charts are essential tools that support ELs and reference important concepts they have studied and will be revisiting.

Polygon Hunt

Polygon #	Type of Polygon
1	triangle
2	obtuse triangle
3	isosceles triangle
4	scalene triangle
5	scalene triangle
6	obtuse triangle
7	pentagon
8	quadrilateral
9	quadrilateral
10	right triangle
11	acute triangle
12	obtuse triangle
13	right triangle
14	acute triangle

FIGURE 7-3. Julia was able to identify all 14 polygons in Archimedes' Puzzle.

Right Triangle		A three-sided polygon with one right angle
Pentagon		A five-sided polygon

FIGURE 7-4. Class Vocabulary Chart.

"How about number seven?" Luz continued.

"It's a pentagon," Sonya answered.

"Right. It's a pentagon because it has five sides, but it's irregular because the sides are not the same length," Luz responded, adding to Sonya's response and modeling academic language. She then added a pentagon to the vocabulary chart. (See Figure 7–4.)

Luz continued with the class discussion for a few more minutes. She noticed that students were able to distinguish between different types of triangles such as scalene, isosceles, and equilateral triangles. She also found that the review of the names of polygons was helpful, because some students struggled to recall the names of certain polygons.

For the next task, students had to combine the puzzle pieces to form more polygons. They then recorded them on the reverse side of the Polygon Hunt recording sheet titled "Combining Polygons." (See Figure 7–5, and Reproducible 7–3B at the end of the book.)

"Using the puzzle pieces from your zip-top bag, you are going to combine two or more polygons to form a new polygon," Luz explained. "Just like in the first activity, you will record the numbers of the polygons and then the name of the new polygon you create. Let's do one together first. Let's combine polygon numbers twelve, thirteen, and fourteen."

Students used their puzzle pieces to fit the three polygon pieces together.

Polygon Hunt

Combine Polygons	Type of Polygon

FIGURE 7-5. Excerpt of Polygon Hunt Recording Sheet.

"What shape did you create? Luz asked.

Lauren volunteered, "A quadrilateral. It's a trapezoid."

"Why is it a trapezoid?" Luz asked, taking the opportunity to push for an explanation.

"Because it has four sides and two parallel lines," Lauren answered.

"Correct," Luz replied while recording the information on the Polygon Hunt recording sheet she had displayed for students to see.

Although this task was a fairly simple one that many native speakers would understand with just oral directions, Luz knows that modeling is a way for ELs to "see" the task expected of them so they can complete it.

In addition, the use of the puzzle pieces gave students a direct experience in creating new shapes. ELs can use manipulatives to model abstract mathematical thinking and to gain access to the core curriculum. They can demonstrate their understanding with concrete materials even if they don't yet have the English skills to explain their insights with words.

Students continued to make new polygons for about five minutes, recording their findings on the Polygon Hunt recording sheet.

> English learners can use manipulatives to model abstract mathematical thinking and to gain access to the core curriculum. They can demonstrate their understanding with concrete materials even if they don't yet have the English skills to explain their insights with words.

Combine Polygons	Type of Polygon
1, 2, 3	Right Triangle
9, 11	Acute Triangle
8, 10	Trapezoid
1, 2, 3, 4, 5, 6, 7, 9, 11	Pentagon

FIGURE 7-6. Kenny identified two different kinds of triangles—a right triangle and an acute triangle—as well as other polygons.

As Luz circulated the room, she heard students identifying polygons and explaining to their partners how they constructed their new shapes.

"Numbers one, two, and three make a right triangle," Kenny said. (See Figure 7–6.)

"We made a quadrilateral with numbers eight and ten," Omid contributed. (See Figure 7–7.)

Sangeeta shares, "Numbers nine and eight are a hexagon." (See Figure 7–8.)

While monitoring students during this task, Luz felt comfortable that students could identify many different kinds of polygons, an important content standard that she knew students needed to learn. Based on her formative assessment, Luz decided that the students were ready to review how to find the area of different polygons. She called the class back together.

"You were able to create many different kinds of polygons combining the puzzle pieces," Luz said. "What kind of a polygon will I have if I combine all the puzzle pieces, numbers one through fourteen?" Luz displayed a copy of Archimedes' Puzzle for all students to see.

"A square!" several students responded.

"Yes, it is a square," Luz affirmed. "Who knows how to find the area of this square?"

Many hands shot up. Luz assumed that quite a few students would use the formula length times width as a way to figure out the area

Combine Polygons	Type of Polygon
2,3	Triangle
8,10	Quadrilateral
12,13	Quadrilateral
13,10,8	Triangle
1,4,9,12	Triangle
14,12,13	Quadrilateral
5,6,7,11,14	Triangle; equilateral, acute triangle
4,9	Quadrilateral
1,4	Triangle
2,3,5,6,7,11,14	Right triangle; Isosceles

FIGURE 7-7. Omid used the generic names such as triangle and quadrilateral to identify the polygons he constructed.

of a square. However, she knew there were many different ways to approach this task, especially because the pieces of Archimedes' Puzzle were superimposed on grid paper. Luz was interested in determining whether the students could think flexibly and find several ways to solve the problem.

Combine Polygons	Type of Polygon
2,3	Triangle
1,4	Triangle
4,9	Quadrilateral
6,7	Pentagon
9,8	Hexagon
7,11	Pentagon
11,14	Triangle
12,14	Triangle
14,12,13	Quadrilateral
5,6	Triangle

FIGURE 7-8. Sangeeta identified four different types of polygons.

"Before I have you share, I want you to work with a partner or in small groups of three or four to find at least two different ways to find the area," Luz explained.

The students got right to work and immediately began to converse. As Luz circulated, she noticed that most began by sharing the formula for finding the area of a square: length times width. With encouragement, many students thought of different approaches for finding the area.

Rodrigo raised his hand for help. He was confused and did not understand the task. Rodrigo is a newcomer to the United States and, although he has very little English language knowledge, he does have a strong background in mathematics. Earlier in the lesson, Luz noticed that one of Rodrigo's table partners, Naisha, was instrumental in helping him understand some of the tasks and concepts. Luz asked Naisha to share with Rodrigo how she would explain finding the area of the entire puzzle.

Naisha spoke slowly to Rodrigo and traced her finger along the length of the square and said, "Length." She then did the same procedure with the width of the square. Rodrigo echoed her words. Naisha then wrote the formula for area on a piece of paper, stating aloud the meaning of each symbol (*l* and *w*) as she went. Immediately after Naisha shared this information, Rodrigo recognized the formula for area, and said *"área"* while running his pencil across the inside of the puzzle. He said, *"área"* in Spanish, recognizing the same label for the concept of area in his primary language. Luz affirmed that *area* and *área* were cognates and have the same meaning. When Luz asked Rodrigo if he knew what "area" meant, Rodrigo nodded and indicated, with his pencil moving across the puzzle, that it meant the entire surface of the puzzle.

After a few minutes of discussion time, Luz called the group back together. "Who would like to share a strategy they used for finding the area of a square? I'd like you to come to the front of the class to show us how you figured it out."

Having demonstrations of mathematical thinking provides additional access to the math content for ELs. By illustrating or showing thinking instead of just using an oral explanation, ELs, as well as other students, can see how others approach the problem. It also gives ELs a scaffold, by providing them with a concrete model upon which to explain their strategies.

Yung volunteered. Using a copy of *Archimedes' Puzzle*, he explained his approach, demonstrating the steps as he spoke. "You can divide the square into two equal rectangles. Then you find the area of one rectangle and multiply by two."

Luz recorded Yung's idea with words and visuals on chart paper for all students to see.

"How did you find the area of the rectangle?" Luz asked, looking for clarification of one of Yung's steps.

"You do length times width," replied Roberto, Yung's partner.

Luz invited Roberto to the front of the class to show what he meant by length and width. Roberto ran his finger down the side and across the bottom of the square, saying each term as he demonstrated. Luz recorded the terms *length* and *width*, labeling a square she had drawn on the chart paper. She then wrote the mathematical expression $l \times w = area$.

"How about another way?" Luz asked the class.

"You can count the number of squares on each side and then multiply them," explained Sonya, as she demonstrated her method for finding area to the class.

"Any other ways?" Luz probed while recording Sonya's idea on the chart.

"You could count all of the squares in the inside of the square," Jason added.

"You mean like this?" Luz asked. She started to point to the squares inside, counting them one by one. Jason nodded in agreement.

"How about length times width?" Quiana ventured.

"Yes. That formula also works," Luz replied. (See Figure 7–9.) "Do all of these strategies give us the same answer?"

Students nodded in agreement and some called out that the area was 144 square units.

"Now that you know the area, I want you to explain to a partner the specific steps you used to find the area of the square. You can use any of the strategies listed or, if you did it another way, you may share that," Luz said. "Here are some sentence starters to help you describe your steps." Sentence starters are different from sentence frames in that they provide the language for beginning a sentence. Luz displayed the sentence starters for all to see.

"I am going to read the starters to you so you can hear how to use them," Luz explained. Modeling how to use the language is a critical step if ELs are to use the linguistic scaffolds we have developed for

---

Strategies for Finding the Area of a Square

✦ *Divide the square into two equal rectangles*
  ✦ *The area of one rectangle = $l \times w$*
  ✦ *Multiply the area of the rectangle by 2*
✦ *Count the number of units on each side*
  ✦ *Area of a square = $l \times l$*
             = length squared
✦ *Length $\times$ width*

FIGURE 7-9. The class's strategies for finding the area of a square.

them. Without hearing how to construct the grammatically correct sentences, some ELs may grapple with their oral language production.

Luz read the sentence starters aloud while referencing each one.

First, _____ .

Then, _____ .

Finally, _____ .

"Here is another way to describe your steps," Luz said showing students the second, more sophisticated set of sentence starters.

At first, _____ .

Following that, _____ .

Next, _____ .

As a last step, _____ .

Providing several frames or starters is a way to differentiate language by proficiency levels and to provide some variation in language production. Different frames can provide students with a variety of ways to express ideas and can help alleviate stilted or robotic language.

Different frames can provide students with a variety of ways to express ideas and can help alleviate stilted or robotic language.

"With a partner, please share the steps you took to find the area of the square using either set of sentence starters," Luz directed the class.

Students paired up and began their conversations. Luz visited Nancy and Lauren as they discussed their different approaches.

Nancy started, "At first, see what kind of square it is. Following that, see the sides of the figure. Next, use length times width and times them. As a last step, you get the area of one hundred forty-four square units."

Lauren then shared her approach. "First, I counted the cubic units of the length. Then, I counted the cubic units for width. Finally, I multiplied the width times the length. Then, I got the answer."

"Lauren, are you sure the squares inside the puzzle are 'cubic units'?" Luz asked. Luz wondered whether Lauren knew that cubic units are related to three-dimensional shapes and that square units are for two-dimensional shapes.

"I'm not sure. I remember studying cubic units as a way to find the measurement of shapes," Lauren replied.

"Do you remember if the shapes were two dimensional like a square or three dimensional like a cube?" Luz probed.

"That's when we were working with cubes," Lauren mused.

"Three-dimensional shapes are measured in cubic units whereas two-dimensional shapes are measured in square units. What's the square?" Luz asked.

"It's two dimensional, so that means the area is one hundred forty-four square units," Lauren concluded.

Luz moved on and listened in as Kenny and Omid worked.

Omid began, "First, I count half the units on the shape. Then, I multiply it by two and finally, I have my answer for the area."

Next, Jason recounted his procedure for finding the area. "First, I found the length which was twelve units. Then I found the width. That was also twelve units. Finally, I multiplied them together and got the area one hundred forty-four."

Summarizing ✦ **Part 1**

As Luz circulated, she heard students describe a variety of strategies used to find the area. Although finding the area of a square was a familiar task for the students, this first part of the lesson was designed to review important concepts (names of polygons, figuring area) and to practice the linguistic structures students need in their discussions later in the lesson. Pleased with the students' success in Part 1 of the lesson, Luz went on to Part 2: Finding the Area of Other Polygons.

Archimedes' Puzzle: Part 2

Finding the Area of Other Polygons

"You have described in detail the steps you took to find the area of a square. Now we are going to work on finding the area of a triangle," Luz began. "We're going to start with puzzle piece number ten. Please find triangle number ten and talk with a partner about ways to find the area. See if you can find at least two ways."

The noise level in the room rose as students began discussing with their partners ways to find the area of a triangle. Luz intentionally chose triangle number ten because it included a right angle, a feature that might make it easier for students to work with initially.

Luz listened in as Roberto explained his idea to the students at his table. "I counted the squares in the triangle. For the squares that weren't whole I combined them with other pieces of squares to count them as one square. I got three squares as the area, but I'm not sure if it's right."

Roberto's explanation is a good example of how students use language to unveil their thinking about mathematical concepts and the uncertainties they may have.

"I did base times height divided by two," Naisha told her partner.

Similar conversations were occurring at tables around the classroom. After a few minutes of discussion, Luz called the class back together. She wanted them to share their ideas with one another using new sentence starters for describing their strategies as well as create a strategies chart to which the students could refer.

"Before you share how you found the area of the triangle, I want to show you some other ways to share your strategies," Luz said. She displayed these two new sentence frames:

I found the area by _____.

In order to find the area, _____.

Luz read the sentence starters aloud and directed students to say them to their partner to practice before sharing with the whole class.

"Who would like to explain one strategy they used for finding the area of a triangle?" Luz asked. "Remember to use the sentence frames we just practiced or those used earlier with the square."

Sonya raised her hand. "First, I made it a rectangle."

Luz interrupted Sonya, realizing that much value would be gained by having her demonstrate her strategies instead of just describing them orally. "Sonya, could you come and show the class what you mean by that?" Showing, rather than just telling, is especially beneficial for ELs.

Sonya made her way to the front of the class with her copy of Archimedes' Puzzle. She demonstrated how she enclosed the triangle inside a rectangle. "Then, I found the length and width of the sides of

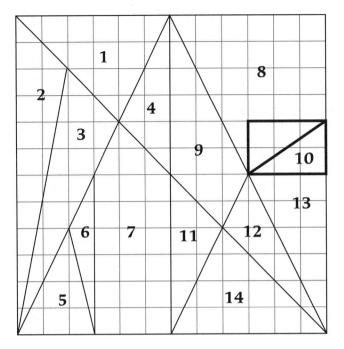

FIGURE 7-10. An illustration of Sonya's steps with *Archimedes' Puzzle*.

the rectangle and multiplied to get the area of the rectangle. After that, I divided by two." (See Figure 7–10.)

Luz recorded Sonya's steps on a chart called "Strategies for Finding the Area of a Triangle." This chart was displayed in the front of the class for all to see.

"Thank you, Sonya," Luz replied. "That's one way to find the area. I heard some of you talk about how the triangle can be reflected. What does that mean?"

Luz prompted the class to share what they remembered about the *reflection property* of symmetry. She takes advantage of every opportunity to revisit mathematical concepts previously introduced so students have multiple chances to understand and apply them.

"Reflection is when the same shape is on the other side to create symmetry," Kenny shared.

"How does that work with finding the area of a triangle?" Luz probed.

"The triangle is half the rectangle so if we see that there is a reflection of a triangle, we can make a rectangle and just find the area of a rectangle and divide it by two."

Luz called Kenny up to the front of the class and asked him to demonstrate what he meant by reflection. He traced a triangle in the rectangle and indicated how the triangle was reflected in the other half of the rectangle.

"Interesting," Luz said. "Any other ways to find the area of a triangle?"

Omid made his way to the front of the class to demonstrate his method. "We used base times height divided by two," he said, while pointing out the base and height of the triangle and showing how he calculated the formula by dividing the product of those two measurements by two.

Luz recorded Omid's strategy on the chart (Figure 7–11) and asked him to use the sentence frames they had practiced earlier.

"In order to find the area of triangle ten, I used base times height divided by two, which is three times two divided by two. I simplified that and got three," Omid explained.

"You have described a number of strategies for finding the areas of regular rectangles and triangles," Luz said, addressing the class. "For our next activity, you are going to combine pieces of Archimedes' Puzzle like we did earlier and find the area of irregular polygons."

Summarizing ✦ **Part 2**

Taking the time for students to discover and share a variety of strategies for finding the area of regular polygons created a foundation for finding the area of irregular polygons—Luz's final objective of the lesson. In addition to engaging in problem solving, students were also given an introduction to and time to practice the academic language associated with their task.

Strategies for Finding the Area of a Triangle

✦ $b \times h/2$

✦ *Draw a rectangle (add a visual shape of a rectangle)*
  ✦ *Find the length and width and divide by 2*

✦ *Count the whole square (add a visual of a square)*
  ✦ *Count the small pieces that combined give you a square*
  ✦ *Divide by 2*

FIGURE 7-11. The class's strategies for finding the area of a triangle.

Archimedes' Puzzle

In Part 3 of *Archimedes' Puzzle*, students would find the area of polygons they constructed from various puzzle pieces, and would also write about their process.

Archimedes' Puzzle: Part 3

Writing About *Archimedes' Puzzle*

"In the next part of the lesson, you will be combining two pieces from Archimedes' Puzzle to create an irregular polygon," Luz described. With these directions, Luz distributed a copy of "Writing About Archimedes' Puzzle" to each student. (See Figure 7–12, and Reproducible 7–4 at the end of the book.)

"An irregular polygon is a shape that is a polygon, but one where the sides are not the same length," Luz explained. "Let me give me you an example."

Luz demonstrated how combining pieces 12 and 13 would make an irregular polygon. She asked students what other combinations of pieces that were congruent create irregular polygons. Students contributed many ideas. (Refer back to Figure 7–1.)

Writing About Archimedes' Puzzle Recording Sheet

1. **Combine 2 different polygons** from Archimedes' Puzzle. The new polygon should be an **irregular polygon.**
2. **Trace** the new shape in the space below.
3. Find the **area** of the new polygon.
4. **Important information:**
   ✦   The area of every piece is an **integer**.
   ✦   The area of every piece is a **multiple of 3**.
5. Explain **in writing** how you found the area of the new polygon using any of the following sentence frames.

> *I found the area by _____.*
>
> *In order to find the area, _____.*
>
> *First, _____. Then, _____. Finally, _____.*
>
> *At first, _____. Following that, _____.*
>
> *After that, _____. As a last step, _____.*

FIGURE 7-12. Writing About Archimedes' Puzzle Recording Sheet.

"Six and seven." "Four and nine." "Four, six, and seven"—all suggestions the students made.

Luz felt comfortable that students understood the directions for creating irregular polygons, so she continued with the rest of the directions. "After you have found your shape, trace it on the paper, find the area, and write about the steps you used to find it."

Because students had prior experience with this procedure, their mental energy was focused on problem solving to find the area of the irregular polygons and not as focused on the language demands expected of them.

"Before you begin, I want to share some important information with you. This information will help you check whether you have the correct answer," Luz shared. "The first piece of information is that the area of every piece is an integer. What is an integer? Can you give me some examples?"

Students shared their examples, such as twenty-eight, two, and five, and Luz recorded them on the vocabulary chart displayed for everyone to see. She also wrote the word *integer* alongside the examples.

"Could an integer be three and forty-two hundredths?" Luz asked, looking for clarification.

"No, it has to be a whole number," Sangeeta explained.

"Right. The other piece of important information is that the area of your irregular shape is a multiple of three. What are some multiples of three?" Luz asked.

Omid volunteered, "Six, nine, twelve, thirty, and sixty."

"How do you know they are multiples of three?" Luz probed.

"They are all divisible by three," Quiana replied.

"Now you have all the information you need to begin. As with the other tasks, you may work with a partner or in small groups," Luz directed.

Students started to work on the assignment. They referred to the strategy charts for finding the area of rectangles and triangles, and for ideas on how to find the area of the irregular polygons they constructed.

Rodrigo and Hanh were working together for this activity. As mentioned earlier, Rodrigo is a newcomer to the United States and has only been in the country for a few months. Although he had developed some basic communication skills in English, he still struggled to explain his mathematical thinking. One tool that Rodrigo used to help him communicate with his partner was a dictionary. He and Hanh used the dictionary

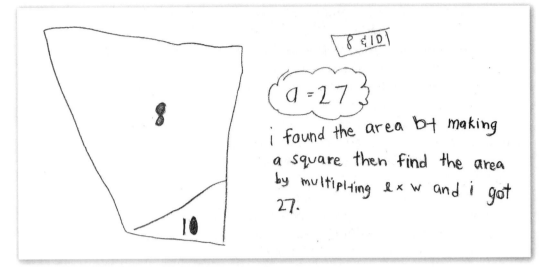

FIGURE 7-13. Rodrigo, a beginning EL, explains how he found the area of polygons 8 and 10 by finding a square within the irregular polygon.

to converse and exchange ideas as they worked on combining polygons 8 and 10. (See Figure 7–13.)

Some students, like Rodrigo and Hanh, decomposed the irregular polygons into regular polygons and then applied formulas to find the area.

Quiana and Sonya worked on the irregular polygon formed from pieces 12 and 13. (See Figure 7–14.)

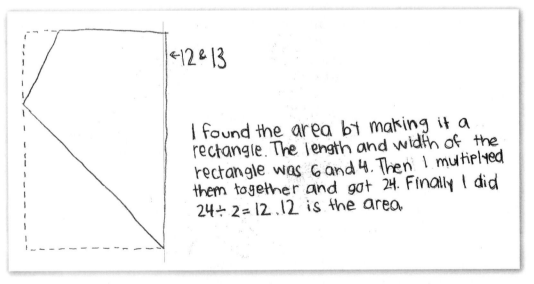

FIGURE 7-14. Quiana explains in detail how she found the area of the irregular shape she created. She uses academic vocabulary and sequence words in her writing.

Other students approached the task in different ways. Jason and Yung told Luz that they were going to divide their irregular polygon into triangles and use the Pythagorean Theorem to find one of the missing sides (either the base or the height) of each triangle. Then, they would apply the formula for finding the area of a triangle to find the total area of the irregular polygon. They were able to articulate the formula $a^2 + b^2 = c^2$, and find all the sides of the triangles; however, when they calculated the formula for the area of a triangle, they got a number that was neither an integer nor a multiple of three. Luz encouraged them to go back and revisit their work, and questioned them about their process along the way. After some time, Jason and Yung decided that they wanted to try a different way for finding the area, because they weren't having any luck following their original strategy.

Luz is aware that many students learn formulas without understanding what they mean. By providing familiar contexts using visuals and manipulatives, Luz hopes to help students learn to understand and apply mathematical formulas when solving problems.

> Luz is aware that many students learn formulas without understanding what they mean . . . and hopes to help students learn to understand and apply mathematical formulas when solving problems.

Some students, like Nancy, counted whole squares and partial squares to find the total square units. (See Figure 7–15.)

Other strategies included creating larger polygons around the irregular shapes, using formulas to find the areas of those shapes, and using reflection to create a regular polygon. (See Figures 7–16 and 7–17.)

After about 10 minutes of work time, Luz called the class back together so students could share their different shapes and strategies. She had each student, or pair of students, come to the front of the class to demonstrate their process. These demonstrations were helpful to all students; the ELs in the class especially benefitted from the visual support.

"You've found many strategies for finding the area of regular and irregular polygons today. Your strategies included more than just using a formula," Luz summarized. "I will post the charts that we created in the class for you to refer to as we continue to study the concept of area."

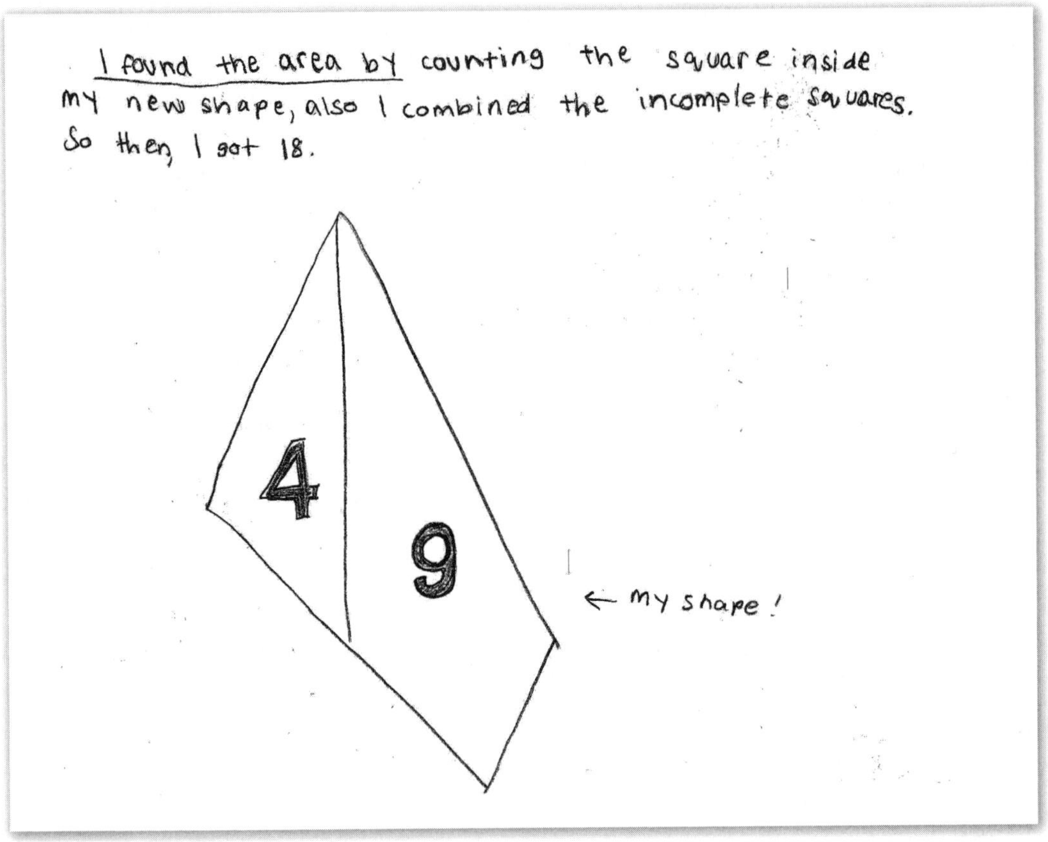

I found the area by counting the square inside my new shape, also I combined the incomplete squares. So then, I got 18.

4

9

← my shape!

FIGURE 7-15. Nancy described how she counted squares to find the area of the new shape.

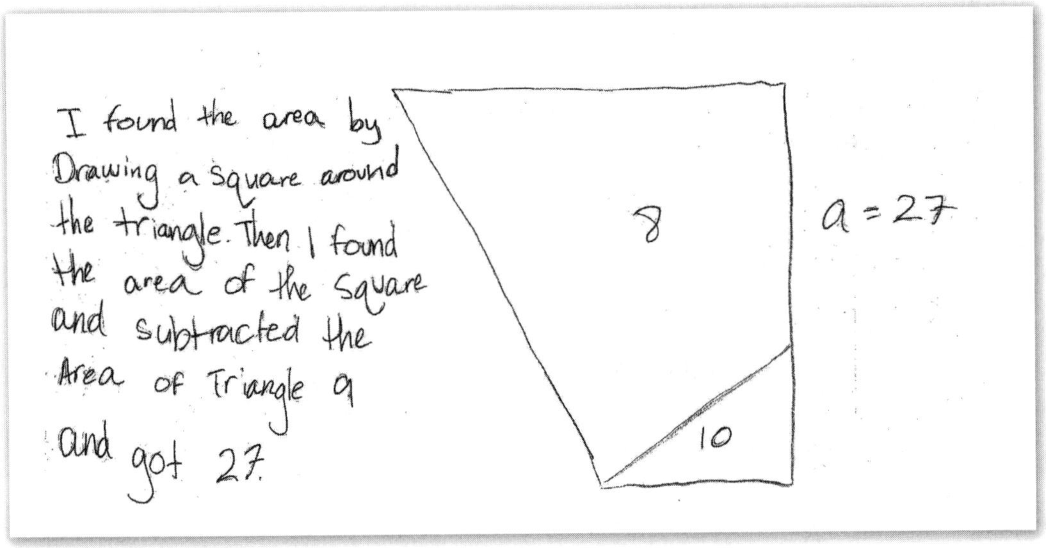

I found the area by Drawing a square around the triangle. Then I found the area of the Square and subtracted the Area of Triangle 9 and got 27.

8

a = 27

10

FIGURE 7-16. Lauren demonstrated her understanding of creating larger, regular polygons around the irregular polygon to find the area.

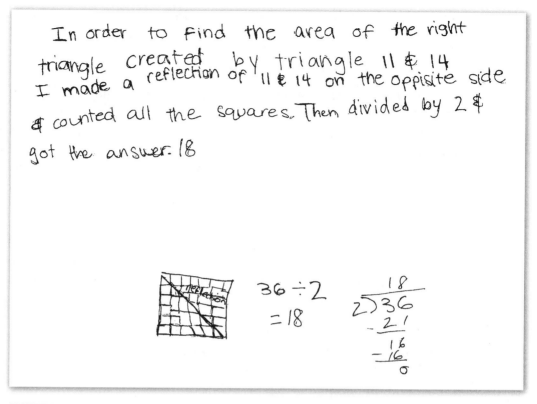

In order to find the area of the right triangle created by triangle 11 & 14 I made a reflection of 11 & 14 on the oppisite side & counted all the squares. Then divided by 2 & got the answer. 18

$36 \div 2 = 18$

FIGURE 7-17. Roberto used the concept of reflection to determine the area of his new shape.

✦ **Summarizing the Lesson: Key English Language Learner Strategies**

Luz incorporated many strategies to help her ELs fully participate in the lesson *Archimedes' Puzzle.*

Strategy 1: Using Manipulative Materials

Students had access to two different copies of Archimedes' Puzzle. One was a complete copy of the puzzle on a piece of 8.5-by-11–inch paper. The other copy was cut-up pieces of the puzzle placed into zip-top plastic bags. By making both forms of the puzzle accessible, ELs had multiple ways to access the core content. They could look at, draw on, and use the complete puzzle when listening to others, and they could refer to the puzzle when they were describing it.

In addition, students could demonstrate their understanding of mathematical problem-solving strategies using the puzzle pieces and minimal English. The manipulative materials served as a concrete representation of their work.

Strategy 2: Modeling and Demonstrating

Luz provided models for both the content and language objectives throughout the lesson. She showed students how to use the puzzle to identify polygons, construct new polygons, and find the area based on students' suggestions. She also modeled how to use the academic language that she wanted students to use when describing their sequence of steps. This modeling provides explicit instruction on how to use the language so ELs aren't left struggling for how to use the language correctly.

Luz wasn't the only one to model during the class. She also asked students to demonstrate for their peers their approach to solving the problems posed. The visual demonstrations gave ELs a chance to see what they were hearing.

Suggestions for Extending the Lesson

Rearrange the Shapes

+   Use the pieces of Archimedes' Puzzle to rearrange the shapes to create the triangle shown here. The figure on the left shows how the pieces must be arranged to form the triangle.

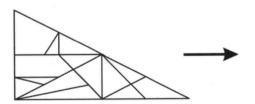 

+   Ask students to talk about how they arranged the pieces. Possible questions include the following:
    +   What strategy did you use?
    +   What did you use from your knowledge about geometry to build the triangle on the right?

Make Other Shapes

+   Other shapes can be made from the pieces of Archimedes' Puzzle. Have students try to make some of the shapes, like this one:

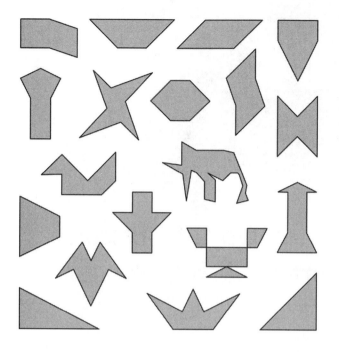

✦ Ask students to talk about how they arranged the pieces. Possible questions include the following:

✦ Which of the shapes were most difficult to create? Which were easiest?

✦ Why are some shapes more difficult to create than others?

✦ What strategy did you use?

✦ What knowledge of shapes, angles, congruent figures, and so on, did you use?

(Adapted from NCTM Illuminations: http://illuminations. nctm.org/ LessonDetail.aspx?id = L720)

Archimedes' Puzzle

8 How to Modify Math Lessons to Support English Learners

Education for ELs in American middle school classrooms has improved greatly during the past few decades as research has provided educators with strategies that make instruction more comprehensible. Math teachers often capitalize on the concrete nature of mathematics through the use of visuals or manipulatives to show students the subject matter content instead of just telling them about it. They simplify language so that ELs can understand explanations more easily. They highlight key terms and often provide students with math journals or math vocabulary terms to be used as reference tools. All this effort goes a long way toward making math lessons more comprehensible for all students, particularly for those whose native language is not English.

Comprehension involves more than access to content, however. The fact that the math achievement of ELs overall has not kept up with that of their English-speaking peers (National Assessment of Educational Progress 2009) suggests that it is not enough that the information is presented concretely and clearly. In order for students to learn the concept being presented, they need to interact with the information and make connections between what is already known and what is being learned. ELs then need to test their new understanding by explaining what they have learned. All these steps in the learning process—interacting with new knowledge, making connections to previous learning, and testing understandings—happen through language. Moreover, these cognitive processes require that students produce language. It is at this point that the process often breaks down for the EL. Without adequate linguistic support, ELs cannot articulate their thinking. And if the concept happens to be a completely new one, the student's very *thinking* is compromised because humans use language to think as well as to communicate with others. As a result, by the time they reach middle school years, not only has the language proficiency level of many ELs stalled at the intermediate level, but significant gaps have also arisen in their understanding of math content.

> All these steps in the learning process—interacting with new knowledge, making connections to previous learning, and testing understandings—happen through language.

Providing appropriate linguistic support involves consideration of the levels of English language proficiency of the students in content-area classrooms. Although the specifics of language development may not be foremost in the mind of the math teacher during a lesson, it is during content instruction that students learn new information and have an authentic need to communicate their understanding. It is also during content instruction that the teacher has a need to assess student learning. Language must be the vehicle, not a roadblock, for both acquiring new information and demonstrating understanding.

> Language must be the vehicle, not a roadblock, for both acquiring new information and demonstrating understanding.

Middle school math teachers may encounter a wide range of language proficiency levels among students in their classes. Teachers often see and hear differences in the way that ELs express themselves orally and in writing, and usually receive some indication of the language proficiency classification of the ELs in their classrooms. Although middle school math teachers may not plan separate lessons for the different proficiency levels in their classes, it is helpful for content teachers to understand how these proficiency levels are determined. It is also useful for content teachers to be able to identify typical linguistic behaviors and instructional needs of students at each level to plan lessons that help ELs both access content and develop academic language.

Most English language development tests place students in one of various levels, typically described as beginning, intermediate, and advanced. Within each level there is still a range of abilities, and because students are generally tested only once a year, the accuracy of the individual score decreases as time passes and as the student progresses. Typically speaking, however, students perform as follows:

> ## Typical Levels of English Learners
>
> **Beginning:** At the beginning level, ELs may respond nonverbally during classroom instruction. They can still participate in tasks that demonstrate comprehension, such as identifying, matching, and categorizing, but may need strong visual and manipulative support.
>
> **Intermediate:** Students at the intermediate level can describe, explain, define, retell, summarize, and make comparisons. Although they may need less concrete support in the form of visual aids, they need linguistic support with vocabulary and syntax as they struggle to find the right words and order them into coherent sentences.
>
> **Advanced:** ELs at the advanced level can perform all the higher level functions that a native speaker can perform, giving opinions, justifying answers, negotiating, debating, persuading, and so on, but they lack experience and practice with the specific ways in which language is used within mathematics discourse in English.

Complicating matters at the middle school level are often wide differences in prior learning experiences of these students. Adolescent ELs come from varied linguistic and experiential backgrounds. Some may be recent immigrants who have developed a high degree of proficiency in mathematics in their native language, whereas others may have experienced interruptions to their education as a result of a variety of factors in their country of origin. In addition to recent immigrants, the population of ELs in middle school classrooms also includes students who have been educated in American schools but who have not acquired full proficiency in English. These students, sometimes referred to as *long-term ELs* (Olsen 2010), may also have experienced lack of access to grade-level math content because of factors ranging from family mobility to inconsistent instructional programs and inadequate professional development for their teachers. Students who have developed a foundation of math knowledge in their native language are able to learn new labels for familiar understandings while acquiring new knowledge. ELs who lack this foundation face the challenge of simultaneously learning new academic language and math concepts while trying to fill in linguistic and conceptual gaps.

Taking all these factors into account, math teachers should become familiar with the descriptions of English language development proficiencies and find out the tested proficiency levels of ELs in their classes to plan lessons that support language as well as content development. The lessons and vignettes in this resource illustrate ways in which teachers can provide support for multiple proficiency levels within a single lesson through the use of sentence frames, intentional grouping practices, and other instructional strategies. However, it is also important for teachers to know something about the life experiences of the students in their classes, including the educational histories and immigration trajectories of ELs, to build upon students' strengths and instructional needs in both language and math.

This resource contains a collection of carefully crafted lessons from several strands of mathematics. The lessons were selected because of their appropriateness across grade levels. They were designed with the range of different language proficiency levels and experiential backgrounds of middle school ELs in mind. Although we hope these lessons allow your ELs to experience more success in math, you, the classroom teacher, are our true audience for this resource. We hope these lessons serve as models for modifying the key lessons you present throughout the course of the academic year. This chapter is designed to help you think about how to approach math instruction to support students successfully who are learning the English language and math simultaneously.

Selecting Lessons for Modification

We are not suggesting that teachers rewrite the entire math curriculum. Although new information is presented in most lessons, the information generally builds on concepts previously introduced. After ELs have a solid understanding of the basic concepts, adding new information is a less onerous process. Providing students with support in the development of the necessary language during introductory lessons allows them to interact with the information, make the necessary connections with prior understanding, and test their thinking as the instruction continues. Some lessons provoke more thinking and communication than others. Therefore, we suggest that you select the key lessons that (1) introduce new concepts in each strand, chapter, or unit of study and that (2) require students to use new vocabulary and language structures to think and communicate. Modifying these lessons will ensure that ELs benefit from your subsequent instruction.

Regardless of whether you decide to try adapting a lesson in the style we have modeled here, our sample lessons should help you think about the role of language in the math classroom. When ELs nod when asked if they understand a concept, it is easy for a teacher to assume incorrectly that learning has occurred. It is more reliable and informative to provide students with the opportunity and the language both to develop and to articulate mathematical understanding. The way teachers question ELs can also affect their level of oral participation. If you ask questions with the range of English language proficiencies of your students in mind, they will be more likely to respond in a way that both solidifies their own understanding and allows you to assess their learning. The lesson vignettes in this resource both address and provide examples of level-appropriate questioning. In addition, focusing on the intricacies of English can help a teacher monitor whether the instruction is comprehensible. The precise mathematical usage of everyday terms can cause confusion for ELs at all proficiency levels. A simple clarification of the intended meaning of a term can help them keep pace with the lesson. A list of multiple-meaning words often used in mathematics is provided in the Appendix.

Modifying a Math Lesson

The lessons in this book have two goals: a math goal and a language goal. The math goal must be determined first, because the language goal supports students' understanding of the math goal. After you have identified the math content you are going to teach, think about what the students would be able to say if they had met the math goal. For example, if the math goal involves learning about functions, after students meet that goal they should be able to *state hypotheses and draw conclusions* about the function rule for a given set of variables. If the math goal is that students solve an equation using an effective strategy that makes sense to them, then they should be able to *describe the sequence of steps* that they used for solving the problem after they meet the goal. If the math goal states that the students will identify irregular polygons, then they will need to use language to *describe the geometric properties* of the figure. Each of these three math goals—*constructing a function, solving an equation,* and *identifying a polygon*—has a logical language goal (or goals) that accompanies it. In these cases, the language goals are *stating hypotheses, drawing conclusions, sequencing steps,* and *describing geometric properties*.

Native English-speaking children are typically able to perform these language functions to articulate their math understanding when prompted with questions like: What do you know about functions? What are your steps for solving an equation? What is an irregular polygon?

However, even native English speakers may need explicit support with comprehending complex mathematical language and expressing understanding as the demands of the curriculum increase during secondary school.

ELs may understand the content of the lesson, but their inexperience with the language can keep them from articulating what they know. It is also possible that their struggles with the language of instruction lead them to partial or inaccurate understanding of the content. Until they verbalize their understanding, what they have learned or not learned remains a mystery to the teacher and may even be unclear to the students themselves. Choosing a language goal, or language function, that matches the math content makes learning more observable to all.

> English learners may understand the content of the lesson, but their inexperience with the language can keep them from articulating what they know.

Choosing the language goal is made easier by using the function chart in Table 8–1. It lists nine common functions of language and describes how they apply to the study of mathematics.

Determining Language Functions and Creating Sentence Frames

As there are purposes, or applications, for the various strands in mathematics, so are there purposes, or functions, for language. We use language to describe, to compare, to contrast, to predict, to categorize. Whether we are describing or categorizing in a particular content area, such as mathematics, the sentence structure we use will be the same. For example, we might say that an element on the periodic table has a particular atomic weight, the main character in a novel has a problem to solve, or an algebraic expression has two variables. Each one of these *describing* statements uses the same basic sentence structure, or syntax: _____ *has* _____. We call this structure a *sentence frame*. Consider the function of cause and effect across content areas: If we add baking soda to vinegar, a gas will be produced; if the president vetoes a bill, Congress must have the votes to override the veto; if a given number is multiplied by two, the product will be equal to $2n$. The sentence frame is the same in all cases: *If* _____, _____ *will* _____. This is also true for skills like

> Sentence frames allow English learners to use key vocabulary terms and to put together complete thoughts that can be connected to prior learning and then confirmed or rejected and revised, and finally understood.

Language Functions and Sentence Frames

Function	Beginning	Intermediate/Advanced
Describing	A _____ has _____.	A _____ has _____ and _____.
Examples	An <u>equilateral triangle</u> has <u>three congruent angles</u>.	An <u>equilateral triangle</u> has <u>three congruent angles</u> and <u>three congruent sides</u>.
Comparing	A _____ has _____. A _____ has _____.	A _____ has _____, but _____ has _____. Although _____ and _____ are the same in that _____, they are different because _____.
Examples	An <u>equilateral triangle</u> has <u>three congruent angles</u>. An <u>isosceles triangle</u> has <u>two congruent angles</u>.	An <u>equilateral triangle</u> has <u>three congruent angles</u>, but <u>an isosceles triangle</u> has <u>two congruent angles</u>. Although <u>an equilateral triangle</u> and <u>an isosceles triangle</u> are the same in that <u>they have three angles</u>, they are different because <u>an equilateral triangle has three congruent angles and an isosceles triangle has two congruent angles</u>.
Categorizing	A _____ is a _____. It is _____, because _____.	A _____ is a _____, because _____ and _____.
Examples	A <u>quadrilateral</u> is a <u>polygon</u>. It is a <u>polygon</u> because <u>it is closed</u>.	A <u>quadrilateral</u> is a <u>polygon</u> because <u>it is closed</u> and <u>has four straight sides</u>.
Sequencing	First, _____. Next, _____.	First, _____ and then _____. After _____, _____. Before _____, _____.
Examples	First, <u>I measured the diameter</u>. Next, <u>I tried different ratios</u>.	First, <u>I measured the diameter</u> and then <u>I tried different ratios</u>. After <u>I measured the diameter</u>, <u>I tried different ratios</u>. Before <u>I tried different ratios</u>, <u>I measured the diameter</u>.

TABLE 8–1. Language functions and sentence frames.

Language Functions and Sentence Frames

Function	Beginning	Intermediate/Advanced
Hypothesizing	If _____, then _____.	I know that for _____, the _____ is _____.
Examples	If <u>the input value is 2</u>, then <u>the output value is 4</u>.	I know that for <u>every input value of n</u>, the <u>output value is 2n</u>.
Predicting	_____ will _____.	I predict that _____ will _____. I predict that _____ will _____, because _____.
Examples	<u>I</u> will <u>roll a 7</u>.	I predict that <u>I</u> will <u>roll a 7</u>. I predict that <u>I</u> will <u>roll a 7</u>, because <u>there are more number combinations that equal 7 than any other sum or number on the die</u>.
Making Inferences	I can infer that _____. I think so because _____.	I can infer that _____, because I know _____.
Examples	I can infer that <u>the number is a fraction</u>. I think so because <u>it is not an integer</u>.	I can infer that <u>the number is a fraction</u>, because I know <u>it is not an integer</u>.
Drawing Conclusions	I think the _____ is _____.	I can conclude that _____. I can conclude that _____, because _____ and _____.
Examples	I think the <u>function</u> is <u>2n</u>.	I can conclude that <u>the function is 2n</u>. I can conclude that <u>the function is 2n</u>, because <u>I multiplied the input value by 2</u> and <u>the output value was 4</u>.
Explaining Cause and Effect	The _____ is _____.	_____ because _____. Because _____ is _____, the _____ is _____. _____ caused _____ to _____.
Examples	The <u>area of triangle 10 is 3</u>.	<u>The area of triangle 10 is 3</u> because <u>if I enclose triangle 10 inside a rectangle, the area of that rectangle is 6</u>. Because <u>the area of triangle 10</u> is <u>one half the area of the rectangle</u>, the <u>area of triangle #10</u> is <u>3</u>. <u>Enclosing triangle 10 inside a rectangle</u> caused <u>the area of triangle 10</u> to <u>be one half the area of the rectangle</u>.

TABLE 8-1. continued

How to Modify Math Lessons to Support English Learners

categorizing. In science, one might say that helium, oxygen, and carbon dioxide are gases, because they are made up of loosely connected molecules. In social science, we say that certain societies are democracies because of their forms of government. And in math, certain figures are polygons because they are closed and have three or more straight sides. In each of these cases, the language is supported by the same sentence frame: _____ is a _____ because _____. These basic sentence structures can be powerful tools in the hands of adolescent students learning the English language. When structured appropriately, these sentence frames are flexible enough to be useful in a variety of contexts. Sentence frames allow ELs to use key vocabulary terms and to put together complete thoughts that can be connected to prior learning and then confirmed or rejected and revised, and finally understood. As these examples illustrate, opportunities to practice with the sentence frames can transfer across content areas and help ELs break through the "intermediate plateau" (Scarcella 2003) that has compromised the academic futures of too many of our nation's students.

Teachers can design sentence frames that are increasingly more sophisticated to help students advance in language and conceptual development. For example, if students are comparing geometric figures in math, individual ELs will be ready to use language to think about and discuss their learning at differing levels. Students with beginning levels of proficiency will be able to describe figures before they can compare them. They might use the frame _____ has _____ to express ideas like: *An equilateral triangle has three congruent angles.* Such a limited frame does not serve intermediate- and advanced-level students. They are ready to make comparisons and to use sentence frames such as _____ has _____, but _____ has _____ to compose sentences like: *An equilateral triangle has three congruent angles, but an isosceles triangle has two congruent angles.* These intermediate- and advanced-level students will eventually be able to refine their language use to include dependent clauses: *Although a* _____ *and a* _____ *are the same in that* _____, *they are different because* _____. Using this frame in the same geometry lesson, an EL might state: *Although an equilateral triangle and an isosceles triangle are the same in that they have three angles, they are different because an equilateral triangle has three congruent angles and an isosceles triangle has two congruent angles.* The goal of the sentence frames is twofold: (1) to provide ELs the linguistic support they need to learn about and demonstrate their knowledge of the math content, and (2) to push simultaneously their English language abilities to higher levels of proficiency.

Although the frames may seem abstract outside the context of the math lesson, ELs almost immediately see the usefulness of them because they help students with the difficult parts of their new language. Before students are asked to use a sentence frame, they learn key vocabulary terms that they can place in the frame to begin to talk about their learning. Frames are also introduced with familiar math concepts before they are used with new information. For example, students might describe familiar polygons using the descriptive frames before they describe more complex polygons. After students understand the concept of the frame, in our experience they often try to use frames above their current proficiency level, realizing that the frames allow them to produce much more complicated sentences than they would ordinarily use. The goal is not to create a fill-in-the-blank sentence that has correct and incorrect answers; rather, the goal of the frames is to provide a scaffold that ELs can use to construct and discuss their thoughts.

Refer to Table 8–1 to determine the language function that students will need to perform to articulate the particular math knowledge you want them to learn. In some cases, it may be advisable to select more than one language function. In the *Guess the Function* lesson included in this book, for example, the language goal included both *hypothesizing* and *drawing conclusions* (page 7). Students used the sentence frame for *hypothesizing* to write their function and the frame for *drawing conclusions* to explain their thinking.

After you have determined the function or functions appropriate to the math goal, choose frames that correspond to the overall range of linguistic proficiencies among your students. Often, you will find that incorporating frames at both beginning and intermediate levels is useful for all your ELs within a given lesson.

Mold the frames to fit the particular math goal. Consider the number of blanks necessary for your frame. This sentence frame is effective for describing a circle: *A _____ has _____.* When describing polygons, however, consider using a sentence frame like this: *_____ have _____, _____, and _____.* What verb tense would be most natural? Do you want students to articulate their thinking in the past, present, future, or conditional tense? When predicting, the future tense is the most logical, because the task involves making educated guesses about an event that has not yet happened. When asking students to sequence the steps they used to solve an equation, setting the frames in the past tense makes more sense. The conditional tense is ideal for hypothesizing: *If I placed the triangles side by side, the result would be a quadrilateral.* Is the subject of the frame singular or plural? The answer to this question affects the article and the verb in the frame. If students are describing a singular object—say, a right triangle—they will need a frame designed for a single object: *A _____ has _____.* If students are describing a series of geometric figures or numbers, they will need a frame designed for multiple items: _____, _____, *and* _____ *have* _____. After you have determined your frame, try it out several times to make sure it is flexible enough to articulate many different examples. If slight modifications are necessary—for example, using both singular and plural subjects—be prepared to alter the frame as the students are using it.

Determining Key Vocabulary

Most math curricula now include a set of key terms for each lesson or unit of study. This is a great place to start determining what words ELs will need to know, but it is by no means an exhaustive list. Because math knowledge is cumulative, students who have spent less time learning in English, as well as those who have experienced instructional gaps, may not know the previously taught mathematical terms that are the foundation for a particular lesson. In addition to content terms, consider some of the language in your frames that may be unfamiliar. For example, if you are asking students to predict, do they know what *predict* means? In addition, middle school-age ELs may be unfamiliar with many everyday terms or multiple-meaning words that are used in math instruction, and may not have used these terms in their own in conversations. Directly teaching key terms that are essential for building and demonstrating knowledge may be a good idea, as is providing brief examples or synonyms of important everyday words used in the frames.

After you have determined the key vocabulary for the lesson, give some thought regarding when to teach each term. Some of the words must be taught at the beginning of the lesson for students to follow along. Other words will not appear until partway through the lesson, and it might be more logical to teach them at that time. For example, Kathy provided multiple opportunities for students to solidify their understanding of the key vocabulary terms *choice* and *chance* before they played the game of *SKUNK* (page 100). The purpose of the game was for students to use an understanding of probability to make and test conjectures about strategies that would help them win a game. As students played *SKUNK*, Kathy then quickly taught the key term *strategy* by asking them to talk about their strategy use in the familiar game of dodgeball. Following this example, students were able to engage in the language goal for the lesson—namely, to *describe the strategies* they used. The students will retain the meanings of only those words for which they have an actual need. Anticipating that need and providing key vocabulary at that moment will have the most impact on student learning.

Introducing Academic Language

Learning math and academic language at the same time is a cognitively demanding endeavor. To support ELs, design an activity that will allow students to try out the frames on familiar math material before they are faced with the academic demands of the grade-level lesson. The plans in the book provide models for such opportunities. For example, when teaching the *Secret Number Puzzles* lesson (page 23), Luz first asked students to use their knowledge of number systems to discover the secret number from clues given to them about whole numbers before giving them clues about decimal numbers. Allowing students to practice the frames first with familiar concepts helps them internalize the structures, builds their confidence in volunteering answers, and prepares them to be successful during the part of the lesson in which new math content is presented.

Building in Opportunities for Talk

Language goals, sentence frames, and key vocabulary are useful to the students only if they have opportunities to talk during the lesson. All these linguistic supports are meant to support student learning during instruction, and allow them to showcase their learning after instruction. Arguably the most important role of the sentence frames is to help students formulate their thinking as they are learning the math content. This thinking must occur throughout the lesson in order for the students to keep pace with the instruction.

> Language goals, sentence frames, and key vocabulary are useful to the students only if they have opportunities to talk during the lesson.

Including opportunities for talk within math lessons may appear to be a daunting task at first, given the amount of material included in the middle school curriculum. In addition, some adolescent students may have come to expect that math is primarily about getting the right answer. These students may have become passive learners who are not used to talking about their thinking in math class. However, in our experience, the more that ELs experience success as they use the sentence frames to participate in lessons and explain their ideas, the more readily they engage in oral language activities.

Building in opportunities for structured and guided talk throughout the lesson does take some additional time. However, the investment of time in these opportunities for student talk will pay off, because it allows you to redirect students if misconceptions or confusions arise. Student engagement in these oral language activities promotes development of mathematical understanding as well as proficiency in academic English. Consider using any or all of the following strategies for facilitating student talk during your lessons.

Partner Talk

After each meaningful chunk of instruction, provide students with time to think about what they have learned, pair up with a partner to discuss their ideas, and then share their ideas with the class. It is important to consider how you will structure partner talk. Depending on a variety of factors, you may wish to encourage students to talk with different partners throughout the course of a lesson or unit of instruction. ELs who speak the same native language might use their primary language for clarifying concepts at the beginning of a lesson, for example. In other situations, you may want to ensure that ELs have the opportunity to interact with native speakers or with other ELs who are at more advanced proficiency levels. Same-sex pairings may also facilitate partner talk for adolescent students. Your knowledge of your students and of the content you are teaching should guide these decisions. However you decide to pair students, you can build all three of these activities by posting, explaining, modeling, and encouraging the use of the sentence frames.

Repeating and Paraphrasing

During the presentation of a lesson, students are exposed to many important concepts. Often these concepts build on one another to achieve the math goal of the lesson. Achievement of that math goal can be improved if teachers hold students responsible for each important chunk of learning throughout the lesson. One way to accomplish this is to ask students either to repeat or to paraphrase key concepts as they are presented. Although repeating may not seem like a high-level task, it is much more active than simply listening to the concepts as they are presented. Repeating also gives adolescent students additional confidence to participate in partner talk or other oral displays of their thinking, because they have the opportunity to hear and practice the way that key terms are pronounced. Following along as the teacher reads key vocabulary and sentence structures also provides opportunities for students to acquire knowledge of spelling. This knowledge in turn supports their construction of written responses. Paraphrasing key information encourages students to express a new concept in their own language, a language we know they understand. Students can repeat or reword statements made by the teacher or by other students. The teacher can also repeat or paraphrase statements made by students to emphasize or clarify information.

> Paraphrasing key information encourages students to express a new concept in their own language, a language we know they understand.

Partner Work and Group Work

When directing students to explore with manipulatives, practice a skill, solve problems, conduct an experiment, draw a figure, create a chart, or compare numbers or figures, it is helpful to ask them to work in pairs to promote language use as they negotiate a task together. Working with a partner creates the need for communication. This is yet another opportunity for students to use sentence frames and key vocabulary to build their content knowledge and their language ability. Attention to factors that influence grouping strategies, such as gender and language proficiency, is important here as well as in opportunities for partner talk. Student interaction is also encouraged by setting up situations in which collaboration is required, such as using a common set of materials to complete a task.

Supportive Questioning

Probably the most common way that teachers invite student participation in a lesson is through questioning. Although inquiring and checking for understanding are a natural part of teaching, simply asking questions may not elicit participation from ELs. Some students with advanced proficiency levels in English may respond easily to questions, as would many native English speakers. Other advanced-level ELs, as well as some native speakers, may lack confidence and experience when talking about their mathematical thinking. These students benefit from structured opportunities to practice with the vocabulary and sentence structures specific to the math classroom. Students with intermediate and beginning proficiency levels may need more support to produce a response. When asked a question such as "What steps did you use to solve the equation?" students with intermediate and beginning proficiency levels must produce so much language just to structure their answer (language to sequence their steps, past-tense verbs, math vocabulary) that they might choose not to answer at all.

A teacher can provide support, however, to elicit responses and improve the participation of students with lower levels of English proficiency. When questioning beginning-level students, for example, teachers can ask a question or provide a prompt that requires a physical response ("Point to the right triangle." "Give a thumbs-up when you think you understand the pattern."), or devise a question with a yes-or-no answer ("Is one line segment longer than the other?"). When asking short-answer questions, build the answers into the questions for additional support: "Is this a right triangle or an isosceles triangle?" "Is your answer an integer or a fraction?" "Should we divide or multiply?"

Students with intermediate and advanced levels of proficiency in English need less support to understand and respond to questions from the teacher, but carefully crafted questions can improve the quality of both their responses and their English. For example, consider a lesson in which students are asked to use their knowledge of proportion to make predictions as marbles of different colors are withdrawn from a bag. Instead of asking an intermediate or advanced-level EL: "What do you predict will happen?" you might phrase your question this way: "What color do you predict we will select if we pull another marble out of the bag?" The second question models the structure of a well-crafted answer: "I predict we will select red if we pull another marble out of the bag." Compare that with the response more likely from the first question: "Red."

> In addition to improving student participation, thoughtful questions can improve the quality of students' responses.

Questioning students lets teachers know what students have learned. Answering questions lets students test, confirm, or modify their own understanding. None of these goals can be met unless the questions are structured in a way that produces a response from the students. In addition to improving student participation, thoughtful questions can improve the quality of students' responses.

Explaining Thinking

When teaching the lesson, make sure to prompt students to explain their thinking. When a student provides either a correct answer or an incorrect answer to a question, the more important information is how the student arrived at that answer. The correct answer may have been a lucky guess. It may also have been the result of good mathematical reasoning or problem solving that could serve as an example for other students. There is no way of knowing unless we ask students to explain their thinking. Likewise, an incorrect answer may have been the result of a careless mistake or it may represent complete confusion on the part of the student. Asking students to explain their thinking makes the learning process more transparent. ELs with intermediate or advanced proficiency may not have had enough opportunities to practice with key math vocabulary and sentence structures to explain their thinking fluently and confidently. Structured opportunities for talk, such as the use of sentence frames, assist such students. Students with beginning levels of proficiency in English may not yet have the language to explain their thinking. Providing manipulatives or visuals so that such students can *show* their thinking can give you insight into their learning.

> Asking students to explain their thinking makes the learning process more transparent.

Writing About Thinking

English language development involves four domains: listening, speaking, reading, and writing. For adolescent ELs, the development of language proficiency across each of these domains may be highly variable depending upon their prior experiences with literacy in their primary language as well as their exposure to English. Generally speaking, when students can verbalize their ideas about the math content using the sentence frames and the key vocabulary, they are ready to stretch to the next level and write down their ideas. Their writing is supported by the frames as well as by the talk. Teachers present language support across domains during a math lesson within this approach, providing students with opportunities to understand and produce both written and oral language. For adolescent ELs, writing often serves as a type of rehearsal that builds confidence and enables them to participate more readily in oral responses.

> For adolescent English learners, writing often serves as a type of rehearsal that builds confidence and enables them to participate more readily in oral responses.

How We Develop Lessons

When designing lessons for ELs in the middle school math class, we follow a few important steps. The process is recursive, of course, as we return to particular sections of each lesson to revise our plan and make it as coherent as possible. The following paragraphs demonstrate how we designed one particular lesson: *Scaling Up!* (page 121).

Identify a Math Goal

We selected the math goal of solving a problem involving scale factors because it involved students in working on multiple concepts, including measuring length and understanding and determining scale, ratio, and proportion. These important concepts are built on topics in mathematics. We also used the Common Core State Standards to guide us. In this case, we knew that students need to be able to use their knowledge of proportional relationships to solve real-world as well as mathematical problems. Last, rich, multifaceted problems such as *Scaling Up!* are highly engaging for students. These activities promote extended language use and critical thinking. Such problems also provide opportunities for students to develop the knowledge and reasoning that serve as a foundation for future math studies.

Choose a Language Goal That Serves the Math Goal

Because we knew that students would be engaged in a complex task with multiple concepts, we decided to focus on sequencing to help them organize their problem-solving strategies. In addition, students were later able to communicate their understanding as they described the steps they took to create the completed scaled drawing.

Determine Key Vocabulary

For this lesson, we decided to limit the number of key vocabulary terms to be taught in comparison with the recommendations in the original lesson. We wanted to provide students with ample opportunities to comprehend and practice with the most important key terms, rather than to cover superficially a long list of unfamiliar words. Instead, we provided quick synonyms or definitions for some words that students might not have encountered before, and focused our instruction on terms that were essential to building and demonstrating understanding of the math goal. Our selection of key vocabulary was also influenced by the fact that the classroom in which we would be implementing the lesson contained a number of ELs from Spanish-speaking backgrounds. Some of the key terms we selected are cognates, such as *scale* (*escala*), *similar* (*similar*), and *proportion* (*proporción*). The use of cognates was a way to build on prior knowledge and to facilitate participation by Spanish-speaking ELs during the lesson, particularly for students who were new to English. We also recognized that some of the terms were multiple-meaning words that can be confusing for ELs, as well as for native speakers in some instances. For example, students may be familiar with using a *scale* at home or in the doctor's office to determine someone's weight, but not with the term *scale* to indicate the ratio between the size of an object and a representation of it. Or they may be familiar with the terms *scale* and *factor*, but be unable to determine the meaning of the expression *scale factor*. Last, we anticipated that students might need to use different forms of the term *proportion* (*proportional, proportions*) to express their understanding during and at the end of the lesson. It is important for teachers to show explicitly how a term changes when used as a different part of speech. During the lesson, the key vocabulary was presented in context, and explanations of the terms were supported by visuals and modeling. Students pronounced the terms and practiced using them in math conversations at several points during the lesson.

Design Sentence Frames

The lesson was designed for a seventh-grade classroom that included native English-speaking students as well as ELs at the beginning, intermediate, and advanced proficiency levels. We used the function chart (Table 8–1) to guide us as we created frames that would support students in this particular lesson. We anticipated that beginning-level ELs would quickly be able to use a frame like this: *First* _____. *Next* _____. *Then* _____. Students at intermediate and advanced levels would be able to combine clauses and indicate relationships like this: *First,* _____ *and then* _____. *After* _____, *I* _____.

Plan How to Introduce Academic Language

For this lesson, we designed opportunities for students to revisit important mathematical concepts and key vocabulary that students would need to use later to make their scale drawings. During this time, the students had to answer the question "What do you know about _____?" using the key vocabulary. Their answers were recorded in a class vocabulary bank that was referred to later as the students used sentence starters, or sentence frames, to explain the sequence of steps used in constructing a scale drawing. An individual recording sheet was also provided to students for them to use words, pictures, examples, or other means of showing what they knew about the key concepts of *scale, ratio, scale drawing, similar figures,* and *proportion.* Important sequence words (*first, next, then, finally, after*) to be used in the sentence frames were introduced and recorded in a different color in the class vocabulary bank. Posting the key vocabulary terms and sentence frames for sequencing allowed students to read and revisit words at their own pace, extending opportunities for them to acquire new vocabulary and language structures. The use of the recording sheets and oral student answers also enabled the teacher to draw on prior learning, as well as to clarify misconceptions. At the end of the first activity, the teacher modeled using the sentence frames to explain the steps in constructing a scale drawing, using the key vocabulary and student-generated examples. During this part of the lesson, the teacher was careful not to "give away" how to create the proportions, but instead modeled the steps and academic language used to begin the scale drawing.

Build in Opportunities for Talk

Students were provided with ample opportunities to talk throughout the lesson, which meant that part of the planning task involved deciding how students should be grouped. In this case, because we knew that there were varied proficiency levels in both English and mathematical knowledge among the students in the class, we knew that the ways we planned for partner talk and group work would have to be strategic. We modified the usual seating chart so that we could include same-gender groups, and ensured that the groupings were heterogeneous in terms of language proficiency and math skill levels.

After the groupings were arranged, the lesson plan called for students to engage in whole-class discussion and partner talk as they completed the recording sheet and coconstructed the class vocabulary bank with the teacher. Combining oral and written expression during this part of the lesson was an important instructional strategy that provided formative assessment opportunities for the teacher to incorporate in the scale drawing activity.

The main activity involved students working with partners to construct a scale drawing, so talk was a necessity. The use of the sentence frames provided an important scaffold for student thinking and communication. The language function of sequencing helped students organize their ideas and break a complex task into steps as they decided how to go about scaling up their drawing, and provided a way for them to cement their understanding after they completed the activity. Students were also required to document their processes on paper, using the key vocabulary in the sentence frames.

Through the use of the sentence frames, students were able to discover and confront mistakes in their thinking, as well as to restart the task if necessary, when they recognized gaps or errors in their procedures. At the end of the activity, students used the key vocabulary and sentence frames in a discussion to determine whether their final drawings were proportional, and they then recorded their steps in writing.

Design a Writing Prompt

We ended the lesson by asking students to write their steps to construct a scale drawing. The prompt was open-ended; the students were not directed to use the key vocabulary and sentence frames. The sentence frames were not intended to be a fill-in-the-blanks activity, and the students were not tested on definitions of the key vocabulary. Instead, the sentence frames and vocabulary served as scaffolds to support student mathematical thinking and communication, as well as helped them develop academic language. The frames and vocabulary were available to students as they wrote, because we needed to assess their math knowledge, not their language proficiency.

**Now You Try It: Eight Steps to Modifying
a Lesson for English Learners**

1. Identify a math goal.
2. Choose a language goal that serves the math goal.
3. Determine the key vocabulary.
4. Design sentence frames according to proficiency levels.
5. Plan how to introduce academic language.
6. Build in opportunities for talk.
7. Design a writing prompt to conclude the lesson.
8. Simplify the information using a lesson template.

Identify a Math Goal

Select a math goal for your lesson. Remember that you are looking for key concepts that build foundational knowledge, promote critical thinking, and/or involve an extensive use of language.

Choose a Language Goal That Serves the Math Goal

After you have selected an appropriate math lesson for modification, decide what language students need to articulate their learning. Think about what they will say throughout the lesson to demonstrate that they are learning the concept. What language function will they need to perform? Will they need to describe, categorize, compare, contrast, summarize, sequence, give directions, hypothesize, predict, make inferences, draw conclusions, or establish cause and effect?

Determine the Key Vocabulary

What math terms will be introduced in the lesson? What previously introduced terms and everyday words are still unfamiliar to the ELs in your class, given their language proficiency level and prior experience? What multiple-meaning words will appear in the lesson? Are there any other essential words that might cause confusion? List these terms and decide when in the lesson you will introduce each term.

Design Sentence Frames According to Proficiency Levels

Use the Language Functions and Sentence Frames chart (Table 8–1) to find sample sentence frames that match the language function you chose. Work with the frames until they fit the needs of your lesson. Determine which verb tense sounds the most natural. Decide how many blanks to include in each frame and where to put them. Design frames that will fit the range of English proficiency levels represented in your class. You may find it useful to provide sentence frames at both beginning and intermediate/advanced levels, and allow students to choose the frames they will use at times to differentiate learning opportunities within a whole-group lesson. The key is to use your own knowledge (1) of your students and (2) of the math content to design frames that allow students to verbalize the key lesson concepts and to extend their language proficiency.

Plan How to Introduce Academic Language

After you have created your sentence frames, decide how you will introduce the new academic language with familiar math content. For example, if students will be comparing large or awkward numbers (decimals, fractions, negative integers), have them practice the comparison frames first with smaller, less cumbersome numbers. If students will be summarizing the steps used to solve complicated equations, plan an opportunity for them to use the sentence frames first to summarize the steps in a more basic or familiar problem. Remember that the goal is to familiarize the students with the sentence frames and key vocabulary so that when new content is presented they can devote their thinking to the math content rather than to the vocabulary and sentence structures.

Build in Opportunities for Talk

Throughout the lesson, build in opportunities for students to talk to one another and to you about their learning. These opportunities should include (1) discussions that build background knowledge and allow students to make connections to what they already know about the topic, (2) exploratory talk that encourages students to hypothesize or make predictions about the new concept, and (3) concluding conversations in which students solidify their new knowledge. Also spend time crafting questions to ensure the participation of students with different proficiency levels. Refer to the suggestions in "Building in Opportunities for Talk" (page 181) to ensure there are a variety of activities and grouping strategies that will keep students engaged and participating.

Design a Writing Prompt to Conclude the Lesson

Although talk allows students to explore their knowledge in a relatively nonthreatening manner, it does not necessarily provide the middle school teacher with information on each individual student's learning. To assess what students have learned, design an open-ended question or prompt and ask students to commit their ideas to paper at the end of the lesson. Refer students to the sentence frames for support with this activity. You may find it useful to encourage students to represent visually what they learned in the form of drawings, charts, or graphs if they are not yet comfortable expressing their ideas through writing in English.

Simplify the Information Using a Lesson Template

The template in Figure 8–1 is designed to help you capture all the information you must consider while designing your lesson. Share this document with colleagues who are looking for ways to support their ELs.

Lesson Template

Math Goal
_____
_____

Language Goal
_____
_____

Key Vocabulary
_____   _____   _____

_____   _____   _____

_____   _____   _____

_____   _____   _____

Materials
_____   _____   _____

_____   _____   _____

Sentence Frames That Support the Language Goal

Beginning:
_____

_____

Intermediate:
_____

_____

Advanced:
_____

_____

Activity Directions for Introducing Academic Language (including opportunities to talk)
1.
2.
3.

Activity Directions for the New Math Concept (including opportunities to talk)
1.
2.
3.
4.
5.

Writing Prompt
_____

_____

FIGURE 8-1.
Lesson
template.

Reflecting on the Modifications

When we wrote the math lessons detailed in this resource, the three of us worked together to design a lesson, and then taught the lesson several times and revised it so that it was the most effective. We also made sure to design and implement lessons in a variety of settings. We implemented lessons in classrooms that followed a block schedule as well as in classrooms with 50-minute math periods. We also taught the lessons in classes in which ELs primarily shared a common native language and English proficiency level, as well as in classes in which students came from a range of linguistic and experiential backgrounds.

Across all these settings, we observed each other's lessons and took notes on the teaching and the learning, and then met to debrief after each lesson. We also examined the work that students produced during and at the conclusion of the lessons. Reflecting on our planning and teaching, as well as on student work, led us to many of the insights we have shared in this resource. We learned what Farrell (2003) meant by saying that experience alone is not as important as reflecting on that experience.

Take the necessary time after teaching a math lesson you have modified to reflect on how successful the lesson was. Use the following questions for guidance.

Reflecting on Your Lesson: Guiding Questions

Did the ELs in your class meet the math goal?

Did they meet the language goal?

Did they participate more than they normally do during math lessons?

Were the sentence frames you created appropriate for the lesson?

Did you use too many sentence frames or too few?

Were the key vocabulary terms that you selected appropriate?

What changes would have made the lesson more successful?

> Middle school teachers will likely find that these structured opportunities for talking and writing assist all students—English learners and native speakers alike—as they deepen their conceptual understanding and acquire academic language as a foundation for success.

The work of modifying math lessons not only to make them comprehensible but also to provide language support to help ELs think about new concepts, experiment with their knowledge, and solidify their understanding is not easy. This work, however, allows ELs to participate fully in their learning community and to reap great benefits from your teaching. Indeed, most middle school teachers will likely find that these structured opportunities for talking and writing assist all students—ELs and native speakers alike—as they deepen their conceptual understanding and acquire academic language as a foundation for success.

Appendix

FAQs

1. The ideas in this book seem like just good teaching. Why is it targeted for English learners (ELs)?

Although it is true that all learners will benefit from the strategies presented in this book, the methods are essential for ELs to have access to the core math curriculum. Without the use of explicit vocabulary instruction, visual aids, and opportunities to communicate during math lessons, ELs could have difficulty understanding the material presented, whether verbal or written. This could create gaps or misunderstandings that, in turn, could prevent students from progressing on to and succeeding in higher level math classes. Without the benefit of higher level math classes, students' opportunities for future academic paths would be limited. To prevent this type of inequity, targeted instruction specifically for ELs is essential.

A second, and equally compelling reason this book is targeted for ELs is the focus on the development of the English language needed to participate fully during math lessons. During the middle school years, participation in class is especially critical because teachers are preparing students for the demands of more abstract mathematical concepts to be presented in algebra and beyond. The implementation of the sentence frames provides ELs with linguistic support so they can communicate mathematically and deepen their learning. When students share their thinking both orally and in writing, it provides us, as teachers, with opportunities for assessment and helps us make pivotal instructional decisions for our students.

2. Do the strategies in this book work for all ELs regardless of their native language?

The strategies in this book will be effective for helping all ELs, whatever their native language. Most teachers find that students who have strong oral skills in their primary language have an easier time acquiring a second language—in this case, English. However, regardless of the level students are at in their primary language, all ELs benefit from direct, explicit instruction in English; simply being in an all-English environment is not enough to help them process material and understand it.

In addition, as students advance through middle school, academic language demands increase, thus creating a compelling reason to continue to develop language even if students seem at a fairly advanced level of English proficiency. The strategies in this book will help your ELs develop math content and acquire English, regardless of their primary language.

3. What if I only have a few ELs in my class and they are all at different language levels? Will this affect my native English-speaking students?

This is a common concern, because many teachers are in this exact situation. Although ELs may receive additional support in English as a Second Language classes, they may be in regular education classes for math. We have found that it is very appropriate to teach these lessons to the whole group, and that the majority of students benefit from the additional attention to English. For example, native English-speaking students tend to use the advanced sentence frames, which have more complex academic language than they are used to using. Although they may have been able to explain their mathematical thinking without the use of the frames, native English speakers will acquire a more sophisticated way of doing so—a way that may be more aligned to assessments. ELs at different proficiency levels seem to self-regulate their use of the frames, which is why all students are introduced to all the frames regardless of their level of English proficiency. Providing all students access to the frames increases their level of metalinguistic reflections (their thinking about their language use) and helps them mediate their language learning. As the content in math classes in middle school and beyond increases in complexity, so does the language to accompany it. All students will benefit from attention to developing academic language.

4. I have students in my class who are at different of levels of English proficiency and speak different languages. What can I do to support these students?

It is not uncommon to have students at a range of proficiency levels in your math classes. However, most students who are new to English are more than likely placed in a sheltered math class that provides consistent linguistic support. Yet, a regular classroom teacher could still have students that range from an intermediate proficiency level of English to the fully proficient native English speaker. This diversity, although rich and dynamic, can create quite a challenge for a teacher trying to ensure that all students have equal access to content.

One seventh-grade teacher used a number of strategies to assist her ELs when teaching a lesson on multiplying and dividing positive and negative integers. Juan was a student at the intermediate level of English proficiency. Although he understood most of the teacher's instruction, there were times that he relied on visual clues or clarification from his peers to help him understand the lesson. The teacher recognized that Juan could benefit from some strategic support.

First, she had Juan sit next to Leticia, a native Spanish speaker with an advanced level of English. Leticia was able to clarify or even translate for Juan, thereby using a student's primary language as a resource. By being intentional in seating assignments and promoting cooperative learning, the teacher was building in support for her ELs.

As often as possible, the teacher used concrete materials or visual representations of concepts to help the ELs understand concepts. For example, in the lesson on multiplying and dividing positive and negative integers, the students created a graphic using symbols for positive (+) and negative (−), and for multiplication (×) and division (÷) to help them when using procedures to compute. The graphic was copied by students and also posted in the classroom to provide support.

Last, the teacher had some background information about Juan as a learner. She knew that he came to math with a solid foundation in basic mathematical operations. So when it came time to compute mathematical equations, the teacher often chose Juan to highlight his math strengths and build his confidence and proficiency in English.

5. My ELs seem to struggle more in math than my other students. Should I adjust my expectations for these students?

The adjustments need to occur in the presentation of material and not in what is expected of students. It is critical, as stated earlier, that students in middle school have full access to learning the mathematics at their grade level to prepare them for future, more abstract, rigorous courses. If ELs are struggling in math class, it does not necessarily indicate that they are less capable than the other students in your class or that you should lower your expectations for them. What you are witnessing may be a language barrier that is preventing your ELs from demonstrating their understanding of the material. Language difficulties may be masking the good mathematical thinking that ELs are capable of and could possibly express in their primary language.

We need to adjust our instruction to find out what our students know, and to value the experiences they do have. When we know more about our students, we can then design instruction to make sure we are providing them with an equitable education and allowing them access to the entire curriculum that native English-speaking students receive on a daily basis. It is our professional obligation to modify our lessons so that all students meet grade-level standards.

6. What is academic language and how is it different from social language?

Academic language is defined as the language used in schools. But what exactly does that mean? It is the language that we use in formal learning environments connected to specific subject matter. For example, we may direct students to *summarize* a story, make a *causal statement* about the Civil War, or *draw conclusions* about a scientific experiment. The cognitive functions are correlated to a certain type of language structure that students need to understand (whether material is presented orally or in text) and must be able to produce orally and in writing. In addition to the text structure, word order (syntax) and vocabulary (topic-specific terms related to a subject) are also part of academic language. Academic language is usually related to content and is often highly decontextualized, which increases the chance for difficulty in understanding and applying it. Acquiring academic language is key to success in school and access to higher education.

With regard to the math lessons in this book, the language goals listed for each lesson are the language functions that we identified as the key cognitive tasks that students would be doing in the lessons. For example, when students have to make conjectures about strategies that will help them win the game *SKUNK* (Chapter 5), the academic language they will need to know to be able to participate fully in the lesson is that for describing strategies such as, *I am going to* _____ , *because* _____ and *A* _____ *strategy is* _____ . In addition, there are specific vocabulary words that students should use to demonstrate their understanding of probability such as *choice, chance, likely,* and *unlikely.* Not only did students use the language orally, but they also had to write about the strategies they used in the game.

In contrast, social language is easier to acquire because it is often used in everyday interactions surrounding common activities and topics. We don't always need specific terminology when speaking in social situations because we can usually refer to the topic at hand, such as the show on TV or the drama happening at the lunch tables. We also can use other ways to communicate besides language, such as gestures, phrases, and colloquial words, to participate in discussions. In addition, because of the frequency with which we interact in informal situations, there are many opportunities for practicing the language of socializing or everyday activities. Many times our ELs seem very adept with English, but we should always be checking to see whether their fluency is with the social use of English or the demands of academic English.

7. Some of my ELs are really good at solving mathematical equations. Math is the only time that they can be successful without having to speak English. Why the emphasis on talking during math class?

Providing time for productive talk in math class can improve students' ability to solve complex mathematical equations. Being good at solving for variables or finding the correct mathematical expression requires the kind of flexibility in thinking that enables a student to choose an efficient strategy for a particular problem to yield a correct answer. In order for students to become flexible problem solvers, they must be aware that numerous strategies for finding an answer may exist. By participating in mathematical discussions, students become aware of a variety of strategies to solve mathematical equations and get a chance to develop their English language skills at the same time.

In order for these rich mathematical discussions to occur, it is imperative that teachers in middle school provide time for students to talk with their peers in small groups, whether it be partner talk or group talk. During the implementation of our lessons, we often found it challenging to build in the time for student talk, but with each implementation, we recognized that student talk was as critical, if not more so, than giving students time to work independently on a page of problems. Listening to students talk about their thinking gave us insights into their understanding, and provided us with ongoing opportunities for formative assessment.

8. This book is for grades 6 through 8. Will the lessons, as written, work for all three grades?

This book is meant to demonstrate how to modify math lessons for the ELs in your class and to provide some examples in the various math strands taught in middle school classrooms. We suggest drawing on these lessons as guides, using the ones in the book as highly structured activities that you can try out and implement immediately with your students. Teachers should also take a look at their own textbooks and at the core standards to extend or modify the lessons for each grade level. At the end of each chapter, there are ideas for extensions of the lessons that you can peruse to see what best matches the instructional needs of your classroom.

After experimenting with the lessons and strategies, you can begin to apply the strategies in the book to modify your own math lessons. Moreover, you know your students best, so you will be the most adept in deciding whether the lesson content is appropriate to your group of students and in determining the amount of adjustments you will have to make.

9. I noticed that you spend time practicing the sentence frames with simple math content at the beginning of the lesson. I'm worried about time and whether this is needed for middle school students. Is the oral language practice really necessary?

One of the things we know about teaching is that there never seems to be enough time for everything we would like to do in a period. Adding more to our class periods just seems impossible. We constantly need to scrutinize our teaching to make sure we are maximizing learning time for our students. In this case, we do need to make the time for the oral language practice before getting involved with the more complex math content.

Our brains can only process so much new information. To ensure that ELs can learn both academic language and math content, we need to create a balance in our lessons. By providing time for practice with language before we introduce complex mathematical ideas, students' brains can focus on learning the new language. This upfront investment in language learning will have a payoff later during the lesson, because students will be able to understand more of the math content and participate in class discussions. The time invested in oral language practice prior to the lesson will improve student learning and thereby save time that would have been spent reteaching the math concepts later.

One may wonder how middle school students react when they are asked to repeat words and phrases or practice sentence frames. Surprisingly, during our implementation of lessons, students responded to this new focus on language by participating readily and responding positively to the support we offered them. Providing models and time for oral practice is critical if students are to use language correctly.

Last, oral practice gives teachers opportunities to provide corrective feedback to students about their use of English. While listening to students interact with one another, teachers can monitor the language students are using and provide immediate feedback. As with any other content area, providing feedback to students in a timely and sensitive manner will help them develop their skills in English.

10. Do students get confused when there are too many sentence frames? How many sentence frames should I present at a time?

Students can easily become confused with too many sentence frames and frames that are not presented well. Ideally, we would suggest one sentence frame for the key mathematical concept, differentiated for all the levels in your class. Differentiating the frames is one of the most important elements in ensuring that you are helping students develop their academic language and not holding them back from progressing to the next proficiency level. A good example of this is in the lesson *Archimedes' Puzzle* (Chapter 7). The sentence frames for this lesson were used to support students in describing and sequencing the steps they used to find the area of shapes. Four sentence frames were introduced to give all students an entry point for participation in the lesson. For students at the intermediate levels of English, the frames were

> *First, _____. Then, _____.*
> *Finally, _____.*

> *I found the area by _____.*

For the more advanced ELs and native English speakers, these frames were provided:

> *At first, _____. Following that, _____.*
> *Next, _____. As a last step, _____.*

> *To find the area, _____.*

The teacher modeled how to use the frames and then directed students to use them in their discussions with their partners or small groups to ensure that students had authentic experiences using the language.

11. *In algebra, we mostly use symbols and not words during class. How will the strategies in this book support my ELs?*

As with all math lessons, students benefit from discussing their thinking and understanding of math concepts. Even in algebra, where so much of the content is presented with symbolic representations, it is important that students have multiple entry points into the lesson and a variety of ways to demonstrate their understanding. One idea to support ELs in algebra is to show different ways to represent the main concepts such as using words, numbers, pictures, graphs, and tables or charts. By eliciting multiple representations of the content, ELs can "see" the patterns and functions. Furthermore, sentence frames and small-group discussions help students use their language to understand algebraic expressions better. Because algebra is an important gateway to higher level math classes, it is essential that ELs experience success in this important area of mathematics.

Multiple-Meaning Words in Mathematics

acute	inscribe	rational
altitude	intersection	ray
base	irrational	reflection
change	key	relative
chord	left	right
closed	mass	root
combination	mean	round
composite	median	ruler
coordinate	multiple	scale
count	negative	segment
degree	net	set
difference	obtuse	side
digit	odd	similar
edge	open	slide
even	operation	solution
expression	origin	space
face	period	sum
factor	plane	table
fair	plot	term
figure	point	times
foot	power	translation
formula	prime	union
function	product	unit
identity	proper	value
improper	property	volume
inequality	range	yard

The following recording sheet can be reproduced for use during the lesson. It is simple enough that it can be used with any function. Refer back to this chapter for models of how a teacher used it. The student work displayed in this chapter provides examples of how students used the recording sheet with the two different problems presented in the lesson.

Guess the Function

Input		Output

Sentence Frame #1:

If the _____ value is _____, then the _____ value is _____.
　　　(input/output)　　　　　　　　　　　(input/output)

Sentence Frame #2:

I know that for every input value n, the value of the output value is _____.
　　　　　　　　　　　　　　　　　　　　　　　　　　　　　　　　(function)

Sentence Frame #3:

I can conclude that the function is _____, because _____.

Reproducible 4-1A *Cats and Birds:* **Math Vocabulary Review**

Vocabulary Word	This is my explanation:
Times	
Divisible	
Factor	
Multiple	
Altogether	
Expression	
Solution	

Reproducible 4-1B *Cats and Birds:* **A Quick Review of Some Algebraic Expressions**

Use your own words, draw diagrams, or give examples to explain what you know.

Expression	This is my explanation:
There are 3 times as many apples as there are oranges.	
The total number of apples and oranges share common factors.	
The total number of oranges is a multiple of 4.	
The total number of apples is divisible by 3.	

Cats and Birds

Clue Card 1

Ms. Lang keeps cats and birds.
She has 25 heads to pet.
How many cats and birds does
she have?

Cats and Birds

Clue Card 4

Ms. Lang keeps cats and birds.
The total number of cat paws is a
multiple of 5.
How many cats and birds does she
have?

Cats and Birds

Clue Card 2

Ms. Lang keeps cats and birds.
She counted 3 times as many cat
paws as bird feet.
How many cats and birds does
she have?

Cats and Birds

Clue Card 5

Ms. Lang keeps cats and birds.
The total of the number of cat paws
and bird feet is divisible by 2, 4, 8, 10,
20, 40, and 80.
How many cats and birds does she
have?

Cats and Birds

Clue Card 3

Ms. Lang keeps cats and birds.
The number of cat paws and the
number of bird feet share common
factors.
How many cats and birds does
she have?

Cats and Birds

Clue Card 6

Ms. Lang keeps cats and birds.
The total number of bird feet is a
multiple of 5.
How many cats and birds does she
have?

Octopi and Sea Stars

Clue Card 1

Sara keeps sea stars (with 5 arms each) and octopi (with 8 arms each). How many sea stars and octopi does Sara have?

Octopi and Sea Stars

Clue Card 4

Sara keeps sea stars (with 5 arms each) and octopi (with 8 arms each). The difference between the number of octopus arms and the number of sea star arms is 10.
How many sea stars and octopi does Sara have?

Octopi and Sea Stars

Clue Card 2

Sara keeps sea stars (with 5 arms each) and octopi (with 8 arms each). Sara has 24 mouths to feed.
How many sea stars and octopi does Sara have?

Octopi and Sea Stars

Clue Card 5

Sara keeps sea stars (with 5 arms each) and octopi (with 8 arms each). The number of sea star arms is a multiple of the number of octopus mouths. How many sea stars and octopi does Sara have?

Octopi and Sea Stars

Clue Card 3

Sara keeps sea stars (with 5 arms each) and octopi (with 8 arms each). Sara counted a total of 150 arms on the sea creatures.
How many sea stars and octopi does Sara have?

Octopi and Sea Stars

Clue Card 6

Sara keeps sea stars (with 5 arms each) and octopi (with 8 arms each). The difference between the number of sea stars and octopi is less than 10. How many sea stars and octopi does Sara have?

Reproducible 4-4 *Farmer Eddie:* **Clues**

Farmer Eddie

Clue Card 1

Farmer Eddie keeps cows and chickens.
How many cows and chickens does he have?

Farmer Eddie

Clue Card 4

Farmer Eddie keeps cows and chickens.
There are four times as many cow feet as there are cows.
How many cows and chickens does he have?

Farmer Eddie

Clue Card 2

Farmer Eddie keeps cows and chickens.
Altogether, Farmer Eddie has 45 cows and chickens to feed.
How many cows and chickens does he have?

Farmer Eddie

Clue Card 5

Farmer Eddie keeps cows and chickens.
There is a difference of 30 between the number of chicken feet and the number of cow feet.
How many cows and chickens does he have?

Farmer Eddie

Clue Card 3

Farmer Eddie keeps cows and chickens.
Farmer Eddie knows that these creatures have a total of 110 feet.
How many cows and chickens does he have?

Farmer Eddie

Clue Card 6

Farmer Eddie keeps cows and chickens.
The number of cows is divisible by 2.
How many cows and chickens does he have?

The Tran Family

Clue Card 1

There are 6 children in the Tran family.
Each child has either a bicycle or a tricycle.
How many bicycles and tricycles does the family have?

The Tran Family

Clue Card 4

There are 6 children in the Tran family.
Next year, Dan will be old enough to ride a bicycle. Then there will be a total of 13 wheels.
How many bicycles and tricycles does the family have?

The Tran Family

Clue Card 2

There are 6 children in the Tran family.
No child has both a bicycle and a tricycle.
How many bicycles and tricycles does the family have?

The Tran Family

Clue Card 5

There are 6 children in the Tran family.
Only the children have bicycles or tricycles in the Tran family.
How many bicycles and tricycles does the family have?

The Tran Family

Clue Card 3

There are 6 children in the Tran family.
The oldest child says there are exactly 14 wheels altogether.
How many bicycles and tricycles does the family have?

The Tran Family

Clue Card 6

There are 6 children in the Tran family.
The number of tricycles in the Tran family is a factor of the number of bicycles.
How many bicycles does the family have?

Cycles

Clue Card 1

Lisa wants to make unicycles, bicycles, and tricycles with spare wheels and bike seats.
How many of each can she make?

Cycles

Clue Card 4

Lisa wants to make unicycles, bicycles, and tricycles with spare wheels and bike seats.
Lisa can make more bicycles than other types of cycles.
How many of each can she make?

Cycles

Clue Card 2

Lisa wants to make unicycles, bicycles, and tricycles with spare wheels and bike seats.
Lisa has 26 seats to use.
How many of each can she make?

Cycles

Clue Card 5

Lisa wants to make unicycles, bicycles, and tricycles with spare wheels and bike seats.
The number of wheels Lisa puts on bicycles is close to the number of wheels she puts on tricycles.
How many of each can she make?

Cycles

Clue Card 3

Lisa wants to make unicycles, bicycles, and tricycles with spare wheels and bike seats.
Lisa has 60 wheels to use.
How many of each can she make?

Cycles

Clue Card 6

Lisa wants to make unicycles, bicycles, and tricycles with spare wheels and bike seats.
Lisa does not use very many wheels to make unicycles.
How many of each can she make?

Reproducible 5-1 **Directions for Playing the Game *SKUNK* with the Entire Class**

Objective: *The object of SKUNK is to accumulate the greatest possible point total over five rounds. The rules for play are the same for each of the five rounds.*

Overview: *SKUNK is a game created by Dan Brutlag. The game of SKUNK involves five rounds (thus the letters S, K, U, N, K) during which a pair of dice is rolled. The sum of the numbers on the dice determines how many points students can accumulate (or lose) during the game.*

1. To start the game, all students must make a score sheet like the one presented here.

S	K	U	N	K

2. Each letter of SKUNK represents a different round of the game. Play begins with the S column and continues through the K column.
3. At the beginning of each round, every player stands up. The teacher rolls a pair of dice. (*Important*: Everyone playing uses that roll of the dice.)
4. All students figure the total (sum) of the dice and record it in the appropriate column on their score sheets, using the following guidelines:

   ✦ If a 1 comes up, play is over for that round and all the player's points in that column are wiped out.
   ✦ If double 1s come up, all points accumulated in prior columns are wiped out as well.
   ✦ If a 1 does not come up, students consider the sum as points and may choose either to try for more points on the next roll (by continuing to stand up) or to stop and keep what they have accumulated (by sitting down).

Note: If a 1, or double 1s, occurs on the very first roll of a round, then that round is over and the game starts again. Students should record their scores in the next column.

Reproducible 6-1A **Scaling Up! Recording Sheet**

The following recording sheet can be reproduced for use during Part 1: Introducing Academic Language, of the lesson.

Scale (think ratio):

Scale drawing:

Similar figures:

Proportions:

Reproducible 6-1B **Scaling Up! Directions**

1. The **goal** is to **scale up** the original picture, and to draw its **larger version (as exact as possible)** on the graphing paper.

2. With your partner, figure out **a scale/ratio** that will make you draw a picture big enough to cover most of the graphing paper.

3. The **scaled up (larger)** picture has to be **proportional** to the original picture.

4. **Measure at least five** parts of the original picture so that you can draw its larger version.

From *Supporting English Language Learners in Math Class, Grades 6–8* by Kathy Melanese, Luz Chung, and Cheryl Forbes.
© 2011 by Scholastic Inc. Permission granted to photocopy for nonprofit use in a classroom or similar place dedicated to face-to-face educational instruction.

Scale Table

Scale Factor

Part 1 original size	Part 1 new size (scaled up)
Part 2 original size	Part 2 new size (scaled up)
Part 3 original size	Part 3 new size (scaled up)
Part 4 original size	Part 4 new size (scaled up)
Part 5 original size	Part 5 new size (scaled up)

This recording sheet is an optional tool for students to use during the lesson.

Reproducible 7-1 **Archimedes' Puzzle: Description and Picture**

For the teacher only.

The *Stomachion* (also known as *Archimedes' Puzzle*) is an ancient tangram-type puzzle. Believed by some to have been created by Archimedes, it consists of 14 pieces cut from a square. The pieces can be rearranged to form other interesting shapes. In this lesson, students learn about the history of the puzzle, use the pieces to create other figures, review general properties of polygons, and investigate the areas of the pieces.

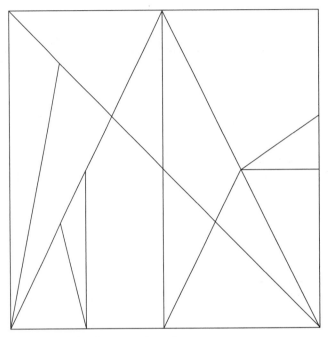

About Archimedes' Puzzle (*Stomachion*)

The *Stomachion* is an ancient puzzle that is at least 2,200 years old. It consists of 14 pieces that can be cut from a 12 by 12-inch square. As with its cousin the *tangram*, the object of the *Stomachion* is to rearrange the pieces to form interesting shapes. Some of the many shapes that can be formed are shown here.

It is not known whether Archimedes developed the *Stomachion*, although the puzzle was definitely known by the ancient Greeks. Because Archimedes wrote about the puzzle extensively, however, two of its alternative names are *Loculus of Archimedes* and *Archimedes' Puzzle*.

Adapted from NCTM Illuminations: http://illuminations.nctm.org/LessonDetail.aspx?id=L720.

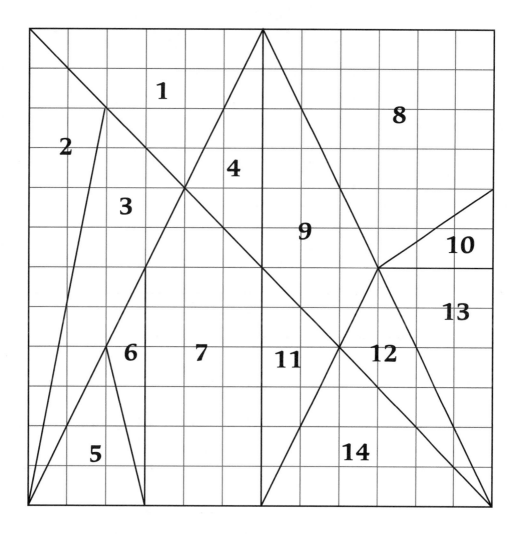

Polygon Hunt

Polygon #	Type of Polygon
1	
2	
3	
4	
5	
6	
7	
8	
9	
10	
11	
12	
13	
14	

Polygon Hunt

Combine Polygons	Type of Polygon

1. **Combine 2 different polygons** from Archimedes' Puzzle. The new polygon should be an **irregular polygon.**
2. **Trace** the new shape in the space below.
3. Find the **area** of the new polygon.
4. **Important information:**
   - ✦ The area of every piece is an **integer.**
   - ✦ The area of every piece is a **multiple of 3.**
5. Explain **in writing** how you found the area of the new polygon using any of the following sentence frames.

> *I found the area by _____.*
>
> *In order to find the area, _____.*
>
> *First, _____. Then, _____. Finally, _____.*
>
> *At first, _____. Following that, _____. After that, _____. As a last step, _____.*

Math Goal

_____
_____

Language Goal

_____
_____

Key Vocabulary

_____   _____   _____
_____   _____   _____
_____   _____   _____
_____   _____   _____

Materials

_____   _____   _____
_____   _____   _____

Sentence Frames That Support the Language Goal
Beginning:

_____
_____

Intermediate:

_____
_____

Advanced:

_____
_____

Activity Directions for Introducing Academic Language (including opportunities to talk)
1.
2.
3.

Activity Directions for the New Math Concept (including opportunities to talk)
1.
2.
3.
4.
5.

Writing Prompt

_____

References

Anderson, Rick. 2007. Being a mathematics learner: Four faces of identity. *The Mathematics Educator* 17 (1): 7–14.

Brutlag, Dan. 1994. Choice and chance in life: The game of SKUNK. *Mathematics Teaching in the Middle School* 1 (1): 28–33.

California Department of Education. 2010. *Language Census Data, 2008–2009.* www.cde.ca.gov.

Chapin, Suzanne H., and Art Johnson. 2006. *Math matters: Understanding the math you teach, grades K–8.* 2nd ed. Sausalito, CA: Math Solutions Publications.

Chapin, Suzanne H., Catherine O'Connor, and Nancy Canavan Anderson. 2003. *Classroom discussions: Using math talk to help students learn, grades 1–6.* Sausalito, CA: Math Solutions Publications.

Cobb, Paul, Ada Boutfi, Kay McClain, and Joy Whitenack. 1997. Reflective discourse and collective reflection. *Journal for Research in Mathematics Education* 28 (3): 258–77.

Cummins, Jim. 2003. Supporting ESL students in learning the language of mathematics. *Issues and Trends in Mathematics.* Chicago, IL: Pearson Education/Scott Foresman.

Dacey, Linda, and Karen Gartland. 2009. *Math for all: Differentiating instruction, grades 6–8.* Sausalito, CA: Math Solutions.

Dutro, Susana, and California Reading and Literature Project. 2003. *A focused approach to frontloading English language instruction for Houghton Mifflin reading, K–6.* Santa Cruz: Toucan Ed.

Dutro, Susan, and Carrol Moran. 2003. Rethinking English language instruction: An architectural approach. In *English learners: Reading the highest levels of English literacy,* ed. Gilbert G. García, 227–58. Newark, DE: International Reading Association.

Faltis, Christian, and Cathy Coulter. 2008. *Teaching English learners and immigrants in secondary school.* Upper Saddle River, NJ: Pearson Education.

Farrell, Thomas S. C. 2003. *Reflective practices in action: 80 reflection breaks for busy teachers.* Thousand Oaks, CA: Corwin.

Fillmore, Lily Wong, and Catherine E. Snow. 2000. "What teachers need to know about language." www.cal.org/ericll/teachers.pdf.

García, Gilbert G., ed. 2003. *English learners: Reaching the highest level of English literacy*. Newark, DE: International Reading Association.

Garrison, Leslie. 1997. Making the NCTM's standards work for emergent English speakers. *Teaching Children Mathematics* 4 (3): 132–38.

Gibson, Margaret, Patricia Gándara, and Jill Peterson Koyama, eds. 2004. *School connections: U.S.–Mexican youth, peers, and school achievement*. New York: Teachers College Press.

Goldenberg, Claude. 2008. Teaching English language learners: What the research does—and does not—say. *American Educator* (Summer): 8–44.

Hiebert, James, Thomas P. Carpenter, Elizabeth Fennema, Karen C. Fuson, Diana Wearne, and Hanlie Murray. 1997. *Making sense: Teaching and learning mathematics with understanding*. Portsmouth, NH: Heinemann.

Hill, Jane D., and Kathleen M. Flynn. 2006. *Classroom instruction that works with English language learners*. Alexandria, VA: Association for Supervision and Curriculum Development.

Illuminations: Resources for Teaching Math. National Council of Teachers of Mathematics (NCTM). *The game of SKUNK*. Retrieved December 4, 2010, from http://illuminations.nctm.org/LessonDetail .aspx?id = L248.

Khisty, Lena L. 1995. Making inequality: Issues of language and meanings in mathematics teaching with Hispanic students. In *New directions for equity in mathematics education*, ed. Walter G. Secada, Elizabeth Fennema, and Linda B. Adajian, 279–98. New York: Cambridge University Press.

Krashen, Stephen D., and Tracy D. Terrell. 1983. *The natural approach: Language acquisition in the classroom*. Hayward, CA: Alemany.

Kress, Jacqueline E. 1993. *The ESL teacher's book of lists*. West Nyack, NY: Center for Applied Research in Education.

Lampert, Magdalene. 1990. When the problem is not the question and the solution is not the answer: Mathematical knowing and teaching. *American Educational Research Journal* 27 (1): 29–63.

Lawrence, Ann, and Charlie Hennessy. 2002. *Lessons for algebraic thinking*. Sausalito, CA: Math Solutions Publications.

Lawrence, Ann, and Charlie Hennessy. 2007. *Sizing up measurement: Activities for grades 6–8 classrooms*. Sausalito, CA: Math Solutions Publications.

McLaughlin, Barry. 1985. *Second-language acquisition in childhood: Vol. 2: School-age children*. 2nd ed. Hillsdale, NH: Lawrence Erlbaum.

National Assessment of Educational Progress. 2009. "National Assessment of Educational Progress 2009," http://nationsreportcard.gov/math_2009/.

National Center for Education Statistics. 2005. *Digest of education statistics.* www.nces.ed.gov.

National Clearinghouse for English Language Acquisition. 2010. "The growing number of English learner students: 1997-98–2007-08," www.ncela.gwu.edu/files/uploads/9/growingLEP_0708.pdf.

National Council of Teachers of Mathematics. 2000. "Principles and standards for school mathematics," http://standards.nctm.org/.

Olsen, Laurie. 2010. *Reparable harm: Fulfilling the unkept promise of educational opportunity for California's long-term English learners.* Long Beach, CA: Californians Together.

Scarcella, Robin. 2003. *Accelerating academic English: A focus on the English learner.* Oakland, CA: Regents of the University of California.

Teachers of English to Speakers of Other Languages. 2006. *Pre-K–12 English language proficiency standards.* Alexandria, VA: Teachings of English to Speakers of Other Languages.

Thompson, Virginia, and Karen Mayfield-Ingram. 1998. *Family math: The middle school years, algebraic reasoning and number sense.* Berkeley, CA: EQUALS Publications, University of California.

U.S. Department of Education. 2000. "Getting ready for college early: A handbook for parents of students in middle and junior high school years." [Archived information]. www2.ed.gov/pubs/GettingReadyCollegeEarly/index.html.

Wood, Terry. 1999. Creating a context for argument in mathematics class. *Journal for Research in Mathematics Education* 30 (2): 171–91.

Index

Academic language
  and academic
    success, 4
  adolescents' skills in, 6
  development of, 6–7,
    9–12
  encouraging use of, 117
  increasing demand for,
    196
  introduction of, 181,
    187–188
  of mathematics, 12
  sample introduction in
    lesson, 23–33, 49–
    59, 72–81, 100–102,
    123–131, 146–158
  vs. social language, 12,
    126, 198–199
  in textbooks, 12
Accessibility of content,
    strategies for, 14–16
Adolescents
  academic language
    skills of, 6
  peer relationships of,
    3, 123
  self-concept/identity of,
    3, 123
  societal pressures on,
    3–4
Archimedes' Puzzle (les-
    son), 144–169
  elements of, 144–145
  extension of, 168–169
  introduction of aca-
    demic language in,
    146–158

key strategies used in,
    167–168
sentence starters/
    frames for, 145
Assessment
  differentiation of, 142
  formative approach to,
    53, 63, 132–133
  use of questions for,
    142, 184

Background knowledge,
    building of, 146–147.
    See also Prior
    knowledge
Beginning-level English
    learners. *See also*
    English language
    proficiency
  characteristics of, 172
  designing questions/
    prompts for, 19, 142,
    184
  explaining thinking by,
    185
  lesson ideas for, 45–46
Bilingual education, effec-
    tiveness of, 6, 7, 16
Building background
    knowledge, 146–147.
    See also Prior knowl-
    edge

California
  levels of English lan-
    guage proficiency
    used by, 13

"long-term English
    learners" in, 6
  prevalence of English
    learners in, 6
California English Lan-
    guage Development
    Test (CELDT), 13
California Reading and
    Literature Project, 9
Cats and Birds (lesson),
    70–97
  elements of, 70–71
  extension of, 97
  introduction of aca-
    demic language for,
    72–81
  key strategies used in,
    96–97
  sentence frames
    for, 71
CELDT. *See* California
    English Language
    Development Test
Charts and tables, use for
    vocabulary review,
    72–81, 108–109,
    130, 138, 148. *See
    also* Graphics
Choral responses/reading
  as effective strategy,
    17–18
  oral language skills in,
    17–18
  sample use in lesson,
    27, 36, 42, 52, 77,
    104, 105, 116,
    128, 138